一天一点英文
Enjoy a Bit of English Everyday
中英双语，全新完美呈现

# 一天一点英文

刘正/编译

*Enjoy a Bit of English Everyday*

**最散文·光芒星**

Zui Prose·Shinning Star

大连理工大学出版社
DALIAN UNIVERSITY OF TECHNOLOGY PRESS

**图书在版编目(CIP)数据**

最散文·光芒星:英汉对照/刘正编译.—大连:
大连理工大学出版社,2010.3(2010.10重印)
(一天一点英文/刘正编译)
ISBN 978-7-5611-5359-8

Ⅰ.①最… Ⅱ.①刘… Ⅲ.①英语—汉语—对照读物
②散文—作品集—世界 Ⅳ.H319.4:Ⅰ

中国版本图书馆CIP数据核字(2010)第014903号

大连理工大学出版社出版
地址:大连市软件园路80号 邮政编码:116023
发行:0411-84708842 邮购:0411-84703636 传真:0411-84701466
E-mail:dutp@dutp.cn URL:http://www.dutp.cn
大连金华光彩色印刷有限公司印刷 大连理工大学出版社发行
幅面尺寸:160mm×235mm 印张:17 字数:276千字
印数:5001~8000
2010年3月第1版 2010年10月第2次印刷

责任编辑:陈 多 责任校对:杜丽芳
封面设计:联智昭阳

ISBN 978-7-5611-5359-8 定价:32.00元

# 写在前面的话
## Previous Remark

  秉着对英语文学的无比敬意和对汉语翻译的深切尊重,我们酝酿并出版了"一天一点英文"中英双语阅读书系,其中包括《最散文·光芒星》、《最小说·天空城》、《最诗歌·灵之翼》、《最童话·梦幻岛》、《最寓言·新月海》、《最幽默·长乐风》六种,力求以点代面综合凸显英语文学的魅力和汉译的艰辛,使亲爱的读者朋友们有种寓学于乐的感觉。《最散文》形散而神不散,行文斑驳而不失寓意;《最小说》风格多样,人物鲜活,描写细腻而情节引人入胜;《最诗歌》追求情调多样、情浓意厚,新颖和经典并存;《最童话》以求索之心唤醒沉睡的童真,故事老少皆宜;《最寓言》每篇短小而深刻,传统道德中融入现代的审美;《最幽默》气氛轻松惬意,让读者在莞尔一笑中增添生活的智慧。

  在这喧嚣的、快节奏的现代生活中,如果我们能给读者朋友们送去一点点休闲和一点点快乐,那正是我们的心愿,倘若还能多上一点点深刻,我们则求之不得。我们希望此书能成为一部望远镜,把艰难的英文阅读向读者拉近,使之变成一种乐趣。本书系的选材和语言都力求无愧于"最"字,虽然文学之海浩渺无垠、无穷无尽,但是我们坚信,若是读者朋友们能把我们的书系读得通透,定会大受裨益。

  本书系是整个团队合作的结晶,非常感谢参与丛书编译的全体人员,我们共同的努力协作保证了这套书的质量和品位,我们也期待着来自读者的反馈和意见。

"一天一点英文"书系全体编辑

2010.3

# 目 录
## *Contents*

# 第三卷

## 人生路漫漫
## Long Life Road

# 第四卷

## 品味乾坤
## Tasting the Universe

## 第五卷

### 畅言无忌
### Free Speech

## 第六卷

### 奇谈杂论
### Miscellaneous Arguments

# 最散文·光芒星
*Zui Prose Shinning Star*

# 第一卷

山水故园情
# Love for Native Land and Natural Scenery

# 英伦之美
# The Beauty of Britain

【英国】约翰·博恩顿·普里斯特利

## 作者简介

约翰·博恩顿·普里斯特利(1894-1984),英国剧作家,小说家,批评家。他的作品具有温文尔雅的讽刺性特征,表达自由政治观点。《危险的角落》(1932年)奠定了他在戏剧界的地位。小说有:《天使人行道》(1930年)、《河对面的农神》(1961年)、《逝去的帝国》(1965年)等。散文《英伦之美》以细腻的笔触感性地描写了英伦风景之包罗万象,尽显作者为祖国而自豪的情怀。

The beauty of our country—or at least all of its south of the Highlands—is as hard to define as it is easy to enjoy. Remembering other and larger countries, we see at once that one of its charms is that it is immensely varied within a small compass. We have here no vast mountain ranges, no illimitable plains, no leagues of forests, and are deprived of the grandeur that may accompany these things. But we have superb variety. A great deal of everything is packed into little space. I suspect that we are always faintly conscious of the fact that this is a smallish island, with the sea always round the corner. We know that everything has to be neatly packed into a small space. Nature, we feel, has carefully adjusted things—mountains, plains, rivers, lakes—to the scale of the island itself. A mountain 12,000 feet high would be a horrible monster here, as wrong as a plain 400 miles long, a river as broad as the Mississippi. In America the whole scale is too big, except for aviators. There is always too much of everything. There you find yourself in a region that is all mountains, then in another region that is merely part of one colossal plain. You can spend a long, hard day in the Rockies simply traveling up or down one valley. You can wander across prairie country that has the desolating immensity of the ocean. Everything is too big; there is too much of it.

Though the geographical features of this island are comparatively small, and there is astonishing variety almost everywhere, that does not mean that our mountains are not mountains, our plains not plains. Consider that piece of luck of ours, the Lake District. You can climb with ease—as I have done many a time—several of its mountains in one day. Nevertheless, you feel that they are mountains and not mere hills—as a correspondent pointed out in The Times recently. This same correspondent told a story that proves my point. A party of climbers imported a Swiss guide into the Lake District, and on the first morning, surveying the misty, jagged peaks before him, he pointed to a ledge about two thirds of the way up one of them and suggested that the party should spend the night there. He did not know that that ledge was only an hour or two's journey away and that before the light went they would probably have conquered two or three of these peaks. He had not realized the scale of the country. He did not know that he was looking at mountains in miniature. What he did know was that he was certainly looking at mountains, and he was right, for these peaks, some of them less than 3,000 feet high, have all the air of great mountains, like those in the Snowdon country, with their grim slaty faces.

My own favorite country, perhaps because I knew it as a boy, is that of the Yorkshire Dales. For variety of landscape, these Dales cannot be matched on this island or anywhere else. A day's walk among them will give you almost everything fit to be seen on this earth. Within a few hours, you have enjoyed the green valleys, with their rivers, find old bridges, pleasant villages, hanging woods, smooth fields; and then the moorland slopes, with their rushing streams, stone walls, salty winds and crying curlews[1], white farmhouses; and then the lonely heights, which seem to be miles above the ordinary world, with their dark tarns, heather and ling and harebells, and moorland tracks as remote, it seems, as traits in Mongolia. Yet less than an hour in a fast motor will bring you to the middle of some manufacturing town, which can be left and forgotten just as easily as it can be reached from these heights.

With variety goes surprise. Ours is the country of happy surprises. You have never to travel long without being pleasantly astonished. It would not be difficult to compile a list of such surprise that would fill the next fifty pages, but will content myself with suggesting the first few that occur to me. If you go down into the West Country, among rounded hills and soft pastures, you suddenly arrive at the bleak tablelands of Dartmoor and Exmoor, genuine high moors, as if the North had left a piece of itself down there. But before you have reached them you have already been surprised by the queer bit of Fen country you have found in the neighborhood of Glastonbury, as if a former inhabitant had been sent to Cambridge and had brought his favorite fenland walk back from college with him into the West. The long, green walls of the North and South Downs are equally happy surprises. The Weald is another of them. East Anglia has a kind of rough heath country of its own that I for one never expect to find there and am always delighted to see. No doubt it is only natural that East Lincolnshire and that Southeastern spur of Yorkshire should show us an England that looks more than half Dutch, but the transition always comes as a surprise to me. Then, after the easy rolling Midlands, the dramatic Peak District, with its genuine steep fells, never fails to astonish me, for I feel that it has no business to be there. A car will take you all round the Peak District in a morning. It is nothing but a crumpled green pocket handkerchief. Nevertheless, we hear of search parties going out there to find lost travelers. Again, there has always been something surprising to me about those conical hills that suddenly pop up in Shropshire and along the Welsh border. I have never explored this region properly, and so it remains to me a country of mystery, with a delightful fairy tale quality about its sugar-loaf hills. I could go on with this list of surprises, but perhaps you had better make your own.

Another characteristic of our landscape is its exquisite moderation. It looks like the result of one of those happy compromises that make our social and political plans so irrational and yet so successful. It has been born of a compromise between wildness and tameness, between Nature and Man. In many countries you pass straight from regions where men have left their mark on every inch of ground to other regions that are desolate wildernesses. Abroad, we have all noticed how abruptly most of the cities seem to begin: here, no city; there, the city. With us the cities pretend they are not really there until we are well inside them. They almost insinuate themselves into the countryside. This comes from another compromise of ours, the suburb. There is a great deal to be said for the suburb. To people of moderate means, compelled to live fairly near their work in a city, the suburb offers the most civilized way of life. Nearly all Englishmen are at heart country gentlemen. The suburban villa enables the salesman or the clerk, out of hours, to be almost a country gentleman. (Let us admit that it offers his wife and children more solid advantages.) A man in a newish suburb feels that he has one foot in the city and one in the country. There are, however, things to be said against the suburb. To begin with, now that everybody has a passion—and, in my opinion, a ridiculous passion—for living in detached or semidetached villas, the new suburbs eat into the countryside in the greediest fashion and immensely enlarge the bounds of their cities. Nor is there anything very pleasing in the sight of these villas and bungalows, thickly sown for miles, higgledy-piggledy[2] and messy. Then again, there are disadvantages about being neither completely urban nor completely rural: it might be better if people who work in the cities were more mentally urban, more ready to identify themselves with the life of the city proper. Thus there is something more than cheap snobbery behind that accusing cry of "Suburban!" which we hear so often. It may mean that the accused, with his compromises, has contrived to lose the urban virtues without acquiring the rural ones, and is mentally making the worst of both worlds.

We must return, however, to the landscape, which I suggest is the result of a compromise between wildness and cultivation, Nature and Man. One reason for this is that it contains that exquisite balance between Nature and Man. We see a cornfield and a cottage, both solid evidences of Man's presence. But notice how these things, in the middle of the scene, are surrounded by witnesses to that ancient England that was nearly all forest and heath. The fence and the gate are man-made, but are not severely regular and trim as they would be in some other countries. The trees and hedges, the grass and wild flowers in the foreground, all suggest that Nature has not been dragooned[3] into obedience. Even the cottage, which has an irregularity and coloring that make it fit snugly into the landscape (as all good cottages should do), looks nearly as much a piece of natural history as the trees: you feel it might have grown there. In some countries, that cottage would have been an uncompromising cube of brick which would have declared, "No nonsense one. Man, the drainer, the tiller, the builder, has settled here." In this English scene there is no such direct opposition. Men and trees and flowers, we feel, have all settled down comfortably together.

## 英伦之美
## The Beauty of Britain

The motto is, "Live and let live." This exquisite harmony between Nature and Man explains in part the enchantment of the older Britain, in which whole towns fitted snugly into the landscape, as if they were no more than bits of woodland; and roads went winding the easiest way as naturally as rivers; and it was impossible to say where cultivation ended and wild life began. It was a country rich in trees, birds, and wild flowers, as we can see to this day.

英国之美,至少在高地以南的所有地方的美,难以形容却又易于领略。想想别的更大的国家,我们立刻就能明白我国的一个诱人之处就在于其景致方圆维度虽小,却变幻多端、多姿多彩。我们这儿没有巍峨崔巍的高山,没有一望无际的草原,也没有重翠叠嶂的森林,更加没有高山、草原、森林所带来的那种宏伟壮观。但是,我们的景致却多姿多彩,地方虽小,却包罗万象。我想我们总是很少意识到这是一个四面环海的岛国,万物都被非常精巧地安排在这小小的土地上;自然巧夺天工般地对山脉、草原、河流、湖泊进行了规划,使它们和这个岛国相得益彰。在这里,一座12000英尺高的山峰就会出奇地不相称,一个400英里长的草原也是相当地不适合,更不要说一条像密西西比河那样宽阔的河流了。在美国,除了飞行员以外,人人都会认为整个地方太大,事物也太多。在那里,你来到一个地方,你会发现放眼望去全是山峰;如果你到了另一个地方,你会发现你所在之处只是一个巨大草原的一隅而已。你可以花上一整天,艰苦地在落基山上爬上又爬下;你也可以在如一望无际的、荒凉孤落的大海般的草原上徘徊良久。一切景致都太大也太多。

尽管从地理特征上说,这座岛国相对较小,但所到之处皆多姿多彩、令人惊叹,可这不意味着我们的山不是山,我们的草原不是草原。想想我国那方聚祥纳福的"湖区"宝地吧。你可以悠然自得地在一天中翻越几座小山,我就曾多次地这样做过。不过,你会觉得它们无一例外都是山,而不是沙丘——一个《泰晤士报》的记者最近就这样评价过。这个记者讲述了一件轶事,和我的看法不谋而合。一

最 散文
Zui Prose

群登山爱好者请了一个瑞士的导游来到湖区。第一天早上，在查看了眼前云深雾绕、嶙峋兀列的山峰之后，这位瑞士导游指着离山顶三分之一距离的一块山石说就在那里过夜。他茫然不知到那块山石只有一两个小时的路程，并且，在天黑之前，他们可能已经翻越了两三座这样的山峰。他完全没有意识到这个国家的大小，也不知道他所看到的只是微型的山。他只知道他看到的是山，事实也确实如此，因为这些山虽然都不足3000英尺高，却摆足了大山的气派，这就和斯诺顿地区那些崖岸陡峻的山一样。

我最喜欢的地方是约克郡峡谷，这或许是由于我从小就生活在那里的缘故吧。由于拥有多姿多彩的景致，我们英伦岛内或者世界上其他任何地方都不能与此山谷相比。你花一天时间畅游山谷，它们将会让你看到世界上值得去看的一切景致。在几个小时之内，你就可以有幸领略到苍翠欲滴的谷地里，涓涓小河流淌其中；你同样可以发现精致的古桥、舒适的村落、茂密的森林、平坦的田野；随后就有带着沼地的小山坡，坡儿上有湍泻的小溪、青石古墙、微咸的海风、啼鸣的麻鹬、白色的农舍；再往前就是荒寂的高地，它们比平地高出几英里，上面布满黑色的深潭，遍地都是美丽的石南和蓝铃；最后还有那沼地小径，它们和蒙古一样幽远。可若骑上高速摩托车，不到一个小时，你就能来到某个制造业的小镇，但此等小镇又非常容易被遗忘，因为从高地来到小镇是如此地容易。

与景致的变幻多姿交相辉映的就是风景使人惊喜无限。我们的国家充满着令人无比惬意的惊喜。你从来不用走多远，惊喜就已经接踵而至映入你的眼帘。如果要罗列一下这些惊喜，写满接下来的50页纸，丝毫不费力。现在，我只想把我自己最先知悉的几个惊喜信手拈来、以飨自身。如果你来到西部，游历完锦绣峰峦和茵茵绿野之后，你突然发现自己身处凛冽肃杀、凄切孤寂的达特木尔和埃克木尔台地，它们是真正的沼泽地，好似寒冷的北方在此留下的一块土地。但是在你来到这些台地之前，你就会为在格拉斯顿伯里附近找到的一块奇怪的沼泽而感到大吃一惊，这恰似一个人去了剑桥，临走之时依恋万分，把他最喜欢的散步场所从剑桥带回了西部。而南北丘陵那些绵延、苍翠的壁崖同样也能让人大吃一惊。威尔德就是它们中的一个。东安格利亚崎岖满地、石南遍野，这样一种别具一格的特点别处无从找到，所以，一旦看到，我就无比赏心悦目。毫无疑问，林肯郡东部和约克郡东南部向我们自然地展示了一个和荷兰非常相似的英国景致，然而它们之间的变化和过渡就已经让我无比惊喜了。紧接着微微起伏的米德兰，就是引人入胜的皮克地区，那里悬崖陡峻，非常让我吃惊，因为我认为皮克地区出现在那里本来就不可思议。驾着车,一早上的时间就可以游历完整个皮克地区,因为它小得像一块褶皱的绿色手帕。然而,我们还听说有搜救队去找寻迷路的游客,真是令人吃惊。同时,那些兀然挺拔于什罗普郡和威尔士边陲的锥形小山就足以让我觉得吃惊。我从来没有好好地游历过这个地区,它以其童话般美丽的圆锥形小山让我觉得神秘莫测。这里的惊喜太多,我可以继续写下去,但您最好亲自来领略。

英国景致的另外一个特征就是大小适度、精致绝伦。这些景致似乎是完美和谐的产物,这样的和谐使得我们的社会和政治规划如此缺乏理性、却又如此成功。这是一种野生与文明的和谐,也是人化与自然的和谐。在很多国家,你可以从一个每寸土地都留下人类烙印的地方一下子就来到一个荒无人烟的地方。在别的国家,我们已经发现大多数城市出现得非常突兀:一处,没有城市;下一处,冷不丁地就冒出一座城市。而我们国家的情况是:很多的城市你若没有身处其中,根本就不会发现它们是城市,因为城市与农村已经水乳交融。二者的合二为一源于我们的另外一个妥协和过渡,那就是城市与农村之间的郊区。关于郊区,值得一提的东西太多了。那些中等收入的人们被迫住在城市和他们工作地点相去不远的地方,郊区为他们提供了最文明的生活方式。几乎所有的英国人从根本上说都是乡村绅士。郊区的别墅使得推销员或者公司职员在工作之余得以享受乡村绅士一般的生活情趣(我们还得承认,乡村绅士的生活方式给他们的妻子和孩子带来了更加实惠的好处)。一个新兴郊区的人觉得自己身处城市与农村之间。然而,郊区也有一些不足。首先,既然人们都热衷于住在独立或半独立的别墅里——按照我的观点,这种热衷是荒谬的,所以,新兴的郊区正在用一种最为贪婪的方式吞噬着乡村的土地,并且无限地扩充着城市的边界。同时,如果满目皆是这些杂乱无章、密集排列着的、并且绵延数里的别墅和平房,那就没有什么可以让人赏心悦目了。再者,纯粹的农村或纯粹的城市也有其不足,如果在城市工作的人更加心系城市、更加心甘情愿地过纯粹的城市生活,情况可能会有所好转。但是我们经常听到的一句鄙夷性的话就是"郊区人",这句话的背后只有那种低俗不堪的势利。这句话可能意味着那些被鄙视的对象通过自身的妥协,不但失去了城市人的美德,又没有养成农村人的优点,结果弄得自己不伦不类。

我们现在再回来谈我们的景致,我认为这样的景致是野性与文明、自然与人化和谐统一的产物。原因之一在于它蕴含了自然与人化之间那种巧妙的平衡。我们可以看到一片玉米地和一间农舍,这些都是人类足迹的铁证。但是请注意,在整个景致中,这二者周围都是古英格兰风貌的那种森林满地、石南遍野的气派。农舍的栅栏和大门都是人造的,但却没有其他国家那样规则和整齐。农舍前那些林木、树篱、绿草、野花全都证明了自然没有屈从于人类。而那间农舍,即便是它那不规整的形状和颜色都让它和谐地融入到景致中(所有好的农舍都应该这样),它看起来如颗颗树木一样,好像是真正的自然之物,让你觉得它好像原本就生长在那里。在一些国家,这样一间农舍准会像一块与周围极不和谐的方砖,仿佛在叫嚣:"人,排水工,农夫,建筑工,都已经在此定居了下来,没有给我留下任何余地了!"在我们英国的景致中,这样直接的对立与不和谐绝不存在。我们觉得,人和树木、花草应舒服自在地融在一起。我们的箴言是:"生活与共生。"自然与人化的完美和谐从某种程度上展示了古英国的诱人魅力。在英国,一座座小镇和周围的景致巧妙地交融起来,似乎它们只是森林的一隅而已,道路如河流般蜿蜒通畅,让人无法辨别哪里是人化的终结,哪里是野生的开端。我们的国家就是这样充满了树木、鸟儿、野花,任何时候都可以去欣赏、去领略。

[1] curlew  n. 鹬, 白腰杓鹬
[2] higgledy-piggledy  adj.乱七八糟的, 混乱的
[3] dragoon  v. 迫害, 镇压

# 航程
# The Voyage

【美国】华盛顿·欧文

作者简介

　　华盛顿·欧文(1783-1859),是散文大师、美国文学奠基人之一。被尊为"美国文学之父"。其文笔优雅自然,清新精致,时常流露出温和的幽默。欧文的几部名著早已经林琴南介绍到中国,其中有《柑掌录》(即《见闻札记》),《旅人述异》(即《旅客谈》)和《大食故宫余载》(即《阿尔罕伯拉》)。《航程》一文中,作者记述了航海远离桑梓奔向祖先的欧洲时的复杂心情。读者不禁被这文字吸引着去琢磨:这航程究竟是寻根还是背井?

Ships, ships, I will descrie you,

Amidst the main,

I will come and try you,

What you are protecting,

And projecting?

What's your end and aim?

One goes abroad for merchandise and trading,

Another stays to keep his country from invading,

A third is coming home with rich and wealthy lading.

Hallo! my fancie, whither wilt thou go?

——old poem

To an American visiting Europe, the long voyage he has to make is an excellent preparative. The temporary absence of worldly scenes and employments produces a state of mind peculiarly fitted to receive new and vivid impressions. The vast space of waters that separate the hemispheres is like a blank page in existence. There is no gradual transition by which, as in Europe, the features and population of one country blend almost imperceptibly with those of another. From the moment you lose sight of the land you have left, all is vacancy, until you step on the opposite shore, and are launched at once into the bustle and novelties of another world.

In travelling by land there is a continuity of scene, and a connected succession of persons and incidents, that carry on the story of life, and lessen the effect of absence and separation. We drag, it is true, "a lengthening chain" at each remove of our pilgrimage; but the chain is unbroken; we can trace it back link by link; and we feel that the last still grapples us to home. But a wide sea voyage severs us at once. It makes us conscious of being cast loose from the secure anchorage of settled life, and sent adrift upon a doubtful world. It interposes a gulf, not merely imaginary, but real, between us and our homes—a gulf, subject to tempest, and fear, and uncertainty, rendering distance palpable, and return precarious.

Such, at least, was the case with myself. As I saw the last blue lines of my native land fade away like a cloud in the horizon, it seemed as if I had closed one volume of the world and its concerns, and had time for meditation, before I opened another. That land, too, now vanishing from my view, which contained all most dear to me in life; what vicissitudes might occur in it—what changes might take place in me, before I should visit it again! Who can tell, when he sets forth to wander, whither he may be driven by the uncertain currents of existence; or when he may return; or whether it may be ever his lot to revisit the scenes of his childhood?

I said, that at sea all is vacancy; I should correct the impression. To one given to day-dreaming, and fond of losing himself in reveries, a sea voyage is full of subjects for meditation; but then they are the wonders of the deep and of the air, and rather tend to abstract the mind from worldly themes. I was delighted to loll over the quarter-railing or climb to the main-top, of a calm day, and muse for hours together on the tranquil bosom of a summer's sea; to gaze upon the piles of golden clouds just peering above the horizon, fancy them some fairy realms, and people them with a creation of my own; — to watch the gently undulating billows rolling their silver volumes, as if to die away on those happy shores.

There was a delicious sensation of mingled security and awe with which I looked down, from my giddy height, on the monsters of the deep at their uncouth gambols: shoals of porpoises tumbling about the bow of the ship; the grampus, slowly heaving his huge form above the surface; or the ravenous shark, darting, like a spectre, through the blue waters. My imagination would conjure up all that I had heard or read of the watery world beneath me; of the finny herds that roam its fathomless valleys; of the shapeless monsters that lurk among the very foundations of the earth; and of those wild phantasms that swell the tales of fishermen and sailors.

Sometimes a distant sail, gliding along the edge of the ocean, would be another theme of idle speculation. How interesting this fragment of a world, hastening to rejoin the great mass of existence! What a glorious monument

13

最散文
Zui Prose

of human invention; which has in a manner triumphed over wind and wave; has brought the ends of the world into communion; has established an interchange of blessings, pouring into the sterile regions of the north all the luxuries of the south; has diffused the light of knowledge, and the charities of cultivated life; and has thus bound together those scattered portions of the human race, between which nature seemed to have thrown an insurmountable barrier.

We one day descried some shapeless object drifting at a distance. At sea, every thing that breaks the monotony of the surrounding expanse attracts attention. It proved to be the mast of a ship that must have been completely wrecked; for there were the remains of handkerchiefs, by which some of the crew had fastened themselves to this spar, to prevent their being washed off by the waves. There was no trace by which the name of the ship could be ascertained. The wreck had evidently drifted about for many months; clusters of shell-fish had fastened about it, and long sea-weeds flaunted at its sides. But where, thought I, is the crew? Their struggle has long been over—they have gone down amidst the roar of the tempest—their bones lie whitening among the caverns of the deep. Silence, oblivion, like the waves, have closed over them, and no one can tell the story of their end. What sighs have been wafted after that ship! what prayers offered up at the deserted fireside of home! How often has the mistress, the wife, the mother, pored over the daily news, to catch some casual intelligence of this rover of the deep! How has expectation darkened into anxiety—anxiety into dread—and dread into despair! Alas! not one memento may ever return for love to cherish. All that may ever be known, is that she sailed from her port, "and was never heard of more!"

The sight of this wreck, as usual, gave rise to many dismal anecdotes. This was particularly the case in the evening, when the weather, which had hitherto been fair, began to look wild and threatening, and gave indications of one of those sudden storms that will sometimes break in upon the serenity of a summer voyage. As we sat round the dull light of a lamp, in the cabin, that made the gloom more ghastly, everyone had his tale of shipwreck and disaster. I was particularly struck with a short one related by the captain:

"As I was once sailing," said he, "in a fine, stout ship, across the banks of Newfoundland, one of those heavy fogs that prevail in those parts rendered it impossible for us to see far ahead, even in the daytime; but at night the weather was so thick that we could not distinguish any object at twice the length of the ship. I kept lights at the masthead, and a constant watch forward to look out for fishing smacks, which are accustomed to anchor on the banks. The wind was blowing a smacking breeze, and we were going at a great rate through the water. Suddenly the watch gave the alarm of 'a sail ahead!'—it was scarcely uttered before we were upon her. She was a small schooner, at anchor, with her broadside toward us. The crew were all asleep, and had neglected to hoist a light. We struck her just amidship. The force, the size, and weight of our vessel, bore her down below the waves; we passed over her and were hurried on our course. As the crashing wreck was sinking beneath us, I had a glimpse of two or three half-naked wretches, rushing from her cabin; they just started from their beds to be swallowed shrieking by the waves. I heard their drowning cry mingling with the wind. The blast that bore it to our ears, swept us out of all further hearing. I shall never forget that cry! It was some time before we could put the ship about, she was under such headway. We returned, as nearly as we could guess, to the place where the smack had anchored. We cruised about for several hours in the dense fog. We fired signal-guns, and listened if we might hear the halloo of any survivors: but all was silent—we never saw or heard any thing of them more."

I confess these stories, for a time, put an end to all my fine fancies. The storm increased with the night. The sea was lashed into tremendous confusion. There was a fearful, sullen sound of rushing waves and broken surges. Deep called unto deep. At times the black volume of clouds overhead seemed rent asunder by flashes of lightning which quivered along the foaming billows, and made the succeeding darkness doubly terrible. The thunders bellowed over the wild waste of waters, and were echoed and prolonged by the mountain waves. As I saw the ship staggering and plunging among these roaring caverns, it seemed miraculous that she regained her balance, or preserved her buoyancy. Her yards would dip into the water; her bow was almost buried beneath the waves. Sometimes an impending surge appeared ready to overwhelm her, and nothing but a dexterous movement of the helm preserved her from the shock.

When I retired to my cabin, the awful scene still followed me. The whistling of the wind through the rigging sounded like funereal wailings. The creaking of the masts; the straining and groaning of bulkheads, as the ship labored in the weltering sea, were frightful. As I heard the waves rushing along the side of the ship, and roaring in my very ear, it seemed as if Death were raging around this floating prison, seeking for his prey: the mere starting of a nail, the yawning of a seam, might give him entrance.

A fine day, however, with a tranquil sea and favoring breeze, soon put all these dismal reflections to flight. It is impossible to resist the gladdening influence of fine weather and fair wind at sea. When the ship is decked out in all her canvas, every sail swelled, and careering gayly over the curling waves, how lofty, how gallant, she appears—how she seems to lord it over the deep!

I might fill a volume with the reveries of a sea voyage; for with me it is almost a continual reverie—but it is time to get to shore.

It was a fine sunny morning when the thrilling cry of "land!" was given from the mast-head. None but those who have experienced it can form an idea of the delicious throng of sensations which rush into an American's bosom, when he first comes in sight of Europe. There is a volume of associations with the very name. It is the land of promise, teeming with everything of which his childhood has heard, or on which his studious years have pondered.

From that time, until the moment of arrival, it was all feverish excitement. The ships of war, that prowled like guardian giants along the coast; the headlands of Ireland, stretching out into the channel; the Welsh mountains towering into the clouds;—all were objects of intense interest. As we sailed up the Mersey, I reconnoitred[1] the shores with a telescope. My eye dwelt with delight on neat cottages, with their trim shrubberies and green grass-plots. I saw the mouldering ruin of an abbey overrun with ivy, and the taper spire of a village church rising from the brow of a neighboring hill;—all were characteristic of England.

The tide and wind were so favorable, that the ship was enabled to come at once to her pier. It was thronged with people; some idle lookers-on; others, eager expectants of friends or relations. I could distinguish the merchant to whom the ship was consigned. I knew him by his calculating brow and restless air. His hands were thrust into his pockets; he was whistling thoughtfully, and walking to and fro, a small space having been accorded him by the crowd, in deference to his temporary importance. There were repeated cheerings and salutations interchanged between the shore and the ship, as friends happened to recognize each other. I particularly noticed one young woman of humble dress, but interesting demeanor. She was leaning forward from among the crowd; her eye hurried over the ship as it neared the shore, to catch some wished-for countenance. She seemed disappointed and sad; when I heard a faint voice call her name. It was from a poor sailor who had been ill all the voyage, and had excited the sympathy of every one on board. When the weather was fine, his messmates had spread a mattress for him on deck in the shade, but of late his illness had so increased that he had taken to his hammock, and only breathed a wish that he might see his wife before he died. He had been helped on deck as we came up the river, and was now leaning against the shrouds, with a countenance so wasted, so pale, so ghastly, that it was no wonder even the eye of affection did not recognize him. But at the sound of his voice, her eye darted on his features: it read, at once, a whole volume of sorrow; she clasped her hands, uttered a faint shriek, and stood wringing them in silent agony.

17

最
散文
Zui Prose

All now was hurry and bustle. The meetings of acquaintances–the greetings of friends–the consultations of men of business. I alone was solitary and idle. I had no friend to meet, no cheering to receive. I stepped upon the land of my forefathers–but felt that I was a stranger in the land.

船儿，船儿，你漂向海洋，

我把你遥望，

向你探问，

你守卫什么？

筹划什么？

心向何方？

一船出国贸易经商，

一船留下守卫边疆，

一船自远方归来，财富满舱。

喂，可爱的船儿，你将漂向何方？

——一首古老的诗

　　凡去欧洲观光的美国人，须远涉重洋，但这不失为一个绝妙的准备过程。他将尘世与俗务一时摆脱，心境宁然——此情尤宜于观赏新鲜生动的景象。你看这大海，浩瀚无边，宛如一页现存的白纸，铺于地球当中。举目遥望，尽皆一色；犹如欧洲，各国的风土人情浑然一体，其变化极难觉察。故土一旦从眼前消失，一切便成空白，直至你踏上大海彼岸；此时，你又立即被抛向另一个喧嚣而新奇的世界。

　　陆地旅行，景物连绵不断，所见人事接踵而至，人生的故事得以继续，因此，我们不会有太多离愁别绪。不错，我们在远游中每前进一步，都拉着"一根长长的链条"；这链条节节不离，我们可沿此返回，感到其末端仍把我们与家紧连。但在大海上航行，我们便瞬间脱离一切，仿佛先前还在平稳牢固的锚地，现在忽被解缆，漂向一个疑惑丛生的世界。一片汪洋，把我们与家断然分开——这并非想象，而是千真万确。大海常遭风暴袭击，变幻不定，令人担忧，使你宛如远在天边，难以重返家园。

　　至少我的情形如此。祖国的蓝天，像浮云消失在地平线下；目睹此景，我仿佛觉得关于美国的大书我已就此合上，终于有闲暇作一番悠然的遐想，之后再打开另一本书。那片故土，也正从我视野里消逝；我一生最可爱的东西，无不珍藏其中。当我重返故园，她将发生怎样的变迁？我自己的变化又将如何？——旦起程远航，怎知这翻腾不息的大海要将你漂向何方？至于何时重返故乡，是否有幸再回到童年生活的地方，你均不可得知。

　　如上所述，海上一切皆为空白——此言应予纠正。一个人若喜爱幻想，勤于思索，便能于航行中发现，可供思索的事物比比皆是：不过它们是大海与天空的奇迹，使你把世间置之脑后。我喜欢于夏季风平浪静之日，漫步至船后栏杆，流连忘返，或爬上主桅楼，在大海平静的胸怀里，沉思默想数小时之久；举目凝望一团团金光灿烂的云团从地平线上徐徐显露，将其幻想成美妙仙境，同时把我臆造之物置于其中；注视缓缓起伏的波涛卷起银色浪花，似欲奔向幸福的海岸。

　　我从一个令人眩晕的高度，看海里种种怪物笨拙地嬉戏；我虽并无危险，但仍感畏惧，此种感觉实在有趣。只见群群海豚在船头两边翻滚，虎鲸将巨大身躯漫漫浮出海面，或者，贪婪的鲨鱼像个鬼怪在蓝海上猛冲而过。这时我凭着想象，把曾经听到和读过的一切，幻化入海里——如漫游于深不可测的波谷中的鳍状兽群、潜伏于地球最深处的怪异之物以及渔夫水手颇爱讲述的狂暴幽灵。

　　有时，远处忽现一叶孤帆，沿海边微微滑行，引起我另一番遐想。那片小小的世界，也急于奔赴坚实庞大的土地，多么有趣啊！人类发明了船只，便立下一座荣耀的丰碑：风浪已在一定程度上被征服，天涯海角彼此相连，上帝的恩赐得以互惠——南方一切华贵之物，无不涌入北方贫困地区；知识的光芒普照大地，四处可见文明社会的善行义举；天各一方的人们得以团聚。而昔日，自然似乎让一个巨大障碍横隔其间，无法超越。

　　某日，我们发现一个奇形物体在远处漂浮。海上这片浩瀚的世界，单调沉闷，因此某物一旦出现都会引人注目。原来是一只桅杆，船身必定已彻底毁损，残余的围巾仍依稀可见，一些船员曾用之将自己系于桅上，以免被海浪冲走。船为何名，无迹可查。这失事的船只显然已在海上漂浮数月：一簇簇水生贝壳类动物紧附四周，两侧漂浮着长长的海藻。我想，船员们此刻身在何处呢？他们早已不再挣扎，在咆哮的风暴中葬身海底，尸骨在大海深处发白。寂寞与遗忘，像波涛一样将他们淹没。他们何以遭此厄运，不得而知。怎样的哀叹曾飘随船后，他们凄凉的家中，曾有过怎样的祈祷！情人、妻子和母亲，每天又是怎样时刻关注着他们的消息,以期忽然听到漂泊大海的船只一点音信。然而,期待怎样变得黯然,成为焦虑,成为恐惧,成为绝望。哎呀! 船上可资珍爱的纪念物均无从获得,人们只知船出了港,"从此杳无音信!"

眼前这只破船,一如往常,令人想起许多可悲的往事。尤其在傍晚,晴朗之日突然天昏地暗,十分可怕,一场疾风暴雨将至;先前还一帆风顺,此刻便不得安宁。我们围着一盏孤灯坐下,其光昏然,室内因此更阴森可怖。大家依次讲述关于船只遇难的故事。船长讲的故事虽然不长,但使我尤为感动。

"一次,我乘坐一艘牢固的船,"他说,"沿纽芬兰海岸航行,遇上当地常见的漫天大雾,白天也看不多远。一到夜晚,天气十分阴暗,两船之遥的东西都辨认不清。我点亮桅杆顶部的几盏灯,随时观察,以免碰到前面的小渔船,这些船习惯停在沿岸。风呼呼地猛刮,船飞快行驶。突然,值班海员发出'前面有船!'的惊呼——话一出口两船就撞上了。那是一只停泊的纵帆船,船身正好横对我们。上面的船员都在睡觉,连一盏灯也忘记升起。我们沉重的大船正撞中它胸怀,猛烈地将它撞沉,并从其面上穿越而过,向前驶去。当它在我们身下渐渐沉没时,我瞥见两三个不幸的人半裸着身子,从船舱奔跑出来——他们刚从床上惊起,就在尖叫声中被海浪吞没。我听见风中传来他们被淹没时的哭叫。狂风把这声音卷到我们耳边,随之刮走,再也听不到了。那些哭叫声让我永生难忘! 过了一些时间,我们才得以调回船头,因船速太快。我们尽力返回原地,猜想那只小渔船可能停泊的地方,并在浓雾里四处巡游了几小时。我们又鸣放信号枪,看是否能听到幸存者的呼叫;然而四周一片寂静——他们从我们眼里、耳里彻底消失了!"

我承认,类似故事,使我美好的幻想一时化为乌有。夜愈深,风暴愈猛,使大海波涛汹涌,翻腾不息,发出沉闷可怕的声音。海水一浪高过一浪。有时,头上的阴云似乎被闪电撕裂,只见闪电在滔天的白浪上空震颤,随之而来的黑暗因此更为恐怖。这片汹涌的汪洋之上,雷声轰鸣,在巨浪中回响,连绵不断。我看见船在咆哮的海面摇晃,颠簸,竟保持了平衡,或者说仍未被巨浪卷沉,堪称一奇。帆桁时时沉入水中,船头几乎被波涛淹没。有时一个巨浪迎面冲来,仿佛要将它倾覆,唯有巧妙地把握好舵方能使其免遭重创。

我回到船舱,可怕场面仍萦绕脑际。狂风从帆缆呼啸而过,发出丧葬似的哭声。桅杆吱嘎作响,船在汹涌的海浪中挣扎时,舱壁紧绷,发出呻吟,令人胆颤。我听见海浪一次次猛击船身,在耳边咆哮,好像正围着这漂浮的监狱怒吼,寻捕食物——哪怕一个钉状的小孔,接合处的一点小缝,都会使之乘虚而入。

但有一天,大海平静安宁,和风宜人,一切忧愁顿然消失。天气这样明朗,风儿如此和美,谁不为之欣喜呢。船鼓起风帆,欢快地在微波中乘胜前进,此时它多么傲然,多么英勇——似欲称霸大海!

也许,一次航行,我即可将所思所想记录成书,因思绪几乎连绵不断——不过我该上岸啦。

这天早晨,天气晴朗,阳光明媚。桅头传来"陆地"的叫声,令人激动不已。美国人初见欧洲,总会心潮澎湃,妙不可言,唯有身临其境者,方能心有所悟。只"欧洲"一名,便会使他浮想联翩。这是一个"希望之乡",他童年时之所闻,学生时之所思,无不珍藏其中。

从那时起,直至我亲临欧洲,皆满怀激动。战舰像守护的巨人,悄然潜伏海岸;爱尔兰岬伸入海峡;威尔士大山高耸入云,这些,令我兴味盎然。船驶向默茨河时,我用望远镜观察沿岸。整洁的村舍,置身于美丽的灌木与绿草之中,我凝目遥望,欣喜不已。一座大寺,日见腐朽,成为废墟,常春藤蔓延其上。附近山顶有乡村教堂一座,其尖塔直刺天空。种种景观,无不为英国所特有。

此刻风平浪静,船很快靠住码头。只见人群熙来攘往,有的悠闲自在地旁观,有的热切期待亲友。有个商人似乎颇为精明,眉头紧皱,神情不安,我由此得知他专为接船而来。他两手插入衣兜,若有所思地吹着口哨,来回踱步;见他与众不同,人们专为他让出小道。船上、岸边的朋友不时看见对方,发出欢呼和问候。一个衣着简朴、举止异样的年轻妇女,尤其引起我注意。她从人群中挤出,船靠岸时急切地寻找,看久盼的人儿在何处,显得失望焦虑。忽然,我听见一个微弱的声音在呼唤她。原来是个不幸的水手,此次航行病魔缠身,人人同情。每遇晴朗天气,同伴就在甲板阴凉处为他铺一床垫。但近日他病情加重,整天躺在吊床上,咕哝着,希望死前见妻一面。船沿内河行驶时,他已被扶至甲板,此刻正靠支索,面容消瘦,极其苍白,难怪妻子充满爱意的双眼都没能把他认出。可一听见其声,她就立即转过身去,顿时眼里悲哀有加。她攥紧双手,发出一声轻微的尖叫,默默站着,痛苦万分。

此时周围的人多么匆忙嘈杂。熟人相见,朋友问好,商人交易。唯我一人独处一旁,无所事事。无友人见我,没任何人同我欢呼致意。我踏上了祖先的土地——却感到置身此处,我倒成了一个陌生的人。

---

[1] reconnoitre v. 侦察,勘察

# 《草叶集》序
# Preface to *Leaves of Grass*, 1855

## 作者简介

瓦尔特·惠特曼(1819–1892),美国最伟大的浪漫主义诗人。《草叶集》是他惟一的一部诗集,他创造了"自由诗体"。本文节选自1855年第一版序言的前半部分。《草叶集》序正体现了爱默生的评价:对于才华横溢的《草叶集》,我不是看不见它的价值,我认为它是美国至今所能贡献的最了不起的精华。我一向认为,我们似乎处于贫瘠枯槁的状态,过多的迂缓气质正把我们的智慧变得迟钝而平庸,而《草叶集》的出现正是我们所需要的。

America does not repel the past or what it has produced under its forms or amid other politics or the idea of castes or the old religions...accepts the lesson with calmness... is not so impatient as has been supposed that the slough still sticks to opinions and manners and literature while the life which served its requirements has passed into the new life of the new forms... perceives that the corpse is slowly borne from the eating and sleeping rooms of the house... perceives that it waits a little while in the door... that it was fittest for its days... that its action has descended to the stalwart and wellshaped heir who approaches... and that he shall be fittest for his days.

The Americans of all nations at any time upon the earth have probably the fullest poetical nature. The United States themselves are essentially the greatest poem. In the history of the earth hitherto the largest and most stirring appear tame and orderly to their ampler largeness and stir. Here at last is something in the doings of man that corresponds with the broadcast doings of the day and night. Here is not merely a nation but a teeming nation of nations. Here is action untied from strings necessarily blind to particulars and details magnificently moving in vast masses. Here is the hospitality which forever indicates heroes... Here are the roughs and beards and space and ruggedness and nonchalance that the soul loves. Here the performance disdaining the trivial unapproached in the tremendous audacity of its crowds and groupings and the push of its perspective spreads with crampless and flowing breadth and showers its prolific and splendid extravagance. One sees it must indeed own the riches of the summer and winter, and need never be bankrupt while corn grows from the ground or the orchards drop apples or the bays contain fish or men beget children upon women.

Other states indicate themselves in their deputies... but the genius of the United States is not best or most in its executives or legislatures, nor in its ambassadors or authors or colleges or churches or parlors, nor even in its newspapers or inventors... but always most in the common people. Their manners, speech, dress, friendships—the freshness and candor of their physiognomy—the picturesque looseness of their carriage... their deathless

23

最 散文
Zui Prose

attachment to freedom—their aversion to anything indecorous or soft or mean—the practical acknowledgment of the citizens of one state by the citizens of all other states—the fierceness of their roused resentment—their curiosity and welcome of novelty—their self-esteem and wonderful sympathy—their susceptibility to a slight—the air they have of persons who never knew how it felt to stand in the presence of superiors—the fluency of their speech—their delight in music, the sure symptom of manly tenderness and native elegance of soul... their good temper and openhandedness—the terrible significance of their elections—the President's taking off his hat to them not they to him—these too are unrhymed poetry. It awaits the gigantic and generous treatment worthy of it.

The largeness of nature or the nation were monstrous without a corresponding largeness and generosity of the spirit of the citizen. Not nature nor swarming states nor streets and steamships nor prosperous business nor farms nor capital nor learning may suffice for the ideal of man... nor suffice the poet. No reminiscences may suffice either. A live nation can always cut a deep mark and can have the best authority the cheapest... namely from its own soul. This is the sum of the profitable uses of individuals or states and of present action and grandeur and of the subjects of poets.— As if it were necessary to trot back generation after generation to the eastern records! As if the beauty and sacredness of the demonstrable must fall behind that of the mythical! As if men do not make their mark out of any times! As if the opening of the western continent by discovery and what has transpired since in North and South America were less than the small theatre of the antique or the aimless sleepwalking of the middle ages! The pride of the United States leaves the wealth and finesse of the cities and all returns of commerce and agriculture and all the magnitude of geography or shows of exterior victory to enjoy the breed of fullsized men or one fullsized man unconquerable and simple.

The American poets are to enclose old and new, for America is the race of races. Of them a bard is to be commensurate with a people. To him the other continents arrive as contributions... he gives them reception for their sake and his own sake. His spirit responds to his country's spirit... he incarnates its geography and natural life and rivers and lakes. Mississippi with annual freshets and changing chutes, Missouri and Columbia and Ohio and Saint Lawrence with the falls and beautiful masculine Hudson, do not embouchure where they spend themselves more than they embouchure into him. The blue breadth over the inland sea of Virginia and Maryland and the sea off Massachusetts and Maine and over Manhattan bay and over Champlain and Erie and over Ontario and Huron and Michigan and Superior, and over the Texan and Mexican and Floridian and Cuban seas and over the seas off California and Oregon, is not tallied by the blue breadth of the waters below more than the breadth of above and below is tallied by him. When the long Atlantic coast stretches longer and the Pacific coast stretches longer he easily stretches with them north or south. He spans between them also from east to west and reflects what is between them. On him rise solid growths that offset the growths of pine and cedar and hemlock and liveoak and locust and chestnut and cypress and hickory and limetree and cottonwood and tuliptree and cactus and wildvine and tamarind and persimmon... and tangles as tangled as any canebrake or swamp... and forests coated with transparent ice and icicles hanging from the boughs and crackling in the wind...and sides and peaks of mountains... and pasturage sweet and free as savannah or upland or prairie... with flights and songs and screams that answer those of the wildpigeon and highhold and orchard-oriole and coot and surf-duck and redshouldered-hawk and fish-hawk and white-ibis and indian-hen and cat-owl and water-pheasant and qua-bird and pied-sheldrake and blackbird and mockingbird and buzzard and condor and night-heron and eagle. To him the hereditary countenance descends both mother's and father's. To him enter the essences of the real things and past and present events—of the enormous diversity of temperature and agriculture and mines—the tribes of red aborigines—the weatherbeaten vessels entering new ports or making landings on rocky coast—the first settlements north or south—the rapid stature and muscle—the haughty defiance of '76, and the war and peace and formation of the constitution... the union always surrounded by blatherers and always calm and impregnable—the perpetual coming of immigrants—the wharf hem'd cities and superior marine—the unsurveyed interior—the loghouses and clearings and wild animals and hunters and trappers... the free commerce—the fisheries and whaling and gold-digging—the endless gestation of new states—the convening of Congress every December, the members duly coming up from all climates and the uttermost parts... the noble character of the young mechanics and of all free American workmen and workwomen... the general ardor and friendliness and enterprise—the perfect equality of the female with the male... the large amativeness—the fluid movement of the population—the factories and mercantile life and laborsaving machinery—the Yankee swap—the New-York firemen and the target excursion—the southern plantation life—the character of the northeast and of the northwest and southwest—slavery and the tremulous spreading of hands to protect it, and the stern opposition to it which shall never cease till it ceases or the speaking of tongues and the moving of lips cease. For such the expression of the American poet is to be transcendant and new. It is to be indirect and not direct or descriptive or epic. Its quality goes through these to much more. Let the age and wars of other nations be chanted and their eras and characters be illustrated and that finish the verse. Not so the great psalm of the republic. Here the theme is creative and has vista. Here comes one among the wellbeloved stonecutters and plans with decision and science and sees the solid and beautiful forms of the future where there are now no solid forms.

Of all nations the United States with veins full of poetical stuff most need poets and will doubtless have the greatest and use them the greatest. Their Presidents shall not be their common referee so much as their poets shall. Of all mankind the great poet is the equable man. Not in him but off from him things are grotesque or eccentric or fail of their sanity. Nothing out of its place is good and nothing in its place is bad. He bestows on every object or quality its fit proportions neither more nor less. He is the arbiter of the diverse and he is the key. He is the equalizer of his age and land... he supplies what wants supplying and checks what wants checking. If peace is the routine out of him speaks the spirit of peace, large, rich, thrifty, building vast and populous cities, encouraging agriculture and the arts and commerce— lighting the study of man, the soul, immortality—federal, state or municipal government, marriage, health, free trade, intertravel by land and sea... nothing too close, nothing too far off... the stars not too far off. In war he is the most deadly force of the war. Who recruits him recruits horse and foot... he fetches parks of artillery the best that engineer ever knew. If the time becomes slothful and heavy he knows how to arouse it... he can make every word he speaks draw blood. Whatever stagnates in the flat of custom or obedience or legislation he never stagnates[1]. Obedience does not master him, he masters it. High up out of reach he stands turning a concentrated light... he turns the pivot with his finger... he baffles the swiftest runners as he stands and easily overtakes and envelops them. The time straying toward infidelity and confections and persiflage he withholds by his steady faith... he spreads out his dishes  he offers the sweet firmfibred meat that grows men and women. His brain is the ultimate brain. He is no arguer... he is judgment. He judges not as the judge judges but as the sun falling around a helpless thing. As he sees the farthest he has the most faith. His thoughts are the hymns of the praise of things. In the talk on the soul and eternity and God off his equal plane he is silent. He sees eternity less like a play with a prologue and denouement... he sees eternity in men and women... he does not see men and women as dreams or dots. Faith is the antiseptic of the soul... it pervades the common people and preserves them... they never give up believing and expecting and trusting. There is that indescribable freshness and unconsciousness about an illiterate person that humbles and mocks the power of the noblest expressive genius. The poet sees for a certainty how one not a great artist may be just as sacred and perfect as the greatest

27

最散文
Zui Prose

artist... The power to destroy or remould is freely used by him but never the power of attack. What is past is past. If he does not expose superior models and prove himself by every step he takes he is not what is wanted. The presence of the greatest poet conquers... not parleying or struggling or any prepared attempts. Now he has passed that way see after him! There is not left any vestige of despair or misanthropy[2] or cunning or exclusiveness or the ignominy of a nativity or color or delusion of hell or the necessity of hell... and no man thence forward shall be degraded for ignorance or weakness or sin.

美国没有排斥过去，也没有排斥不同的历史时期、不同的政治条件所造就的一切以及等级观念和古老的宗教信仰……她平心静气地借鉴着过去的得失……她并不像人们想象的那样急不可耐，虽然各种观念、日常的礼仪和文学等仍积重难返，但现实的生活却已步入了一个崭新的历史阶段……她深知腐烂的躯体只能慢慢地从饭厅和卧室里抬走……还要在门口停留一会儿……这样才符合历史的要求……因为她的一言一行已传承到体格强健、威武英俊的年轻一代的身上……这样他们才能无愧于自己的时代。

同其他民族相比，美利坚民族大概是亘古以来最具诗意的民族了。从本质上来说，整个美利坚合众国就是一首气势恢宏的诗篇。纵观人类历史，这里的人们奏出的篇章无论就规模还是就影响力而言，都是无与伦比的。在这里，人们终于成了自己的主人，可以尽情地按照自己的意愿去生活。这里不只生活着一个民族，这里是多个民族融合在一起组成的大家庭。在这里，人们豁达大度、坦荡无私、以诚相见，高贵的气质令人油然而生敬意。在这里，热情好客是永恒的主题，英雄层出不穷……这里天高地广，人民粗犷奔放、质朴无华。在这里，人们以无比巨大的勇力、无所畏惧的闯劲辛勤劳作，获得了丰厚的回报；而对于琐碎无益的小事，他们不屑一顾。经年的收获，人们受之无愧。当田野里稻谷茁壮，果园内硕果累累，河湾中鱼儿肥硕，男人使女人怀上孩子的时候，人们再也不会生活在穷困潦倒之中。

别的国家都凭它们的行政长官为世人所识……但最能展现美利坚民族精神的却并非它的立法或行政机构，并非它的驻外使节、作家，或是大学、教堂和会所，甚至也不是它的报刊和发明家……而往往是普通的民众。他们谈吐自然，衣着不事修饰，珍视彼此之间的友谊。他们的脸上露出活力与率真……他们的马车别致而精巧……他们对自由有着至死不渝的追求……对粗劣鄙俗、软弱无能充满了憎恶……如果一个州的公民权得到承认，它在其他各州也能得到承认……他们敢怒敢言……对新鲜事物充满好奇与渴望……他们充满自尊，且富于同情……他们情感细腻……在上级面前始终保持不卑不亢的作风……他们口才雄辩……他们喜好音乐，男子汉的气度和与生俱来的优雅之风在他们身上体现得淋漓尽致……他们豁达开朗、出手大方……他们的竞选意义深远……他们的总统向他们（而非他们向总统）脱帽致意……这一切，构成了无韵的诗篇。它期待着人们用巨大的热情和宽阔的胸怀去阅读它，它也值得人们为此付出努力。

大自然和一个国家的广袤如果没有慷慨和宽大为怀的民族精神与之相适应，那将是不可想象的。无论是大自然，还是人口密集的各州、各条街道，或是那些汽船，还有繁荣的商业、农场、资本以及学问等都不足以概括人们心中的理想，更不必说诗人的理想。回忆也不足以做到这一点。一个富有生机的民族总是能让自己的民族精神得到最深刻的体现，它能以最简便易行的方式使这种精神发扬光大……那就是让它从每个人的内心深处流露出来。这种精神是每一个人，所有的州以及今天人们的一言一行所创造出的伟大的结晶，是诗人的感怀与吟诵之物——我们没有必要小心翼翼地回到过去，仿佛要一页一页地去重温东方的历史。那些确确实实存在的美丽与神圣必定胜过神话传说中的美景！人类的进步当然是建立在过去的基础之上。西半球的发现以及随后在南北美洲所发生的变化，其影响和重要性当然远胜一出小小的古代喜剧或中世纪漫无目的的梦游！美利坚的光荣和骄傲使得人们置城市的财富与机巧于不顾、撇开商业和农业所带来的巨大回报、疆域的辽阔或对外战争胜利的荣耀，转而去关注并欣赏身心健全的人们的成长，或一个身心健全、纯朴但不屈不挠的人的成长。

美国的诗人们将把过去和未来一同拥抱，因为美利坚民族是各民族融合的大家庭。对一个诗人来说，他与人民脉息相通。他把来自五大洲的移民视为对美洲大陆的贡献……对新来者的款待，既是为着他人，更是出于自身。他血脉中流淌的精神与民族精神一脉相承……他的身上承载着这个国家的地里面貌、自然生活，还有河流和湖泊。密西西比河年复一年的洪水、变幻莫测的激流，密苏里河、哥伦比亚河、俄亥俄河以及圣劳伦斯河上的瀑布，还有那雄浑壮阔的哈德逊河，这一切都显得那么大气磅礴，同时又仿佛沁入了他的心田。弗吉尼亚州和马里兰州广阔的内海、马萨诸塞州和缅因州的沿海、曼哈顿湾、尚普兰湖、伊利湖、安大略湖、休伦湖、密歇根湖以及苏必利尔湖，还有德克萨斯、墨西哥、佛罗里达州和古巴海以及加利福尼亚州与俄勒冈州附近海域接天映日、碧波荡漾，但还是难以企及诗人宽广的胸怀。任凭那大西洋和太平洋的海岸线尽情延伸，他都能够轻易地跨越南北迎头赶上。不仅如此，他还横贯东西，在广阔的空间畅想思索。他挺拔地生长，使得松树、雪松、铁杉、栎树、洋槐、栗树、柏树、山胡桃树、菩提树、棉白杨、鹅掌楸、仙人掌、野藤萝，还有那酸豆树、柿子树的成长显得微不足道……他枝繁叶茂，一如那藤蔓或沼泽……他宛若林中的树，树身上裹着晶莹剔透的冰，树枝上的冰凌在风中嘎嘎作响……他就像山岭与山脊……田园飘香，他的心在自由地驰骋，在那草原上放歌，在高地上飞翔，他的歌声和野鸽、啄木鸟、黄鹂、黑鸭、海凫、红翼鹰、渔鹰、白鹭、麻鸦、猫头鹰、水雉、夜鹭、麻鸭、乌鸫、嘲鸟、秃鹰、苍鹭和雄鹰的叫声遥相呼应。他的容貌来自父母双亲的嫡传。他的体内流动着历史与现实的交汇。他见证了昨天与今天的一切——各地差别迥异的气温、农业，还有矿藏——还有红种人的部落——历尽风雨的船只驶进新建的海港或在岩石密布的海岸登陆——还有大江南北开辟出的第一块殖民地——高大勇武、肌肉强健的人们——1776年的伟大独立，战争、和平，国家宪法的制定……始终被流言和诋毁所包围、却保持镇定自若、岿然不动的联邦政府——移民的不断涌入——沿海城市码头环绕、船只精良；内陆腹地犹如未开垦的处女地，那里有木屋，有旷野，有野兽，还有猎手……自由的商业——渔业、捕鲸业和淘金业——新兴各州不断从中脱胎而出。议会每年十二月召开，来自天南海北的代表届时济济一堂……无论是年轻的机械师，还是享有自由的男女劳工，全都气度不凡。人们对友谊、对事业充满热情；男女之间完全平等……爱欲强烈，人口自由流动，工商业兴起，机械的使用节省了大量的劳力——新英格兰人的交易、纽约的消防队员，还有打靶远足——南方的种植园生活，东北、西北、西南也有着各自的风貌——还有奴隶制，有人曾用颤抖的双手想要庇护它，但也有人对它发出声讨。这种声讨将永不停歇，除非最后奴隶制消亡了，不然，讨伐之声将永不停息。凡此种种足够这位美国诗人纵横驱使，挥洒出全新而超乎想象的篇章。那既不是史诗，也不是直接的描述，但却婉转而意味深长。诗文的内容悠远绵长。让以往的年代和其他民族的战争也载入这一篇章吧！让那些属于他们的时代和各式风流人物在他的笔下重生,以此为这首诗篇划上一个圆满的句号吧！他的诗句,不仅仅是对民众的赞美,也充满了创意,展望了未来。诚然,未来是无法预料的。但从倍受爱戴的石匠中走出的这一位诗人,却凭着毅力和科学的头脑,真真切切地洞见了美好的明天。

在所有的民族中,脉搏里流淌着诗意的美利坚民族最需要诗人,而且,也必将拥有最伟大的诗人,最大限度地发挥他们的才智。他们的诗人是社会道德风气的评判者,这一点甚至连他们的总统也相形见绌。在所有的人当中,伟大的诗人总是心平气和、公正无私。人们在他身上找不到任何荒诞不经、偏执古怪、精神失常的行为。他摒弃所有这一切。在他眼里,顺应其道者无一不善,逆道而行者一无是处。他仔细度量每一个物件或品质,给予适当的评价。他是各类纷争的仲裁者,是解决问题的关键所在。他是时代与国家的协调者、平衡者……他提供人们需要的一切,制止应当制止的行为。如果宁静和平代表了诗人一贯的气质,那么,在他身上体现出的正是这样一种精神。我们的诗人博大、雄浑,又不失简约。他主张建设巨大和人口稠密的城市,鼓励农业、艺术还有商业的发展——提倡人们探求知识、探索灵魂与永恒之道——主张成立联邦政府、州政府和各级地方政府,强调婚姻、健康、自由贸易,以及海陆远游的重要性……他相信没有什么是唾手可得的,也没有什么是遥不可及的……就连天上的星星也并非不可企及。如果开战,他将是战争中最致命的武器。一旦招募到了他,就等于招募到了步兵与马匹……他给大炮腾出炮位,身手之灵敏连机械工程师也为之侧目。如果时间变得慵懒而滞重,他知道如何将它唤醒……他的每一句话都一针见血。一旦出现民风怠惰、法规疏松,他便挺身而出正本清源。顺从不是他的本性,他骄傲而坚决。他高高在上,仿佛一盏明灯……他转动手指,俨然一个挺拔的支点。他和健步如飞的赛跑能手较量,轻而易举地超过他们,将他们笼罩在自己的身影之下。他坚定守真,绝不允许时间在背信弃义、懒洋洋和玩笑打闹中流逝。他捧出佳肴……为男男女女供上美味可口的肉品。他的大脑里藏着终极智慧。他不是一个辩手……而是一个判官。他不像普通的法官那样作出裁决,而是像太阳将光辉洒向无助的生灵那样去裁决。他能看到最远的地方,因而最具坚定的信念。他的思想是赞美万物的诗篇。当他看到人们对灵魂、永生以及上帝的谈论超出了自己的理解范畴,便会选择沉默。他眼中的永恒,并不像一出有头有尾的戏……他在男男女女的身上看到了永恒……他不仅仅将他们看做梦想或点缀。信念是灵魂的防腐剂……它渗透于每个公民,为他们的灵魂提供保护……令他们永不放弃信仰、期待与信任。正因为如此，即使是一个没有文化的粗人也能在不知不觉中，以难以形容的饱满精神将富于言辞的高贵才子嘲弄一番，而使他们自惭形秽。诗人清楚地知道，一个无名的艺术家如何能够做到与最伟大的艺术家一样完美而受人推崇……他娴熟地运用消灭与改造的力量，但绝不使用攻击的力量。过去的一切已成为历史。如果他未能展现出无上的风范，在前进的每一步上都证明他自己，那他也失去了他的价值。最伟大诗人的到来并非要压制和谈、斗争或任何有所准备的企图。如今，他走过的道路已经留在了他的身后！那里没有留下丝毫的失望，也没有对世事的憎恶，没有诡计，也没有孤傲；那里没有他生来的丑行，也没有粉饰，既没有地狱的可怖谵狂，也没有地狱的索命的脚步声……从此以后，再没有会因为无知、孱弱和罪孽而堕落。

---

[1] stagnate  v. 淤塞，沉滞；腐败；失去活力

[2] misanthropy  n. 不愿与人来往，厌世

# 孤独
# Solitude

【美国】亨利·大卫·梭罗

## 作者简介

亨利·大卫·梭罗(1817-1862),美国作家及自然主义者,超验主义哲学大师。其作品主张对不公正的政府进行非暴力抵抗运动,特别是对20世纪产生了广泛的影响。所著《瓦尔登湖》一书一直风行天下。他强调亲近自然、学习自然、热爱自然,追求"简单些,再简单些"的质朴生活,提倡短暂人生因思想丰盈而臻于完美。他投入数十载的时间对野生果实、野草及森林演替进行观察研究,写出了《种子的信念》一书。《孤独》一文是《瓦尔登湖》中最有代表性的一篇,阐明真正孤独的境界能使人精神丰富这一超验主义哲学理念。

This is a delicious evening, when the whole body is one sense, and imbibes delight through every pore. I go and come with a strange liberty in Nature, a part of herself. As I walk along the stony shore of the pond in my shirt—sleeves, though it is cool as well as cloudy and windy, and I see nothing special to attract me, all the elements are unusually congenial to me. The bullfrogs trump to usher in the night, and the note of the whip—poor—will is borne on the rippling wind from over the water. Sympathy with the fluttering alder and poplar leaves almost takes away my breath; yet, like the lake, my serenity is rippled but not ruffled. These small waves raised by the evening wind are as remote from storm as the smooth reflecting surface. Though it is now dark, the wind still blows and roars in the wood, the waves still dash, and some creatures lull the rest with their notes. The repose is never complete. The wildest animals do not repose, but seek their prey now; the fox, and skunk, and rabbit, now roam the fields and woods without fear. They are Nature's watchmen—links which connect the days of animated life.

When I return to my house I find that visitors have been there and left their cards, either a bunch of flowers, or a wreath of evergreen, or a name in pencil on a yellow walnut leaf or a chip. They who come rarely to the woods take some little piece of the forest into their hands to play with by the way, which they leave, either intentionally or accidentally. One has peeled a willow wand, woven it into a ring, and dropped it on my table. I could always tell if visitors had called in my absence, either by the bended twigs or grass, or the print of their shoes, and generally of what sex or age or quality they were by some slight trace left, as a flower dropped, or a bunch of grass plucked and thrown away, even as far off as the railroad, half a mile distant, or by the lingering odor of a cigar or pipe. Nay, I was frequently notified of the passage of a traveller along the highway sixty rods off by the scent of his pipe.

There is commonly sufficient space about us. Our horizon is never quite at our elbows. The thick wood is not just at our door, nor the pond, but somewhat is always clearing, familiar and worn by us, appropriated and fenced in some way, and reclaimed from Nature. For what reason have I this vast range and circuit, some square miles of unfrequented forest, for my privacy, abandoned to me by men? My nearest neighbor is a mile distant, and no house is visible from any place but the hill-tops within half a mile of my own. I have my horizon bounded by woods all to myself; a distant view of the railroad where it touches the pond on the one hand, and of the fence which skirts the woodland road on the other. But for the most part it is as solitary where I live as on the prairies. It is as much Asia or Africa as New England. I have, as it were, my own sun and moon and stars, and a little world all to myself. At night there was never a traveller passed my house, or knocked at my door, more than if I were the first or last man; unless it were in the spring, when at long intervals some came from the village to fish for pouts—they plainly fished much more in the Walden Pond of their own natures, and baited their hooks with darkness—but they soon retreated, usually with light baskets, and left "the world to darkness and to me," and the black kernel of the night was never profaned by any human neighborhood. I believe that men are generally still a little afraid of the dark, though the witches are all hung, and Christianity and candles have been introduced.

Yet I experienced sometimes that the most sweet and tender, the most innocent and encouraging society may be found in any natural object, even for the poor misanthrope and most melancholy man. There can be no very black melancholy to him who lives in the midst of Nature and has his senses still. There was never yet such a storm but it was Aeolian music to a healthy and innocent ear. Nothing can rightly compel a simple and brave man to a vulgar sadness. While I enjoy the friendship of the seasons I trust that nothing can make life a burden to me. The gentle rain which waters my beans and keeps me in the house today is not drear and melancholy, but good for me too. Though it prevents my hoeing them, it is of far more worth than my hoeing. If it should continue so long as to cause the seeds to rot in the ground and destroy the potatoes in the low lands, it would still be good for the grass on the uplands, and, being good for the grass, it would be good for me. Sometimes, when I compare myself with other men, it seems as if I were more favored by the gods than they, beyond any deserts that I am conscious of; as if I had a warrant and surety at their hands which my fellows have not, and were especially guided and guarded. I do not flatter myself, but if it be possible they flatter me. I have never felt lonesome, or in the least oppressed by a sense of solitude, but once, and that was a few weeks after I came to the woods, when, for an hour, I doubted if the near neighborhood of man was not essential to a serene and healthy life. To be alone was something unpleasant. But I was at the same time conscious of a slight insanity in my mood, and seemed to foresee my recovery. In the midst of a gentle rain while these thoughts prevailed, I was suddenly sensible of such sweet and beneficent society in Nature, in the very pattering of the drops, and in every sound and sight around my house, an infinite and unaccountable friendliness all at once like an atmosphere sustaining me, as made the fancied advantages of human neighborhood insignificant, and I have never thought of them since. Every little pine needle expanded and swelled with sympathy and befriended me. I was so distinctly made aware of the presence of something kindred to me, even in scenes which we are accustomed to call wild and dreary, and also that the nearest of blood to me and humanest was not a person nor a villager, that I thought no place could ever be strange to me again.

"Mourning untimely consumes the sad;

Few are their days in the land of the living,

Beautiful daughter of Toscar."

Some of my pleasantest hours were during the long rain-storms in the spring or fall, which confined me to the house for the afternoon as well as the forenoon, soothed by their ceaseless roar and pelting; when an early twilight ushered in a long evening in which many thoughts had time to take root and unfold themselves. In those driving northeast rains which tried the village houses so, when the maids stood ready with mop and pail in front entries to keep the deluge out, I sat behind my door in my little house, which was all entry, and thoroughly enjoyed its protection. In one heavy thunder–shower the lightning struck a large pitch pine across the pond, making a very conspicuous and perfectly regular spiral groove from top to bottom, an inch or more deep, and four or five inches wide, as you would groove a walking–stick. I passed it again the other day, and was struck with awe on looking up and beholding that mark, now more distinct than ever, where a terrific and resistless bolt came down out of the harmless sky eight years ago. Men frequently say to me, "I should think you would feel lonesome down there, and want to be nearer to folks, rainy and snowy days and nights especially." I am tempted to reply to such—This whole earth which we inhabit is but a point in space. How far apart, think you, dwell the two most distant inhabitants of yonder star, the breadth of whose disk cannot be appreciated by our instruments? Why should I feel lonely? Is not our planet in the Milky Way? This which you put seems to me not to be the most important question. What sort of space is that which separates a man from his fellows and makes him solitary? I have found that no exertion of the legs can bring two minds much nearer to one another. What do we want most to dwell near to? Not to many men surely, the depot[1], the post–office, the bar–room, the meeting–house, the school–house, the grocery, Beacon Hill, or the Five Points, where men most congregate, but to the perennial source of our life, whence in all our experience we have found that to issue, as the willow stands near the water and sends out its roots in that direction. This will vary with different natures, but this is the place where a wise man will dig his cellar.... I one evening overtook one of my townsmen, who has accumulated what is called "a handsome property"—though I never got a fair view of it— on the Walden road, driving a pair of cattle to market, who inquired of me how I could bring my mind to give up so many of the comforts of life. I answered that I was very sure I liked it passably well; I was not joking. And so I went home to my bed, and left him to pick his way through the darkness and the mud to Brighton—or Bright–town—which place he would reach some time in the morning.

Any prospect of awakening or coming to life to a dead man makes indifferent all times and places. The place where that may occur is always the same, and indescribably pleasant to all our senses. For the most part we allow only outlying and transient circumstances to make our occasions. They are, in fact, the cause of our distraction. Nearest to all things is that power which fashions their being. Next to us the grandest laws are continually being executed. Next to us is not the workman whom we have hired, with whom we love so well to talk, but the workman whose work we are.

"How vast and profound is the influence of the subtle powers of Heaven and of Earth!"[2]

"We seek to perceive them, and we do not see them; we seek to hear them, and we do not hear them; identified with the substance of things, they cannot be separated from them."

"They cause that in all the universe men purify and sanctify their hearts, and clothe themselves in their holiday garments to offer sacrifices and oblations to their ancestors. It is an ocean of subtle intelligences. They are everywhere, above us, on our left, on our right; they environ us on all sides."

We are the subjects of an experiment which is not a little interesting to me. Can we not do without the society of our gossips a little while under these circumstances—have our own thoughts to cheer us? Confucius says truly, "Virtue does not remain as an abandoned orphan; it must of necessity have neighbors."

With thinking we may be beside ourselves in a sane sense. By a conscious effort of the mind we can stand aloof from actions and their consequences; and all things, good and bad, go by us like a torrent. We are not wholly involved in Nature. I may be either the driftwood in the stream, or Indra in the sky looking down on it. I may be affected by a theatrical exhibition; on the other hand, I may not be affected by an actual event which appears to concern me much more. I only know myself as a human entity; the scene, so to speak, of thoughts and affections; and am sensible of a certain doubleness by which I can stand as remote from myself as from another. However intense my experience, I am conscious of the presence and criticism of a part of me, which, as it were, is not a part of me, but spectator, sharing no experience, but taking note of it, and that is no more I than it is you. When the play, it may be the tragedy, of life is over, the spectator goes his way. It was a kind of fiction, a work of the imagination only, so far as he was concerned. This doubleness may easily make us poor neighbors and friends sometimes.

I find it wholesome to be alone the greater part of the time. To be in company, even with the best, is soon wearisome and dissipating. I love to be alone. I never found the companion that was so companionable as solitude. We are for the most part more lonely when we go abroad among men than when we stay in our chambers. A man thinking or working is always alone, let him be where he will. Solitude is not measured by the miles of space that intervene between a man and his fellows. The really diligent student in one of the crowded hives of Cambridge College is as solitary as a dervish in the desert. The farmer can work alone in the field or the woods all day, hoeing or chopping, and not feel lonesome, because he is employed; but when he comes home at night he cannot sit down in a room alone, at the mercy of his thoughts, but must be where he can "see the folks," and recreate, and, as he thinks, remunerate himself for his day's solitude; and hence he wonders how the student can sit alone in the house all night and most of the day without ennui and "the blues"; but he does not realize that the student, though in the house, is still at work in his field, and chopping in his woods, as the farmer in his, and in turn seeks the same recreation and society that the latter does, though it may be a more condensed form of it.

Society is commonly too cheap. We meet at very short intervals, not having had time to acquire any new value for each other. We meet at meals three times a day, and give each other a new taste of that old musty cheese that we are. We have had to agree on a certain set of rules, called etiquette and politeness, to make this frequent meeting tolerable and that we need not

39

最散文
Zui Prose

come to open war. We meet at the post-office, and at the sociable, and about the fireside every night; we live thick and are in each other's way, and stumble over one another, and I think that we thus lose some respect for one another. Certainly less frequency would suffice for all important and hearty communications. Consider the girls in a factory—never alone, hardly in their dreams. It would be better if there were but one inhabitant to a square mile, as where I live. The value of a man is not in his skin, that we should touch him.

I have heard of a man lost in the woods and dying of famine and exhaustion at the foot of a tree, whose loneliness was relieved by the grotesque visions with which, owing to bodily weakness, his diseased imagination surrounded him, and which he believed to be real. So also, owing to bodily and mental health and strength, we may be continually cheered by a like but more normal and natural society, and come to know that we are never alone.

I have a great deal of company in my house; especially in the morning, when nobody calls. Let me suggest a few comparisons, that some one may convey an idea of my situation. I am no more lonely than the loon in the pond that laughs so loud, or than Walden Pond itself. What company has that lonely lake, I pray? And yet it has not the blue devils, but the blue angels in it, in the azure tint of its waters. The sun is alone, except in thick weather, when there sometimes appear to be two, but one is a mock sun. God is alone—but the devil, he is far from being alone; he sees a great deal of company; he is legion. I am no more lonely than a single mullein or dandelion in a pasture, or a bean leaf, or sorrel, or a horse-fly, or a bumblebee. I am no more lonely than the Mill Brook, or a weathercock, or the north star, or the south wind, or an April shower, or a January thaw, or the first spider in a new house.

I have occasional visits in the long winter evenings, when the snow falls fast and the wind howls in the wood, from an old settler and original proprietor, who is reported to have dug Walden Pond, and stoned it, and fringed it with pine woods; who tells me stories of old time and of new eternity; and between us we manage to pass a cheerful evening with social mirth and pleasant views of things, even without apples or cider—a most wise and humorous friend, whom I love much, who keeps himself more secret than ever did Goffe or Whalley; and though he is thought to be dead, none can show where he is buried. An elderly dame, too, dwells in my neighborhood, invisible to most persons, in whose odorous herb garden I love to stroll sometimes, gathering simples and listening to her fables; for she has a genius of unequalled fertility, and her memory runs back farther than mythology, and she can tell me the original of every fable, and on what fact every one is founded, for the incidents occurred when she was young. A ruddy and lusty old dame, who delights in all weathers and seasons, and is likely to outlive all her children yet.

The indescribable innocence and beneficence of Nature—of sun and wind and rain, of summer and winter—such health, such cheer, they afford forever! and such sympathy have they ever with our race, that all Nature would be affected, and the sun's brightness fade, and the winds would sigh humanely, and the clouds rain tears, and the woods shed their leaves and put on mourning in midsummer, if any man should ever for a just cause grieve. Shall I not have intelligence with the earth? Am I not partly leaves and vegetable mould myself?

What is the pill which will keep us well, serene, contented? Not my or thy great-grandfather's, but our great-grandmother Nature's universal, vegetable, botanic medicines, by which she has kept herself young always, outlived so many old Parrs in her day, and fed her health with their decaying fatness. For my panacea, instead of one of those quack vials of a mixture dipped from Acheron and the Dead Sea, which come out of those long shallow black-schooner looking wagons which we sometimes see made to carry bottles, let me have a draught of undiluted morning air. Morning air! If men will not drink of this at the fountainhead of the day, why, then, we must even bottle up some and sell it in the shops, for the benefit of those who have lost their subscription ticket to morning time in this world. But remember, it will not keep quite till noonday even in the coolest cellar, but drive out the stopples long ere that and follow westward the steps of Aurora. I am no worshipper of Hygeia, who was the daughter of that old herb-doctor Aesculapius, and who is represented on monuments holding a serpent in one hand, and in the other a cup out of which the serpent sometimes drinks; but rather of Hebe, cup-bearer to Jupiter, who was the daughter of Juno and wild lettuce, and who had the power of restoring gods and men to the vigor of youth. She was probably the only thoroughly sound-conditioned, healthy, and robust young lady that ever walked the globe, and wherever she came it was spring.

　　这是一个愉快的傍晚，全身只有一个感觉，每一个毛孔中都浸润着喜悦。我在大自然里以奇异的自由姿态来去，成了她自己的一部分。我只穿衬衫，沿着硬石的湖岸走，虽然天气寒冷，多云又多风，也没有特别分心的事，那时天气对我异常地合适。牛蛙鸣叫，邀来黑夜，夜鹰的乐音乘着吹起涟漪的风从湖上传来。摇曳的赤杨和白杨，激起我的情感使我几乎不能呼吸了；然而像湖水一样，我的宁静只有涟漪而没有激荡。和如镜的湖面一样，晚风吹起来的微波是谈不上什么风暴的。虽然天色黑了，风还在森林中吹着，咆哮着，波浪还在拍岸，一些动物还在用它们的乐音催眠着另外的那一些，宁静不可能是绝对的。最凶狠的野兽并没有安静，现在正找寻它们的牺牲品；狐狸，臭鼬，兔子，也正漫游在原野上、在森林中，它们却没有恐惧，它们是大自然的看守者，——是连接一个个生气勃勃的白昼的链环。

　　等我回到家里时，发现已有访客来过，他们还留下了名片呢，不是一束花，便是一个常春树的花环，或用铅笔写在黄色的胡桃叶或者木片上的一个名字。不常进入森林的人常把森林中的小玩意儿一路上拿在手里玩，有时故意，有时偶然，把它们留下了。有一位剥下了柳树皮，做成一个戒指，丢在我桌上。在我出门时有没有客人来过，我总能知道，不是树枝或青草弯倒，便是有了鞋印，一般来说，从他们留下的微小痕迹里我还可以猜出他们的年龄、性别和性格;有的掉下了花朵,有的抓来一把草,又扔掉,甚至还有一直带到半英里外的铁路边才扔下的呢;有时,雪茄烟或烟斗味道还残留不散。我常常还能从烟斗的香味中注意到六十杆之外公路上行经的一个旅行者。

我们周围的空间该说是很大的了。我们不能一探手就触及地平线。蓊郁的森林或湖沼并不就在我的门口,中间总还有着一块我们熟悉而且由我们使用的空地,多少整理过了,还围了点篱笆,它仿佛是从大自然的手里被夺取得来的。为了什么理由,我能私藏这么大范围和规模的,好多平方英里的没有人迹的,遭人类遗弃的森林呢? 离我最近的邻居在一英里外,看不到什么房子,除非登上那半里之外的小山山顶去瞭望,才能望见一点儿房屋。我的地平线全给森林包围起来,专供我自个儿享受,极目远望只能望见那在湖的一端经过的铁路和在湖的另一端沿着山林的公路边上的篱笆。大体说来,我居住的地方,寂寞得跟生活在大草原上一样。在这里离新英格兰也像离亚洲和非洲一样遥远。可以说,我有我自己的太阳、月亮和星星,我有一个完全属于我自己的小世界。从没有一个人在晚上经过我的屋子,或叩我的门,我仿佛是人类中的第一个人或最后一个人,除非在春天里,隔了很长一段时间,有人从村里来钓鳘鱼,——在瓦尔登湖中,很显然他们能钓到的只是他们自己的多种多样的性格,而钩子只能钩到黑夜而已——他们立刻都撤走了,常常是鱼篓很轻地撤退了,又把"世界留给黑夜和我",而黑夜的核心是从没有被任何人类的邻舍污染过的。我相信,虽然妖巫都给吊死了,基督教和蜡烛火也都已经介绍过来,可人们通常还都有点儿害怕黑暗。

然而我有时经历到,在任何大自然的事物中,都能找出最甜蜜温柔、最天真和鼓舞人的伴侣,即使是对于愤世嫉俗的可怜人和最最忧闷的人也一样。只要生活在大自然之间而且还有五官的话,便不可能有很阴郁的忧虑。对于健全而无邪的耳朵,暴风雨还真是伊奥勒斯的音乐呢。什么也不能正当地迫使单纯而勇敢的人产生庸俗的伤感。当我享受着四季的友爱时,我相信,任什么也不能使生活成为我沉重的负担。今天佳雨洒在我的豆子上,使我在屋里待了整天,这雨既不使我沮丧,也不使我抑郁,对于我可是好得很呢。虽然它使我不能够锄地,但比我锄地更有价值。如果雨下得太久,使地里的种子、低地的土豆烂掉,它对高地的草还是有好处的,既然它对高地的草很好,它对我也是很好的了。有时,我把自己和别人作比较,好像我比别人更得诸神的宠爱,比我应得的似乎还多呢;好像我有一张证书和保单在他们手上,别人都没有,因此我受到了特别的引导和保护。我并没有自称自赞,可是如果可能的话,倒是他们称赞了我。我从不觉得寂寞,也一点不受寂寞之感的压迫,只有一次,在我进了森林数星期后,我怀疑了一个小时,不知宁静和健康的生活是否应当有些近邻,独处似乎不很愉快。同时,我却觉得我的情绪有些失常了,但我似乎也预知我会恢复到正常的。当这些思想占据我的时候,温和的雨丝飘洒下来,我突然感觉到能跟大自然做伴是如此甜蜜、如此受惠,就在这滴答滴答的雨声中,我屋子周围的每一个声音和景象都有着无穷尽无边际的友爱,一下子这个支持我的气氛把我想象中的有邻居方便一点的思潮压下去了,从此之后,我就没有再想到过邻居这回事。每一支小小松针都富于同情心地胀大起来,成了我的朋友。我明显地感到这里存在着我的同类,虽然我是在一般所谓凄惨荒凉的处境中,然而那最接近于我的血统,并最富于人性的却并不是一个人或一个村民,从今后再也不会有什么地方会使我觉得陌生的了。

"不合宜的哀恸消蚀悲哀;

在生者的大地上,他们的日子很短,

托斯卡尔的美丽的女儿啊。"

我最愉快的若干时光在于春秋两季的长时间的暴风雨当中,这弄得我上午下午都被禁闭在室内,只有不停止的大雨和咆哮安慰着我;我从微明的早起就进入了漫长的黄昏,其间有许多思想扎下了根,并发展了它们自己。在那种来自东北的倾盆大雨中,村中那些房屋都受到了考验,女佣人都已经拎了水桶和拖把,在大门口阻止洪水侵入,我坐在我小屋子的门后,只有这一道门,却很欣赏它给予我的保护。在一次雷阵雨中,曾有一道闪电击中湖对岸的一株苍松,从上到下,划出一个一英寸,或者不止一英寸深,四五英寸宽,很明显的螺旋形的深槽,就好像你在一根手杖上刻的槽一样。那天我又经过了它,一抬头看到这一个痕迹,真是惊叹不已,那是八年以前,一个可怕的、不可抗拒的雷霆留下的痕迹,现在却比以前更为清晰。人们常常对我说,"我想你在那儿住着,一定很寂寞,总是想要跟人们接近一下的吧,特别在下雨下雪的日子和夜晚。"我喉咙痒痒的只想这样回答,——我们居住的整个地球,在宇宙之中不过是一个小点。那边一颗星星,我们的天文仪器还无法测量出它有多么大呢,你想想它上面的两个相距最远的居民又能有多远的距离呢?我怎会觉得寂寞?我们的地球难道不在银河之中?在我看来,你提出的似乎是最不重要的问题。怎样一种空间才能把人和人群隔开而使人感到寂寞呢?我已经发现了,无论两条腿怎样努力也不能使两颗心更为接近。我们最愿意和谁紧邻而居呢?人并不是都喜欢车站啊,邮局啊,酒吧间啊,会场啊,学校啊,杂货店啊,烽火山啊,五点区啊,虽然在那里人们常常相聚,人们倒是更愿意接近那生命的不竭之源泉的大自然,在我们的经验中,我们时常感到有这么个需要,好像水边的杨柳,一定向有水的方向伸展它的根。人的性格不同,所以需要也很不相同,可是一个聪明人必须在不竭之源泉的大自然那里挖掘他的地窖……有一个晚上在走向瓦尔登湖的路上,我赶上了一个市民同胞,他已经积蓄了所谓的"一笔很可观的产业",虽然我从没有好好地看到过它,那天晚上他赶着一对牛上市场去,他问我,我是怎么想的,宁肯抛弃这么多人生的乐趣? 我回答说,我确信我很喜欢我这样的生活;我不是开玩笑。就这样,我回家,上床睡了,让他在黑夜泥泞之中走路走到布赖顿去——或者说,走到光亮城里去——大概要到天亮的时候才能走到那里。

对一个死者说来,任何觉醒的或者复活的景象,都使一切时间与地点变得无足轻重。可能发生这种情形的地方都是一样的,对我们的感官是有不可言喻的欢乐的。可是我们大部分人只让外表上的很短暂的事情成为我们所从事的工作。事实上,这些是使我们分心的原因。最接近万物的乃是创造一切的一股力量。其次靠近我们的宇宙法则在不停地发生作用。再其次靠近我们的,不是被我们雇佣的、我们喜欢与其交谈的匠人,而是那个我们自己就是其所创造的作品的匠人。

"神鬼之为德,其盛矣乎。"

"视之而弗见,听之而弗闻,体物而不可遗。"

"使天下之人,斋明盛服,以承祭祀,洋洋乎如在其上,如在其左右。"

我们是一个实验的材料,但我对这个实验很感兴趣。在这样的情况下,难道我们不能够离开我们充满了是非的社会一会儿——只让我们自己的思想来鼓舞我们? 孔子说得好,"德不孤,必有邻。"

有了思想,我们可以在清醒的状态下,欢喜若狂。只要我们的心灵有意识地努力,我们就可以高高地超乎任何行为及其后果之上;一切好事坏事,就像奔流一样,从我们身边经过。我们并不是完全都给纠缠在大自然之内的。我可以是急流中的一片浮木,也可以是从空中望着尘寰的因陀罗。看戏很可能感动了我;而另一方面,和我生命更加攸关的事件却可能不感动我。我只知道我自己是作为一个人而存在的;可以说我是反映我思想感情的一个舞台面,我多少有着双重人格,因此我能够远远地看自己犹如看别人一样。不论我有如何强烈的经验,我总能意识到我的一部分在从旁批评我,好像它不是我的一部分,只是一个旁观者,并不分担我的经验,而是注意到它:正如他并不是你,他也不能是我。等到人生的戏演完,很可能是出悲剧,观众就自己走了。关于这第二重人格,这自然是虚构的,只是想象力的创造。但有时这双重人格很容易使别人难于和我们作邻居,交朋友了。

大部分时间内,我觉得寂寞是有益于健康的。有了伴儿,即使是最好的伴儿,不久也要厌倦,弄得很糟糕。我爱孤独。我没有碰到比寂寞更好的同伴了。到户外置身于人群之中多半比独处室内格外觉得寂寞。一个在思想着或在工作着的人总是单独的,让他爱在哪儿就在哪儿吧。寂寞不能以一个人离开他的同伴的里数来计算。真正勤学的学生,在剑桥学院最拥挤的蜂房内,寂寞得像沙漠上的一个托钵僧一样。农夫可以一整天,独个儿地在田地上,在森林中工作、耕地或砍伐,却不觉得寂寞,因为他有工作;可是到晚上,他回到家里,却不能独自在室内沉思,而必须到"看得见人"的地方去消遣一下,按照他的想法,是用以补偿他一天的寂寞;因此他很奇怪,为什么学生们能整日整夜坐在室内却不觉得无聊与"忧郁";可是他不明白虽然学生在室内,却在他的田地上工作,在他的森林中采伐,像农夫在田地或森林中一样,过后学生也要找消遣,也要社交,尽管那形式可能更加凝炼些。

社交往往廉价。相聚的时间之短促,来不及使彼此获得任何新的有价值的东西。我们在每日三餐的时间里相见,大家重新尝尝我们这种陈腐乳酪的味道。我们都必须同意若干条规则,那就是所谓的礼节和礼貌,使得这种经常的聚首能相安无事,避免公开争吵,以至面红耳赤。我们相会于邮局,于社交场所,每晚在炉火边;我们生活得太拥挤,互相干扰,彼此牵绊,因此我想,彼此已缺乏敬意了。当然,所有重要而热忱的聚会,次数少一点也够了。试想工厂中的女工,——永远不能独自生活,甚至做梦也难于孤独。如果一英里只住一个人,像我这儿,那要好得多。人的价值并不在他的皮肤上,所以我们不必要去碰皮肤。

我曾听说过,有人迷路在森林里,倒在一棵树下,饿得慌,又累得要命,由于体力不济,病态的想象力让他看到了周围有许多奇怪的幻象,他以为它们都是真的。同样,在身体和灵魂都很健康有力的时候,我们可以不断地从类似的,但更正常、更自然的社会得到鼓舞,从而发现我们是不寂寞的。

我在我的房屋中有许多伴侣;特别在早上还没有人来访问我的时候。让我来举几个比喻,或能传达出我的某些状况。我并不比湖中高声大笑的潜水鸟更孤独,我并不比瓦尔登湖更寂寞。我倒要问问这孤独的湖有谁作伴?然而在它的蔚蓝的水波上,却有着不是蓝色的魔鬼,而是蓝色的天使呢。太阳是寂寞的,除非乌云满天,有时候就好像有两个太阳,但那一个是假的。上帝是孤独的,——可是魔鬼就绝不孤独;他看到许多伙伴;他是要结成帮的。我并不比一朵毛蕊花或牧场上的一朵蒲公英寂寞,我不比一张豆叶,一枝酢酱草,或一只马蝇,或一只大黄蜂更孤独。我不比密尔溪,或一只风信鸡,或北极星,或南风更寂寞,我不比四月的雨或正月的溶雪,新屋中的第一只蜘蛛更孤独。

在冬天的长夜里,雪狂飘,风在森林中号叫的时候,一个老年的移民,原先的主人,不时来拜访我,据说瓦尔登湖还是他挖了出来,铺了石子,沿湖种了松树的;他告诉我旧时的和新近的永恒的故事;我们俩这样过了一个愉快的夜晚,充满了交际的喜悦,交换了对事物的惬意的意见,虽然没有苹果或苹果酒,——这个最聪明而幽默的朋友啊,我真喜欢他,他比谷菲或华莱知道更多的秘密;虽然人家说他已经死了,却没有人指出过他的坟墓在哪里。还有一个老太太,也住在我的附近,大部分人根本看不见她,我却有时候很高兴到她的芳香的百草园中去散步,采集药草,又倾听她的寓言;因为她有无比丰富的创造力,她的记忆一直追溯到神话以前的时代,她可以把每一个寓言的起源告诉我,哪一个寓言是根据了哪一个事实而来的,因为这些事都发生在她年轻的时候。一个红润的、精壮的老太太,不论什么天气什么季节她都兴致勃勃,看样子要比她的孩子活得还长久。

太阳,风雨,夏天,冬天,——大自然的不可描写的纯洁和恩惠,它们永远提供这么多的康健,这么多的欢乐!对我们人类这样地同情,如果有人为了正当的原因悲痛,那大自然也会受到感动,太阳黯淡了,风像活人一样悲叹,云端里落下泪雨,树木到仲夏脱下叶子,披上丧服。难道我不该与土地息息相通吗?我自己不也是一部分绿叶与青菜的泥土吗?

是什么药使我们健康、宁静、满足的呢?不是你我的曾祖父的,而是我们的大自然曾祖母的,全宇宙的蔬菜和植物的补品,她自己也靠它而永远年轻,活得比汤麦斯·派尔还更长久,用他们的衰败的脂肪更增添了她的康健。不是那种江湖医生配方的用冥河水和死海海水混合的药水,装在有时我们看到过装瓶子用的那种浅长形黑色船状车子上的药瓶子里,那不是我的万灵妙药;还是让我来喝一口纯净的黎明空气。黎明的空气啊!如果人们不愿意在每日之源喝这泉水,那么,啊,我们必须把它们装在瓶子内;放在店里,卖给世上那些失去黎明预订券的人们。可是记着,它能冷藏在地窖下,一直保持到正午,但要在那以前很久就打开瓶塞,跟随曙光的脚步西行。我并不崇拜那司健康之女神,她是爱斯库拉彼斯这古老的草药医师的女儿,在纪念碑上,她一手拿了一条蛇,另一只手拿了一个杯子,而蛇时常喝杯中的水;我宁可崇拜朱庇特的执杯者希勃,这青春的女神,为诸神司酒行觞,她是朱诺和野生莴苣的女儿,能使神仙和人返老还童。她也许是地球上出现过的最健康、最强壮、身体最好的少女,无论她到哪里,哪里便成了春天。

[1] depot n. 火车站;公共汽车站
[2] 此段和下两自然段出自《中庸》第十六章,为孔子所说。梭罗所引用的英译并非完全照原文的直译,而是溶入了些意译。

# 林湖重游
# Once More to the Lake

【美国】E. B. 怀特

## 作者简介

　　E·B·怀特(1899-1985),美国当代著名散文家、评论家,以散文名世,"其文风冷峻清丽,辛辣幽默,自成一格"。散文中,《林湖重游》最为世人称道。被誉为"二十世纪最伟大的美国随笔作家"。他一手奠定了影响深远的"《纽约客》文风"。除了终生挚爱的随笔之外,他还为孩子们写了三本书:《精灵鼠小弟》、《夏洛的网》与《吹小号的天鹅》,同样成为儿童与成人共同喜爱的文学经典。《林湖重游》把深彻的父子之情表现在平凡的林湖情景中,平中见奇的生命律动发人深省。

One summer, along about 1904, my father rented a camp on a lake in Maine and took us all there for the month of August. We all got ringworm from some kittens and had to rub Pond's Extract on our arms and legs night and morning, and my father rolled over in a canoe with all his clothes on; but outside of that the vacation was a success and from then on none of us ever thought there was any place in the world like that lake in Maine. We returned summer after summer—always on August 1st for one month. I have since become a salt-water man, but sometimes in summer there are days when the restlessness of the tides and the fearful cold of the sea water and the incessant wind which blows across the afternoon and into the evening make me wish for the placidity of a lake in the woods. A few weeks ago, this feeling got so strong I bought myself a couple of bass hooks and a spinner and returned to the lake where we used to go, for a week's fishing and to revisit old haunts.

I took along my son, who had never had any fresh water up his nose and who had seen lily pads only from train windows. On the journey over to the lake I began to wonder what it would be like. I wondered how time would have marred this unique, this holy spot—the coves and streams, the hills that the sun set behind, the camps and the paths behind the camps. I was sure that the tarred road would have found it out and I wondered in what other ways it would be desolated. It is strange how much you can remember about places like that once you allow your mind to return into the grooves which lead back. You remember one thing, and that suddenly reminds you of another thing. I guess I remembered clearest of all the early mornings, when the lake was cool and motionless, remembered how the bedroom smelled of the lumber it was made of and of the wet woods whose scent entered through the screen. The partitions in the camp were thin and did not extend clear to the top of the rooms, and as I was always the first up I would dress softly so as not to wake the others, and sneak out into the sweet outdoors and start out in the canoe, keeping close along the shore in the long shadows of the pines. I remembered being very careful never to rub my paddle against the gunwale for fear of disturbing the stillness of the cathedral.

The lake had never been what you would call a wild lake. There were cottages sprinkled around the shores, and it was in farming although the shores of the lake were quite heavily wooded. Some of the cottages were owned by nearby farmers, and you would live at the shore and eat your meals at the farmhouse. That's what our family did. But although it wasn't wild, it was a fairly large and undisturbed lake and there were places in it which, to a child at least, seemed infinitely remote and primeval.

I was right about the tar: it led to within half a mile of the shore. But when I got back there, with my boy, and we settled into a camp near a farmhouse and into the kind of summertime I had known, I could tell that it was going to be pretty much the same as it had been before—I knew it, lying in bed the first morning, smelling the bedroom, and hearing the boy sneak quietly out and go off along the shore in a boat. I began to sustain the illusion that he was I, and therefore, by simple transposition, that I was my father. This sensation persisted, kept cropping up all the time we were there. It was not an entirely new feeling, but in this setting it grew much stronger. I seemed to be living a dual existence. I would be in the middle of some simple act, I would be picking up a bait box or laying down a table fork, or I would be saying something, and suddenly it would be not I but my father who was saying the words or making the gesture. It gave me a creepy sensation.

We went fishing the first morning. I felt the same damp moss covering the worms in the bait can, and saw the dragonfly alight on the tip of my rod as it hovered a few inches from the surface of the water. It was the arrival of this fly that convinced me beyond any doubt that everything was as it always had been, that the years were a mirage and there had been no years. The small waves were the same, chucking the rowboat under the chin as we fished at anchor, and the boat was the same boat, the same color green and the ribs broken in the same places, and under the floor-boards the same freshwater leavings and debris—the dead helgramite, the wisps of moss, the rusty discarded fishhook, the dried blood from yesterday's catch. We stared silently at the tips of our rods, at the dragonflies that came and wells. I lowered the tip of mine into the water, tentatively, pensively dislodging the fly, which darted two feet away, poised, darted two feet back, and came to rest again a little farther up the rod. There had been no years between the ducking of this dragonfly and the other one—the one that was part of memory. I looked at the boy, who was silently watching his fly, and it was my hands that held his rod, my eyes watching. I felt dizzy and didn't know which rod I was at the end of.

We caught two bass, hauling them in briskly as though they were mackerel, pulling them over the side of the boat in a businesslike manner without any landing net, and stunning them with a blow on the back of the head. When we got back for a swim before lunch, the lake was exactly where we had left it, the same number of inches from the dock, and there was only the merest suggestion of a breeze. This seemed an utterly enchanted sea, this lake you could leave to its own devices for a few hours and come back to, and find that it had not stirred, this constant and trustworthy body of water. In the shallows, the dark, water-soaked sticks and twigs, smooth and old, were undulating in clusters on the bottom against the clean ribbed sand, and the track of the mussel was plain. A school of minnows[1] swam by, each minnow with its small, individual shadow, doubling the attendance, so clear and sharp in the sunlight. Some of the other campers were in swimming, along the shore, one of them with a cake of soap, and the water felt thin and clear and insubstantial. Over the years there had been this person with the cake of soap, this cultist[2], and here he was. There had been no years.

Up to the farmhouse to dinner through the teeming, dusty field, the road under our sneakers was only a two-track road. The middle track was missing, the one with the marks of the hooves and the splotches of dried, flaky manure. There had always been three tracks to choose from in choosing which track to walk in; now the choice was narrowed down to two. For a moment I missed terribly the middle alternative. But the way led past the tennis court, and something about the way it lay there in the sun reassured me; the tape had loosened along the backline, the alleys were green with plantains and other weeds, and the net (installed in June and removed in September) sagged in the dry noon, and the whole place steamed with midday heat and hunger and emptiness. There was a choice of pie for dessert, and one was blueberry and one was apple, and the waitresses were the same country girls, there having been no passage of time, only the illusion of it as in a dropped curtain—the waitresses were still fifteen; their hair had been washed, that was the only difference—they had been to the movies and seen the pretty girls with the clean hair.

Summertime, oh summertime, pattern of life indelible, the fade proof lake, the woods unshatterable, the pasture with the sweet fern and the juniper forever and ever, summer without end; this was the background, and the life along the shore was the design, the cottages with their innocent and tranquil design, their tiny docks with the flagpole and the American flag floating against the white clouds in the blue sky, the little paths over the roots of the trees leading from camp to camp and the paths leading back to the outhouses and the can of lime for sprinkling, and at the souvenir counters at the store the miniature birch-bark canoes and the post cards that showed things looking a little better than they looked. This was the American family at play, escaping the city heat, wondering whether the newcomers at the camp at the head of the cove were "common" or "nice," wondering whether it was true that the people who drove up for Sunday dinner at the farmhouse were turned away because there wasn't enough chicken.

It seemed to me, as I kept remembering all this, that those times and those summers had been infinitely precious and worth saving. There had been jollity and peace and goodness. The arriving (at the beginning of August) had been so big a business in itself, at the railway station the farm wagon drawn up, the first smell of the pine-laden air, the first glimpse of the smiling farmer, and the great importance of the trunks and your father's enormous authority in such matters, and the feel of the wagon under you for the long ten-mile haul, and at the top of the last long hill catching the first view of the lake after eleven months of not seeing this cherished body of water. The shouts and cries of the other campers when they saw you, and the trunks to be unpacked, to give up their rich burden. (Arriving was less exciting nowadays, when you sneaked up in your car and parked it under a tree near the camp and took out the bags and in five minutes it was all over, no fuss, no loud wonderful fuss about trunks.)

Peace and goodness and jollity. The only thing that was wrong now, really, was the sound of the place, an unfamiliar nervous sound of the outboard motors. This was the note that jarred, the one thing that would sometimes break the illusion and set the years moving. In those other summertimes, all motors were inboard; and when they were at a little distance, the noise they made was a sedative, an ingredient of summer sleep. They were one-cylinder and two-cylinder engines, and some were make-and-break and some were jump-spark, but they all made a sleepy sound across the lake. The one-lungers throbbed and fluttered, and the twin-cylinder ones purred and purred, and that was a quiet sound too. But now the campers all had outboards. In the daytime, in the hot mornings, these motors made a petulant[3], irritable sound; at night, in the still evening when the afterglow lit the water, they whined about one's ears like mosquitoes. My boy loved our rented outboard, and his great desire was to achieve single-handed mastery over it, and authority, and he soon learned the trick of choking it a little (but not too much), and the adjustment of the needle valve. Watching him I would remember the things you could do with the old one-cylinder engine with the heavy flywheel, how you could have it eating out of your hand if you got really close to it spiritually. Motor boats in those days didn't have clutches, and you would make a landing by shutting off the motor at the proper time and coasting in with a dead rudder. But there was a way of reversing them, if you learned the trick, by cutting the switch and putting it on again exactly on the final dying revolution of the flywheel, so that it would kick back against compression and begin reversing. Approaching a dock in a strong following breeze, it was difficult to slow up sufficiently by the ordinary coasting method, and if a boy felt he had complete mastery over his motor, he was tempted to keep it running beyond its time and then reverse it a few feet from the dock. It took a cool nerve, because if you threw the switch a twentieth of a second too soon you would catch the flywheel when it still had speed enough to go up past center, and the boat would leap ahead, charging bull-fashion at the dock.

We had a good week at the camp. The bass were biting well and the sun shone endlessly, day after day. We would be tired at night and lie down in the accumulated heat of the little bedrooms after the long hot day and the breeze would stir almost imperceptibly outside and the smell of the swamp drift in through the rusty screens. Sleep would come easily and in the morning the red squirrel would be on the roof, tapping out his gay routine. I kept remembering everything, lying in bed in the mornings—the small steamboat that had a long rounded stern like the lip of a Ubangi, and how quietly she ran on the moonlight sails, when the older boys played their mandolins and the girls sang and we ate doughnuts dipped in sugar, and how sweet the music was on the water in the shining night, and what it had felt like to think about girls then. After breakfast we would go up to the store and the things were in the same place—the minnows in a bottle, the plugs and spinners disarranged and pawed over by the youngsters from the boys' camp, the fig newtons and the Beeman's gum. Outside, the road was tarred and cars stood in front of the store. Inside, all was just as it had always been, except there was more Coca Cola and not so much Moxie and root beer and birch beer and sarsaparilla[4]. We would walk out with a bottle of pop apiece and sometimes the pop would backfire up our noses and hurt. We explored the streams, quietly, where the turtles slid off the sunny logs and dug their way into the soft bottom; and we lay on the town wharf and fed worms to the tame bass. Everywhere we went I had trouble making out which was I, the one walking at my side, the one walking in my pants.

One afternoon while we were there at that lake a thunderstorm came up. It was like the revival of an old melodrama that I had seen long ago with childish awe. The second-act climax of the drama of the electrical disturbance over a lake in America had not changed in any important respect. This was the big scene, still the big scene. The whole thing was so familiar, the first feeling of oppression and heat and a general air around camp of not wanting to go very far away. In mid-afternoon (it was all the same) a curious darkening of the sky, and a lull in everything that had made life tick; and then the way the boats suddenly swung the other way at their moorings with the coming of a breeze out of the new quarter, and the premonitory rumble. Then the kettle drum, then the snare, then the bass drum and cymbals, then crackling light against the dark, and the gods grinning and licking their chops in the hills. Afterward the calm, the rain steadily rustling in the calm lake, the return of light and hope and spirits, and the campers running out in joy and relief to go swimming in the rain, their bright cries perpetuating the deathless joke about how they were getting simply drenched, and the children screaming with delight at the new sensation of bathing in the rain, and the joke about getting drenched linking the generations in a strong indestructible chain. And the comedian who waded in carrying an umbrella.

When the others went swimming my son said he was going in too. He pulled his dripping trunks from the line where they had hung all through the shower, and wrung them out. Languidly, and with no thought of going in, I watched him, his hard little body, skinny and bare, saw him wince slightly as he pulled up around his vitals the small, soggy[5], icy garment. As he buckled the swollen belt suddenly my groin felt the chill of death.

大概是在一九〇四年的夏天,父亲在缅因州的某湖上租了一间露营小屋,带了我们去消磨整个八月。我们从一批小猫那儿染上了金钱癣，不得不在臂腿间日日夜夜涂上旁氏浸膏，父亲则和衣睡在小划子里；但是除了这些，假期过得很愉快。自此之后，我们中无人不认为世上再没有比缅因州这个湖更好的去处了。一年年夏季我们都回到这里来——总是从八月一日起，逗留一个月时光。这样一来，我竟成了个水手了。夏季里有时候湖里也会兴风作浪，湖水冰凉，阵阵寒风从下午刮到黄昏，使我宁愿在林间能另有一处宁静的小湖。就在几星期前，这种渴望越来越强烈，我便去买了一对钓鲈鱼的鱼钩，一只能旋转的盛鱼饵器，启程回到我们经常去的那个湖上，预备在那儿垂钓一个星期，再去看看那些梦魂萦绕的老地方。

我把儿子带了去，他从来没有让水没过鼻梁，他也只有从列车的车窗里，才看到过莲花池。在去湖边的路上，我不禁想象这次旅行将是怎样的一次。我缅想时光的流逝会如何毁损这个独特的神圣的地方——险阻的海角和潺潺的小溪，在落日掩映中的群山，露营小屋和小屋后面的小路。我缅想那条容易辨认的沥青路，我又缅想那些已显荒凉的其他景色。一旦让你的思绪回到旧时的轨迹时，简直太奇特了，你居然可以记忆起这么多的去处。你记起这件事，瞬间又记起了另一件事。我想我对于那些清晨的记忆是最清楚的，彼时湖上清凉，水波不兴，记起木屋的卧室里可以嗅到圆木的香味，这些味道发自小屋的木材，和从纱门透进来的树林的潮味混为一气。木屋里的间隔板很薄，也不是一直伸到顶上的，由于我总是第一个起身，便轻轻穿戴以免惊醒了别人。然后偷偷溜出小屋去到清爽的气氛中，驾起一只小划子，沿着湖岸上一长列松林的荫影里航行。我记得自己十分小心不让划桨在船舷上碰撞，惟恐打搅了湖上大教堂的宁静。

这处湖水从来不是什么渺无人迹的地方。湖岸上处处点缀着零星小屋，这里是一片耕地，而湖岸四周树林密布。有些小屋为邻近的农人所有，你可以住在湖边而到农家去就餐，那就是我们家的办法。虽然湖面很宽广，但湖水平静。没有什么风涛，而且，至少对一个孩子来说，有些去处看来是无穷遥远和原始的。

我谈到沥青路是对的，就离湖岸不到半英里。但是当我和我的孩子回到这里，住进一间离农舍不远的小屋，就进入我所稔熟的夏季了，我还能说它与旧日了无差异——我知道，次日一早躺在床上，一股卧室的气味，还听到孩子悄悄地溜出小屋，沿着湖岸去找一条小船。我开始幻觉到他就是小时候的我，而且，由于换了位置，我也就成了我的父亲。这一感觉久久不散，在我们留居湖边的时候，不断显现出来。这并不是全新的感情，但是在这种场景里越来越强烈。我好似生活在两个并存的世界里。在一些简单的行动中,在我拿起鱼饵盒子或是放下一只餐叉,或者在我谈到另外的事情时,突然发现这不是我自己在说话,而是我的父亲在说话或是摆弄他的手势。这给我一种悚然的感觉。

次日早晨我们去钓鱼。我感到鱼饵盒子里的蚯蚓同样披着一层苔藓,看到蜻蜓落在我的钓竿上,在水面几英寸处飞翔,蜻蜓的到来使我毫无疑问地相信一切事物都如昨日一般,流逝的年月不过是海市蜃楼,一无岁月的间隔。水上的涟漪如旧,在我们停船垂钓时,水波拍击着我们的船舷有如窃窃私语,而这只船也就像是昔日的划子,一如过去那样漆着绿色,折断的船骨还在旧处,舱底更有陈年的水迹和碎屑——死掉的翅虫蛹,几片苔藓,锈了的废鱼钩和昨日捞鱼时的干血迹。我们沉默地注视着钓竿的尖端;那里蜻蜓飞来飞去。我把钓竿伸向水中,短暂而又悄悄地避过蜻蜓,蜻蜓已飞出二英尺开外,平衡了一下又栖息在钓竿的梢端。今日戏水的蜻蜓与昨日的并无年限的区别——不过两者之一仅是回忆而已。我看看我的儿子,他正默默地注视着蜻蜓,而这就如我的手替他拿着钓竿,我的眼睛在注视一样。我不禁目眩起来,不知道哪一根是我握着的钓竿。

我们钓到了两尾鲈鱼,轻快地提了起来,好像钓的是鲭鱼,把鱼从船边提出水面完全像是理所当然的事,而不用什么抄网,接着就在鱼头后部打上一拳。午餐前当我们再回到这里来游泳时,湖面正是我们离去时的老地方,连码头的距离都未改分厘,不过这时却已刮起一阵微风。这地方看来完全是使人入迷的海湖。这个湖你可以离开几个钟点,听凭湖里风云多变,而再次回来时,仍能见到它平静如故,这正是湖水的经常可靠之处。在水浅的地方,如水浸透的黑色枝枝桠桠,陈旧又光滑,在清晰起伏的沙底上成丛摇晃,而蛤贝的爬行踪迹也历历可见。一群小鱼游了过去,游鱼的影子分外瞩目,在阳光下是那样清晰和明显。另外还有来宿营的人在游泳,沿着湖岸,其中一个拿着一块肥皂,水便显得模糊和非现实的了。多少年来总有这样的人拿着一块肥皂,这个有洁癖的人,现在就在眼前。年份的界限也跟着模糊了。

上岸后到农家去吃饭,穿过丰饶的满是尘土的田野,在我们橡胶鞋脚下踩着的只是条两股车辙的道路,原来中间那一股不见了,本来这里布满了牛马的蹄印和薄薄一层干透了的粪土。那里过去是三股道,任你选择步行的;如今这个选择已经减缩到只剩两股了。有一刹那我深深怀念这可供选择的中间道。小路引我们走过网球场,蜿蜒在阳光下再次给我信心。球网的长绳放松着,小道上长满了各种绿色植物和野草,球网(从六月挂上到九月才取下)这时在干燥的午间松弛下

最 散文
Zui Prose

垂,日中的大地热气蒸腾,既饥渴又空荡。农家进餐时有两道点心可供选择,一是紫黑浆果做的馅饼,另一种是苹果馅饼;女侍还是过去的普通农家女,那里没有时间的间隔,只给人一种幕布落下的幻象——女侍依旧是十五岁,只是秀发刚洗过,这是惟一的不同之处——她们一定看过电影,见过一头秀发的漂亮女郎。

夏天,啊夏天,生命的印痕难以磨灭,那永远不会失去光泽的湖,那不能摧毁的树林,牧场上永远永远散发着香蕨木和红松的芬芳,夏天是没有终了的;这只是背景,而湖岸上的生活才真是一幅图画,带着单纯恬静的农舍,小小的停船处,旗杆上的美国国旗衬着飘浮着白云的蓝天在拂动,沿着树根的小路从一处小屋通向另一处,小路还通向室外厕所,放着那铺洒用的石灰,而在小店出售纪念品的一角里,陈列着仿制的桦树皮独木舟和与实景相比稍有失真的明信片。这是美国家庭在游乐,逃避城市里的闷热,琢磨琢磨住在小湖湾那头的新来者是"一般人"呢还是"有教养的"人,寻思寻思星期日开车来农家的客人会不会因为小鸡不够供应而吃了闭门羹。

对我说来,因为我不断回忆往昔的一切,那些时光那些夏日是无穷宝贵而永远值得怀念的。这里有欢乐、恬静和美满。到达(在八月的开始)本身就是件大事情,农家的大篷车一直驶到火车站,第一次闻到空气中松树的清香,第一眼看到农人的笑脸,还有那些重要的大箱子和你父亲对这一切的指手划脚,然后是你座下的大车在十里路上的颠簸不停,在最后一重山顶上看到湖面的第一眼,魂牵梦绕的这汪湖水,已经有十一个月没有见面了。其中宿营人看见你去时的欢呼和喧哗,还有那为了放掉富足的重负而待打开的箱子。(今天抵达已经较少兴奋了。你一声不响地把汽车停在树下近小屋的地方,下车取了几个行李袋,只要五分钟一切就都收拾停当,一点没有骚动,没有搬大箱子时的高声叫唤了。)

恬静、美满和愉快。这儿现在惟一不同于往日的,是这地方的声音,真的,就是那不平常的使人心神不宁的舱外推进器的声音。这种刺耳的声音,有时候会粉碎我的幻想而使年华飞逝。在那些旧时的夏季里,所有马达是装在舱里的,当船在远处航行时,发出的喧嚣是一种镇静剂,一种催人入睡的含混不清的声音。这是些单汽缸或双汽缸的发动机,有的用通断开关,有的是电花跳跃式的。但是都产生一种在湖上回荡的催眠声调。单汽缸噗噗震动,双汽缸则咕咕噜噜,这些也都是平静而单调的声响。但是现在宿营人用的都是舱外推进器了。在白天,在闷热的早上,这些马达发出急躁刺耳的声音。夜间,在静静的黄昏里,落日余晖照亮了湖面,这声音在耳边像蚊子那样哀诉。我的孩子钟爱我们租来使用舱外推进器的小艇,他最大的愿望是独自操纵,成为小艇的权威,他要不了多久就学会稍稍关闭一下开关(但并不关得太紧),然后调整针阀的诀窍。注视着他使我记起在那种单汽缸而有沉重飞轮的马达上可以做的事情,如果你能摸熟它的脾性,你就可以应付自如。那时的马达船没有离合器,你登岸就得在恰当的时候关闭马达,熄了火用方向舵滑行到岸边。但也有一种方法可以使机器开倒车,如果你学到这个诀窍,先关一下开关然后再在飞轮停止转动前,再开一下,这样船就会承受压力而倒退过来。在风力强时要接近码头,若用普通靠岸的方法使船慢下来就很困难了,如果孩子认为他已经完全主宰马达,他应该使马达继续发动下去,然后退后几英尺,靠上码头。这需要镇定和沉着的操作,因为哪怕你只提前了二十分之一秒就把开关打开了,你就必须在飞轮以足够快的速度升越中线时抓紧它,船就会猛然向前一跃,像公牛一样冲向码头。

我们过了整整一星期的露营生活,鲈鱼上钩,阳光照耀大地,永无止境,日复一日。晚上我们疲倦了,就躺在为炎热所蒸晒了一天而显得闷热的湫隘卧室里,小屋外微风吹拂使人嗅到从生锈了的纱门透进的一股潮湿味道。睡意总是很快来临,每天早晨红松鼠一定在小屋顶上嬉戏,招到伴侣。清晨躺在床上——那个汽船像非洲乌班基人嘴唇那样有着圆圆的船尾,她在月夜里又是怎样平静航行,当青年们弹着曼陀铃姑娘们跟着唱歌时,我们则吃着撒着糖沫的多福饼,而在这到处发亮的水上夜晚乐声传来又多么甜蜜,使人想起姑娘时又是什么样的感觉。早饭过后,我们到商店去,一切陈设如旧——瓶里装着鲦鱼,塞了和钓鱼的旋转器混在牛顿牌无花果和皮姆牌口香糖中间,被宿营的孩子们移动得杂乱无章。店外大路已铺上沥青,汽车就停在商店门前。店里,与往常一样,不过可口可乐更多了,而莫克西水、药草根水、桦树水和菝葜水不多了,有时汽水会冲了我们一鼻子,而使我们难受。我们在山间小溪探索,悄悄地,在那儿乌龟在太阳曝晒的圆木间爬行,一直钻到松散的土地下,我们则躺在小镇的码头上,用虫子喂食游乐自如的鲈鱼。随便在什么地方,都分辨不清当家做主的我,和与我形影不离的那个人。

有天下午我们在湖上。雷电来临了,又重演了一出为我儿时所畏惧的闹剧。这出戏第二幕的高潮,在美国湖上的电闪雷鸣下所有重要的细节一无改变,这是个宏伟的场景,至今还是幅宏伟的场景。一切都显得那么熟稔,首先感到透不过气来,接着是闷热,小屋四周的大气好像凝滞了。过了下午的傍晚之前(一切都是一模一样),天际垂下古怪的黑色,一切都凝住不动,生命好像夹在一卷布里,接着从另一处来了一阵风,那些停泊的船突然向湖外漂去,还有那作为警告的隆隆声。之后铜鼓响了，接着是小鼓，然后是低音鼓和铙钹，再以后乌云里露出一道闪光，霹雳跟着响了，诸神在山间咧嘴而笑，舔着他们的腮帮子。之后是一片安静，雨滴打在平静的湖面上沙沙做响。光明、希望和精神头儿又回来了。宿营人欢笑着轻快地跑出小屋，冒着雨去游泳。他们明快的喊叫声把关于他们怎样被雨淋透的无尽笑语定格为永恒。孩子们在雨中淋浴，这种新鲜的感觉使他们愉快地尖叫着。大家说着那把几代人像用一条强韧得坚不可摧的锁链连接起来的关于遭受雨淋的笑话。有位滑稽惹笑的家伙竟撑着把伞趟水而来。

当其他人去游泳时，我的儿子也说要去。他把水淋淋的游泳裤从绳子上拿下来，这条裤子在雷雨时就一直在外面淋着，孩子把水拧干了。我无精打采一点也没有要去游泳的心情，只注视着他，他的硬朗的小身子，瘦骨嶙峋，看到他皱皱眉头，穿上那条又小又潮湿、冰凉的裤子，当他扣上泡涨了的腰带时，我的下腹突然打起死一样的寒颤来。

[1] minnow  n. 鲤科小鱼
[2] cultist  n. 狂热地迷恋于某物或某种理念的人
[3] petulant  adj. 暴躁的，难以取悦的，易生气的
[4] sarsaparilla  n. 撒尔沙植物；沙士汽水(一种碳酸饮料)
[5] soggy  adj. 潮湿的；沉闷的；有湿气的

# 巨人树
# The Giant Redwood Trees

【美国】约翰·斯坦贝克

## 作者简介

约翰·斯坦贝克(1902-1968)美国作家。斯坦贝克一生写了17部小说,许多短篇故事、电影和电视剧本,以及非小说作品。由于他"通过现实主义的、富于想象的创作,表现出富于同情的幽默和对社会敏感的观察",1962年获得诺贝尔文学奖。《巨人树》选自游记《偕查理旅行》(1962),以巨人树这宏大的生命赞叹大自然的永恒。

There's a cathedral hush here. Perhaps the thick soft bark absorbs sound and creates a silence. The trees rise straight up to zenith; there is no horizon. The dawn comes early and remains dawn until the sun is high. Then the green fernlike foliage so far up strains the sunlight to a green gold and distributes it in shafts or rather in stripes of light and shade. After the sun passes zenith it is afternoon and quickly evening with a whispering dusk as long as was the morning.

Thus time and the ordinary divisions of the day are changed. To me dawn and dusk are quiet times, and here in the redwoods nearly the whole of daylight is a quiet time. Birds move in the dim light or flash like sparks through the stripes of sun, but they make little sound. Underfoot is a mattress of needles deposited for over two thousand years. No sound of footsteps can be heard on this thick blanket. To me there's a remote and cloistered feeling here. One holds back speech for fear of disturbing something ... what? From my earliest childhood I've felt that something was going on in the groves, something of which I was not a part. And if I had forgotten the feeling, I soon got it back.

At night, the darkness is black ... only straight up a patch of gray and an occasional star. And there's a breathing in the black, for these huge things that control the day and inhabit the night are living things and have presence, and perhaps feeling, and, somewhere in deep-down perception, perhaps communication. I have had lifelong association with these things. (Odd that the word "trees" does not apply). I can accept them and their power and their age because I was early exposed to them. On the other hand, people lacking such experience begin to have a feeling of uneasiness here, of danger, of being shut in, enclosed and overwhelmed. It is not only the size of these redwoods but their strangeness that frightens them. And why not? For these are the last remaining members of a race that flourished over four continents as far back in geologic time as the upper Jurassic period. Fossils of these ancients have been found dating from the Cretaceous era while in the Eocene and Miocene they were spread over

England and Europe and America. And then the glaciers moved down and wiped the Titans out beyond recovery. And only these few are left ... a stunning memory of what the world was like once long ago. Can it be that we do not love to be reminded that we are very young and callow[1] in a world that was old when we came into it? And could there be a strong resistance to the certainty that a living world will continue its stately way when we no longer inhabit it?

　　这儿只有一种大教堂式的肃穆。也许是那厚厚的软树皮吸收了声音才造成这寂静的吧！巨人树耸立着，直到天顶，看不到地平线。黎明来得很早，直到太阳升得老高，辽远天空中的羊齿植物般的绿叶才把阳光过滤成金绿色，分作一道道、一片片的光和影。太阳刚过天顶，便是下午了，紧接着黄昏也到了。黄昏带来一片寂静的阴影，跟上午一样，很漫长。

　　这样时间变了，平时的早晚划分也变了。我一向认为黎明和黄昏是安静的。在这儿，在这座水杉林里，整天都很安静。鸟儿在朦胧的光影中飞动，在片片阳光里穿梭，像点点火花，却很少喧哗。脚下是一片积聚了两千多年的针叶铺成的垫子。在这厚实的绒毯上听不见脚步声。我在这儿有一种远离尘世的隐居感。在这儿人们都凝神屏气不敢说话，深怕惊扰了什么——怕惊扰了什么呢？我从孩提时代起，就觉得树林里有某种东西在活动——某种我所不理解的东西。这种似乎淡忘了的感觉又立即回到我的心里。

　　夜黑得很深沉，头顶上只有一小块灰白和偶然的一颗星星。黑暗里有一种呼吸，因为这些控制了白天、占有了黑夜的巨灵是活的，是存在的，有感觉的，在它们深处的知觉里或许能够彼此交感！我和这类东西(奇怪，我总无法把它们叫作树)来往了大半辈子了。我从小就赤裸裸地接触它们。我能懂得它们——它们的强力和古老。但没有经验的人类到这儿来却感到不安。他们怕危险，怕被关闭、封锁起来。怕抵抗不了那过分强大的力。他们害怕，不但因为巨衫的巨大，而且因为它的奇特。怎能不害怕呢？这些树是早侏罗纪的一个品种的最后的子遗，那是在遥远的地质年代里,那时巨衫曾蓬勃繁衍在四个大陆之上,人们发现过白垩纪初期的这种古代植物的化石。它们在第三纪始新纪和第三纪中新纪曾覆盖了整个英格兰、欧洲和美洲。可是冰河来了,巨人树无可挽回地灭绝了,只有这一片树林幸存下来。这是个令人目眩神骇的纪念品,纪念着地球洪荒时代的形象。在踏进森林里去时,巨人树是否提醒了我们:人类在这个古老的世界上还是乳臭未干、十分稚嫩的,这才使我们不安了吗? 毫无疑问,我们死去后,这个活着的世界还要庄严地活下去,在这样的必然性面前,谁还能作出什么有力的抵抗呢?

[1] callow adj. 年轻而无经验的、未生羽毛的

# 远处的青山
# A Green Hill Far Away

【英国】约翰·高尔斯华绥

作者简介

约翰·高尔斯华绥(1867–1933)是英国小说家、剧作家。其作品以十九世纪后期和二十世纪初期的英国社会为背景,描写了英国资产阶级的社会和家庭生活,以及盛极而衰的历史。他的作品语言简练,形象生动,讽刺辛辣,为20世纪英国现实主义小说三杰之一。1932年,高尔斯华绥"因其描述的卓越艺术——这种艺术在《福尔赛世家》中达到高峰"而获得诺贝尔文学奖。《远处的青山》写于一战后,它赋予自然景物以浓情,尽情歌颂和平,诅咒战争。

Was it indeed only last March, or in another life, that I climbed this green hill on that day of dolour, the Sunday after the last great German offensive began? A beautiful sun-warmed day it was, when the wild thyme on the southern slope smelled sweet, and the distant sea was a glitter of gold. Lying on the grass, pressing my cheek to its warmth, I tried to get solace for that new dread which seemed so cruelly unnatural after four years of war-misery.

"If only it were all over!" I said to myself; "and I could come here, and to all the lovely places I know, without this awful contraction of the heart, and this knowledge that at every tick of my watch some human body is being mangled or destroyed. Ah, if only I could! Will there never be an end?"

And now there is an end, and I am up on this green hill once more, in December sunlight, with the distant sea a glitter of gold. And there is no cramp in my heart, no miasma[1] clinging to my senses. Peace! It is still incredible. No more to hear with the ears of the nerves the ceaseless roll of gunfire, or see with the eyes of the nerves drowning men, gaping wounds, and death. Peace, actually Peace! The war has gone on so long that many of us have forgotten the sense of outrage and amazement we had, those first days of August, 1914, when it all began. But I have not forgotten, nor ever shall.

In some of us—I think in many who could not voice it—the war has left chiefly this feeling: "If only I could find a country where men cared less for all that they seem to care for, where they cared more for beauty, for nature, for being kindly to each other. If only I could find that green hill far away!" Of the songs of Theocritus, of the life of St. Francis, there is no more among the nations than there is of dew on grass in an east wind. If we ever thought otherwise, we are disillusioned now. Yet there is Peace again, and the souls of men fresh-murdered are not flying into our lungs with every breath we draw.

Each day this thought of Peace becomes more real and blessed. I can lie on this green hill and praise Creation that I am alive in a world of beauty. I can go to sleep up here with the coverlet of sunlight warm on my body, and not wake to that old dull misery. I can even dream with a light heart, for my fair dreams will not be spoiled by waking, and my bad dreams will be cured the moment I open my eyes. I can look up at that blue sky without seeing trailed across it a mirage of the long horror, a film picture of all the things that have been done by men to men. At last I can gaze up at it, limpid and blue, without a dogging melancholy; and I can gaze down at that far gleam of sea, knowing that there is no murk of murder on it any more.

And the flight of birds, the gulls and rooks and little brown wavering things which flit out and along the edge of the chalk-pits, is once more refreshment to me, utterly untempered. A merle is singing in a bramble thicket; the dew has not yet dried off the bramble leaves. A feather of a moon floats across the sky; the distance sends forth homely murmurs; the sun warms my cheeks. And all of this is pure joy. No hawk of dread and horror keeps swooping down and bearing off the little birds of happiness. No accusing conscience starts forth and beckons me away from pleasure. Everywhere is supreme and flawless beauty. Whether one looks at this tiny snail shell, marvellously chased and marked, a very elf's horn whose open mouth is coloured rose; or gazes down at the flat land between here and the sea, wandering under the smile of the afternoon sunlight, seeming almost to be alive, hedgeless, with its many watching trees, and silver gulls hovering above the mushroom-coloured "ploughs" and fields green in manifold hues; whether one muses on this little pink daisy born so out of time, or watches that valley of brown-rose-grey woods, under the drifting shadows of low-hanging chalky clouds—all is perfect, as only Nature can be perfect on a lovely day, when the mind of him who looks on her is at rest.

On this green hill I am nearer than I have been yet to realisation of the difference between war and peace. In our civilian lives hardly anything has been changed—we do not get more butter or more petrol, the garb and machinery of war still shroud us, journals still drip hate; but in our spirits there is all the difference between gradual dying and gradual recovery from sickness.

At the beginning of the war a certain artist, so one heard, shut himself away in his house and garden, taking in no newspaper, receiving no visitors, listening to no breath of the war, seeing no sight of it. So he lived, buried in his work and his flowers—I know not for how long. Was he wise, or did he suffer even more than the rest of us who shut nothing away? Can man, indeed, shut out the very quality of his firmament, or bar himself away from the general misery of his species?

This gradual recovery of the world—this slow reopening of the great flower, Life—is beautiful to feel and see. I press my hand flat and hard down on those blades of grass, then take it away, and watch them very slowly raise themselves and shake off the bruise. So it is, and will be, with us for a long time to come. The cramp of war was deep in us, as an iron frost in the earth. Of all the countless millions who have fought and nursed and written and spoken and dug and sewn and worked in a thousand other ways to help on the business of killing, hardly any have laboured in real love of war. Ironical, indeed, that perhaps the most beautiful poem written these four years, Julian Grenfell's[2] "Into Battle!" was in heartfelt praise of fighting! But if one could gather the deep curses breathed by man and woman upon war since the first bugle was blown, the dirge of them could not be contained in the air which wraps this earth.

And yet the 'green hill', where dwell beauty and kindliness, is still far away. Will it ever be nearer? Men have fought even on this green hill where I am lying. By the rampart[3] markings on its chalk and grass, it has surely served for an encampment. The beauty of day and night, the lark's song, the sweet-scented growing things, the rapture of health, and of pure air, the majesty of the stars, and the gladness of sunlight, of song and dance and simple friendliness, have never been enough for men. We crave our turbulent fate. Can wars, then, ever cease? Look in men's faces, read their writings, and beneath masks and hypocrisies note the restless creeping of the tiger spirit! There has never been anything to prevent the millennium except the nature of the human being. There are not enough lovers of beauty among men. It all comes back to that. Not enough who want the green hill far away—who naturally hate disharmony, and the greed, ugliness, restlessness, cruelty, which are its parents and its children.

Will there ever be more lovers of beauty in proportion to those who are indifferent to beauty? Who shall answer that question? Yet on the answer depends peace. Men may have a mint of sterling qualities—be vigorous, adventurous, brave, upright, and self-sacrificing; be preachers and teachers; keen, cool-headed, just, industrious—if they have not the love of beauty, they will still be making wars. Man is a fighting animal, with sense of the ridiculous enough to know that he is a fool to fight, but not sense of the sublime enough to stop him. Ah, well! We have peace!

It is happiness greater than I have known for four years and four months, to lie here and let that thought go on its wings, quiet and free as the wind stealing soft from the sea, and blessed as the sunlight on this green hill.

不仅仅是在这刚刚过去的三月里,但已恍如隔世,在一个充满着痛苦的日子——德国发动它最后一次总攻的那个星期天,我还登上过那座青山吗？正是那个阳光美好的天气,南坡上的野茴香浓郁扑鼻,远处的海面一片金黄。我俯身草上,暖着面颊,一边因为那新的恐怖而寻找安慰,这进攻发生在连续四年的战祸之后,益发显得酷烈出奇。

"但愿这一切快结束吧!"我自言自语道,"那时我就又能到这里来,到一切我熟悉的可爱的地方来,而不至这么神伤揪心,不至随着我的表针的每下滴答,就有一批生灵惨遭涂炭。啊,但愿我又能——难道这事便永无完结了吗?"

现在总算有了完结,于是我又一次登上这座青山,头顶上沐浴着十月的阳光,远处的海面一片金黄。这时心头不再感到痉挛,身上也不再有毒氛侵袭。和平了,仍然有些难以相信。不过再不用过度紧张地去倾听那永无休止的隆隆炮声,或去观看那些倒毙的人们、张裂的伤口与死亡。和平了,真的和平了!战争继续了这么长久,我们不少人似乎已经忘记了一九一四年八月战争全面爆发之初的那种盛怒与惊愕之感。但是我却没有,而且永远不会。

在我们的一些人中——我以为实际在相当多的人中,只不过他们表达不出罢了——这场战争主要给他们留下了这种感觉:"但愿我能找到这样一个国家,那里人们所关心的不再是我们一向所关心的那些,而是美丽,是自然,是彼此仁爱相待。但愿我能找到那座远处的青山!"关于忒俄克里托斯的诗篇,关于圣弗兰西斯的高风,在当今的各个国家里,正如东风里草上的露珠那样,早已渺不可见。即或过去我们的想法不同,现在我们的幻想也破灭。不过和平终归已经到来,那些新近屠杀掉的人们的幽魂总不至再随着我们呼吸而充塞在我们胸臆。

和平之感在我们的思想上正一天天变得愈益真实和愈益与幸福相连。此刻我已能在这座青山之上为自己还能活在这样一个美好的世界而赞美造物主。我能在这温暖阳光的覆盖之下安然睡去,而不会醒后又是过去那种恹恹欲绝。我甚至能心情欢快地去做梦,不至醒后好梦打破,而且即使做了噩梦,睁开眼睛后也就一切消失。我可以抬头仰望那碧蓝的晴空而不会突然瞥见那里拖曳着一长串狰狞可怖的幻象,或者人对人所干出的种种伤天害理的惨景。我终于能够一动不动地凝视着晴空,那么澄澈与蔚蓝,而不会时刻受着悲愁的拘牵;或者俯视那光艳的远海,而不至担心波面上再会浮起屠杀的血污。

天空中各种禽鸟的飞翔,海鸥、白嘴鸭以及那些往来徘徊于白垩坑边的棕色小东西对我都是欣慰,它们是那样自由自在,不受拘束。一只画眉正鸣啭在黑莓丛中,那里叶间还晨露未干。轻如蝉翼的新月依然隐浮在天际;远处不时传来熟悉的声籁;而阳光正暖着我的脸颊。这一切是多么愉快。这里见不到凶猛可怕的苍鹰飞扑而下,把那快乐的小鸟攫去。这里不再有歉疚不安的良心把我从这逸乐之中唤走。到处都是无限欢欣,完美无瑕。这时张目四望,不管你看看眼前的蜗牛甲壳,雕镂刻画得那般精致,恍如童话里小精灵头上的细角,而且角端作薇薇色;还是俯瞰从此处至海上的一带平芜,它浮游于午后阳光的微笑之下,几乎活了起来,这里没有树篱,一片空旷,但有许多炯炯有神的树木,还有那银白的海鸥,翱翔在色如蘑菇的耕地或青葱翠绿的田野之间;不管你凝视的是这株小小的粉红雏菊,慨叹它的生不逢时,还是注目那棕红灰褐的满谷林木,上面乳白的流云低低悬垂,暗影浮动——一切都是那么美好,这是只有大自然在一个风和日丽的天气,而且那观赏大自然的人的心情也分外悠闲的时候,才能见到的。

在这座青山之上,我对战争与和平的区别也认识得比往常更加透彻。在我们的一般生活中,一切几乎没有发生多大改变——我们并没有领得更多的奶油或更多的汽油,战争的外衣与装备笼罩着我们,报刊杂志上还充溢着敌意和仇恨;但是精神情绪上我们确已感到了巨大差别,那久病之后逐渐死去还是逐渐恢复的巨大差别。

据说,此次战争爆发之初,曾有一位艺术家闭门不出,把自己关在家中和花园里面,不订报纸,不会宾客,耳不闻杀伐之声,目不睹战争之形,每日惟以作画赏花自娱——只不知他这样继续了多久。难道他这样做便是聪明,还是他所感到的痛苦比那些不知躲避的人更加厉害?难道一个人连自己头顶上的苍穹也能躲得开吗?连自己同类的普遍灾难也能无动于衷吗?

整个世界的逐渐恢复——生命这株伟大花朵的慢慢重放——在人的感觉与

印象上的确是再美不过的事了。我把手掌狠狠地压在草叶上,然后把手拿开,再看看那草叶慢慢直了过来,脱去它的损伤。我们自己的情形也正是如此。战争的创伤已深深侵入我们身心,正如严霜侵入土地那样。在为了杀人流血这桩事情而在战斗、护理、宣传、文字、工事,以及计数不清的各个方面而竭力努力的人们当中,很少人是出于对战争的真正的热忱才去做的。但是,说来奇怪,这四年来写的一篇最优美的诗歌亦即朱利安·格伦菲尔的《投入战斗!》竟是纵情讴歌战争之作! 但是如果我们能把自那第一声战斗号角之后一切男女对战争所发出的深切诅咒全都聚集起来,那些哀歌之多恐怕连笼罩地面的高空也盛装不下。

然而那美与仁爱所在的"青山"离我们还很遥远。什么时候它会更近些? 人们甚至在我所偃卧的这座青山也打过仗。根据在这里白垩与草地上的工事的痕迹,这里还曾住宿过士兵。白昼与夜晚的美好、云雀的欢歌、花香与芳草、健康的愉悦、空气的澄鲜、星辰的庄严,阳光的和煦,还有那轻歌与曼舞、淳朴的友情,这一切都是人们渴求不餍的。但是我们却偏偏要去追逐那浊流一般的命运。所以战争能永远停止吗? 好好看看人们的一张张面孔,读一读他们写下的文章,注意一下潜藏在面具和伪善下面那骚动不安、悄悄爬行着的恶虎精神吧! 从来不会有什么能阻止太平盛世的存在,唯有人的本性能阻止。人类中热爱美的人数量不够。一切都归到这一点。没有足够多的人要那远处的青山。没有足够多的人出自于秉性去憎恶不和谐,去痛恨那些产生了不和谐并由不和谐所产生的,贪婪的、丑陋的、不安的、残忍的行径。

对应于那些对美漠视的人,会有更多的热爱美的人吗? 谁会回答这个问题呢? 可和平与否恰恰取决于这个答案。人可能会具备很多优秀的素质——精力充沛、勇于冒险、英勇无畏、正直诚实、自我牺牲;口若悬河足以布道、侃侃而谈可为人师;热切、冷静、公正、勤奋。可人如果没有对美的挚爱,他们就依旧在制造着战争。人是种喜好打仗的动物,倒能感知得到何谓荒唐可笑之事,这足以使他知晓自己是个去打仗的傻瓜,可他却不能感知到足以阻止他去打仗的崇高卓越之事。啊,好吧,我们现在拥有和平!

这是四年零四个月以来我再没有领略过的快乐,现在我躺在草上,听任思想自由飞翔,那安祥如海面上轻轻袭来的和风,那幸福如这座青山上的晴光。

---

[1] miasma  n. 毒气,沼气
[2] Julian Grenfell  n. 英国第一次欧战期间著名诗人。初对战争讴歌,后又充满绝望。对战争有着十足的矛盾心理和糊涂认识。
[3] rampart  n. 垒, 城墙、壁垒; 防御物

# 第二卷

思海拾趣
Interesting Thoughts

# 访绸商
# A Visit to a Silk-Merchant

【英国】奥利佛·葛斯密

### 作者简介

奥利佛·葛斯密(1730-1774),是盎格鲁爱尔兰的诗人、作家与医生,以小说《威克菲德的牧师》,诗歌《废弃的农村》(1770)及剧本《好人》(1768)和《屈身求爱》(1773)闻名。同时他还创作了经典的童话故事《两只小好鞋的故事史》。《访绸商》以让人稍微觉得不好受的方式道出了商人之奸猾与圆通。

The shops of London are as well furnished as those of Peking. Those of London have a picture hung at their door, informing the passengers what they have to sell, as those at Peking have a board to assure the buyer that they have no intention to cheat him.

I was this morning to buy silk for a nightcap: immediately upon entering the mercer's shop, the master and his two men, with wigs plastered with powder, appeared to ask my commands. They were certainly the civilest people alive; if I but looked, they flew to the place where I cast my eye; every motion of mine sent them running round the whole shop for my satisfaction. I informed them that I wanted what was good, and they showed me not less than forty pieces, and each was better than the former the prettiest pattern in nature, and the fittest in the world for nightcaps. "My very good friend," said I to the mercer. "You must not pretend to instruct me in silks; I know these in particular to be no better than your mere flimsy[1] Bungees"—"That may be," cried the mercer, who, I afterwards found, had never contradicted a man in his life; "I cannot pretend to say but they may; but I can assure you, my Lady Trail has had a sack from this piece this very morning." – "But, friend," said I, "though my lady has chosen a sack from it, I see no necessity that I should choose a sack from it, I see no necessity that I should wear it for a nightcap." "That may be," returned he again, "Yet what becomes a pretty lady, will at any time look well on a handsome gentleman." This short compliment was thrown in so very seasonably upon my ugly face, that even though I disliked the silk, I desired him to cut me off the pattern of a nightcap.

While this business was consigned to his journeymen, the master himself took down some pieces of silk still finer than any I had yet seen, and spreading them before me. "There," cries he, "there's beauty; my Lord Snakeskin has bespoke the fellow to this for the birth night this very morning; it would look charmingly in waistcoats."—"But I don't want a waistcoat." replied I. "Not want a waistcoat!" returned the mercer, "then I would advise you to buy one; when waistcoats are wanted, you may depend upon it they will come dear. Always buy before you want and you are sure to be well used, as they say in Cheapside." There was so much justice in his advice, that I could not refuse taking it; besides, the silk, which was really a good one, increased the temptation; so I gave orders for that too.

As I was waiting to have my bargains measured and cut, which, I know not how, they executed but slowly, during the interval the mercer entertained me with the modern manner of some of the nobility receiving company in their morning gowns; "Perhaps, Sir," adds he, "you have a mind to see what kind of silk is universally worn." Without waiting for my reply, he spreads a piece before me, which might be reckoned beautiful even in China. "If the nobility," continues he, "were to know I sold this to any under a Right Honourable, I should certainly lose their custom; you see, my lord, it is at once rich, tasty, and quite the thing."— "I am no lord," interrupted I.—"I beg pardon." cried he, "but be pleased to remember, when you intend buying a morning gown, that you had an offer from me of something worth money. Conscience, sir, conscience is my way of dealing; you may buy a morning gown now, or you may stay till they become dearer and less fashionable; but it is not my business to advise." In short, most reverend Fum, he persuaded me to buy a morning gown also, and would probably have persuaded me to buy a morning gown also, and would probably have persuaded me to have bought half the goods in his shop, if I had stayed long enough, or was furnished with sufficient money.

Upon returning home, I could not help reflecting, with some astonishment, how this very man, with such a confined education and capacity, was yet capable of turning me as he thought proper, and moulding me to his inclinations! I know he was only answering his own purpose, even while he attempted to appear solicitous about mine; yet, by a voluntary infatuation, a sort of passion, compounded of vanity and good-nature, I walked into the snare with my open eyes open, and put myself to future pain in order to give him immediate pleasure. The wisdom of the ignorant somewhat resembles the instinct of animals; it is diffused in but a very narrow sphere, but within that circle it acts with vigor, uniformity and success.

伦敦的店铺与北京的一样,布局非常优雅。北京的铺子常常挂着牌匾,以示
童叟无欺;而在伦敦,店门口常挂一幅图像,告知顾客所售之物。

今天上午我去买做睡帽的丝绸。一踏进店门,头戴敷粉假发的店主和两个
伙计赶忙迎上来,询问我的需求。他们一定是世界上最文明最礼貌的人了;只要
我稍看一眼,他们便飞奔到目光所落之处;我的一举一动让他们在店里团团转,去
探寻我想要之物。我说我要上等料子,他们马上拿来不下四十种。每一种都比前
一种要好,都是天底下最漂亮的图案,世界上最适合做睡帽的材料。"我说朋友,"
我对店主说,"不必向我兜售您的丝绸知识了,这些明明连你那些不结实的本吉丝
都不如。"——"这倒有可能,"店主叫道,据我后来所知,这个人一生都没顶过谁,
"我也不能硬说这不可能;但我可以告诉您,就今天上午,翠莱夫人还买了一袋这
种料子。""但是朋友,"我说,"翠莱夫人买了不见得我就非得买它来做睡帽吧?"
"那倒是,但一位夫人穿起来漂亮的东西,在一位英俊的先生身上也总会不错的
吧!"这简短的恭维适时地向我不雅的面孔扑来,尽管不喜欢那丝绸,我还是让他
为我剪下睡帽所需的料子。

把这活儿交给伙计之后,店主拿出比刚才所看的都要好的一匹丝绸,在我面
前展开来。"瞧,多漂亮;今早斯耐克斯金爵爷刚为自己的生日晚会预定了这种材
料。这做件背心可太妙了。""但我不需要背心。"我答到。"不需要? 那我可要劝您
买一件了;等到人人都想要背心时,价格保证就涨上去了。套用吉普赛那地方的
一句话,不要等到用到了再去买。"他的话听起来蛮有道理的,我都不好意思拒
绝。而且那丝绸也的确不错,这也增加了不少诱惑。于是我就订了一块。

我等着他们为我裁量丝绸,但不知为何,他们的动作总是慢腾腾的。就在这
工夫,店主又与我谈起如今一些贵族喜爱穿睡袍见客的风尚。"或许,先生,您也想
看看现在人们都在穿的绸缎。"不等我回答,他早已把面料摊在我面前。这料子就
是在中国也算得上考究的。"如果贵族们知道我把这料子卖给身份不符的人,"他
继续道,"我会失去这些老主顾的。爵爷,您瞧,这料子真是非常华丽非常有品味,
货真价实呀!"——"我不是什么爵爷,"我打断他的话。"真不好意思,"他喊道,"但
如果您打算做一件睡袍的话,一定要记得我这里的货物可是物有所值的。良心
啊,先生,良心就是我的生意经。您可以现在买一件睡袍,也可以等它贵了再来

买，这都由您，我也不能劝您。"总之，敬爱的福沫先生，他说得我又买了一件睡衣的料子。如果我再呆下去或者口袋里的钱再多一些，他可能会让我把半个店都买下来。

回家之后，我不禁思索起来，吃惊地发现，一个缺乏教育、能力有限的人居然使我任由他摆布，玩弄于股掌。我知道，即使他对我百般殷勤，也只是想满足自己的私欲；然而，由于自己的糊涂，由于虚荣与善良渗杂的性情，我眼睁睁地走进他们的圈套，用我未来之痛博得他们一时之乐。无知者的智慧有点像动物的本能；它只存在于狭小的领域，但是只要在那个范围之内，它又猛又准，所向披靡。

[1] flimsy  adj. 易坏的；浅薄的；脆弱的

# 鬼屋
# A Haunted House

【英国】弗吉尼亚·伍尔芙

### 作者简介

　　弗吉尼亚·伍尔芙(1882—1941)，英国著名女作家，在小说创作和文学评论方面都有卓越的贡献。世界三大意识流作家之一，女权主义运动的先驱人物。深受弗洛伊德心理学、女性主义及同性恋运动影响。主要著作有：风格独特的长篇"意识流小说"《达洛威夫人》《到灯塔去》《奥兰多》《自己的房间》和《海浪》等。《鬼屋》是篇意识流散文，情感在过去和现在间交替展现，让人的思绪萦回起伏。

Whatever hour you woke there was a door shutting. From room to room they went, hand in hand, lifting here, opening there, making sure—a ghostly couple.

"Here we left it," she said. And he added, "Oh, but here too!" "It's upstairs," she murmured. "And in the garden," he whispered. "Quietly," they said, "or we shall wake them."

But it wasn't that you woke us. Oh, no. "They're looking for it; they're drawing the curtain," one might say, and so read on a page or two. "Now they've found it, one would be certain, stopping the pencil on the margin. And then, tired of reading, one might rise and see for oneself, the house all empty, the doors standing open, only the wood pigeons bubbling with content and the hum of the threshing machine sounding from the farm." "What did I come in here for? What did I want to find?" My hands were empty. "Perhaps it's upstairs then?" The apples were in the loft. And so down again, the garden still as ever, only the book had slipped into the grass.

But they had found it in the drawing room. Not that one could ever see them. The windowpanes reflected apples, reflected roses; all the leaves were green in the glass. If they moved in the drawing room, the apple only turned its yellow side. Yet, the moment after, if the door was opened, spread about the floor, hung upon the walls, pendant from the ceiling—what? My hands were empty. The shadow of a thrush crossed the carpet; from the deepest wells of silence the wood pigeon drew its bubble of sound. "Safe, safe, safe" the pulse of the house beat softly. "The treasure buried; the room..." the pulse stopped short. Oh, was that the buried treasure?

A moment later the light had faded. Out in the garden then? But the trees spun darkness for a wandering beam of sun. So fine, so rare, coolly sunk beneath the surface the beam I sought always burned behind the glass. Death was the glass; death was between us, coming to the woman first, hundreds of years ago, leaving the house, sealing all the windows; the rooms were darkened. He left it, left her, went North, went East, saw the stars turned in the Southern sky; sought the house, found it dropped beneath the Downs. "Safe, safe, safe," the pulse of the house beat gladly. "The Treasure yours."

The wind roars up the avenue. Trees stoop and bend this way and that. Moonbeams splash and spill wildly in the rain. But the beam of the lamp falls straight from the window. The candle burns stiff and still. Wandering through the house, opening the windows, whispering not to wake us, the ghostly couple seek their joy.

"Here we slept," she says. And he adds, "Kisses without number." "Waking in the morning—" "Silver between the trees—" "Upstairs—" "In the garden—" "When summer came—" "In winter snowtime—" "The doors go shutting far in the distance, gently knocking like the pulse of a heart."

Nearer they come, cease at the doorway. The wind falls, the rain slides silver down the glass. Our eyes darken, we hear no steps beside us; we see no lady spread her ghostly cloak. His hands shield the lantern. "Look," he breathes. "Sound asleep. Love upon their lips."

Stooping, holding their silver lamp above us, long they look and deeply. Long they pause. The wind drives straightly; the flame stoops slightly. Wild beams of moonlight cross both floor and wall, and, meeting, stain the faces bent; the faces pondering[1]; the faces that search the sleepers and seek their hidden joy.

"Safe, safe, safe," the heart of the house beats proudly. "Long years—" he sighs. "Again you found me." "Here," she murmurs, "sleeping; in the garden reading; laughing, rolling apples in the loft. Here we left our treasure—" Stooping, their light lifts the lids upon my eyes. "Safe! safe! safe!" the pulse of the house beats wildly. Waking, I cry "Oh, is this your buried treasure? The light in the heart."

　　无论你何时醒来,总会听到关门声。他们手拉着手,从一个房间穿过另一个房间,找找这里,翻翻那里,那么仔细,仿佛一对幽灵。

　　"这里,我们是把它留在这里。"他说。"还有那里!"他补充。"在楼上。"她低喃。"还有在花园。"他微絮。"轻点儿,"他们同声说,"不然我们会把他们吵醒。"

　　不,不是你们吵醒了我们,哦,不是。"他们正在四处寻找;他们正把窗帘拉闭。"她好像在说什么,又好像在读书。"他们现在找着了,"她确信地说,手中做注记的铅笔停止了移动。她觉得累了,站起身,四处寻找,屋里空空的,什么也没有,门都大开着,只有野鸽子满意的咕咕叫声和农庄里传来的打谷机的轰鸣。"我来这里做什么? 我想找寻什么?"我的两手空空。"难道会在楼上?"苹果放在阁楼里。她走下楼,花园仍似原来那样沉静,只有书滑在草地上。

　　他们还是在客厅里找着了,但不是他们曾经见过的。窗玻璃里映着苹果,映着玫瑰,映着叶子一片碧绿,如果他们在客厅里换个角度,就只会看见苹果那黄色的一面。若是再晚一点儿,若是那扇门开着,光线穿过地板,铺到墙上,悬挂到天花板上——然而我到底要寻找什么? 我的两手空空。乌鸦阴暗的投影掠过地毯;野鸽子在死井般的沉寂里,拖着长调,咕咕不停,"安息、安息、安息,"房子的脉搏轻轻地跳动。"财富已被埋葬;这房间……"脉动突然停止,财富,哦,那就是被埋葬的财富吗?

　　片刻之后,光线在减弱。是在外面的花园里吗? 漫游的阳光透过树木伸展的枝蔓,筛向地面。那么细美,那么珍贵,那么凉爽。这就是我一直追寻的那束阳光,它在窗玻璃后面燃烧。死亡就是这玻璃;死亡就在我们之间,许多年以前,首先走向女人,离开了这所房子,关闭了所有的窗户;屋里一片黑暗。他辞别了它,撇下了她,到北方,到东方,看星辰在南方的天空运转;找寻这所房子,发现它座落在南部丘陵的草原上。"安息、安息、安息,"房子的脉搏在愉快地跳动。"财富是属于你的。"

　　风呼呼地扫过地面,树随风向左右摇摆。月光在风雨中狂乱地倾泻。一束烛光从窗户里射来。蜡烛在平静地燃烧。迷游着,从房间里穿过,打开窗户,轻絮着不要惊醒我们,这对幽灵在寻找他们往日的欢乐。

　　"这里,我们睡过。"她说。"亲吻过无数次。"他补充道。"清晨醒来——""银色的光洒满林间。""在楼上——""在花园——""在夏日来临之际——""在冬雪飘飞之时——"门在遥远的地方关上,轻轻地碰撞仿佛心脏的跳动。

他们越走越近,停在门口。风减弱了,银丝般的雨从窗玻璃上滑落,我们的双眼模糊;我们听不见脚步声;也看不见女士展开她那幽灵般的披风。他用手遮住烛光。"瞧,"他悄声说,"他们睡熟了。爱印在他们的唇上。"

他们弯着腰,把银色的烛灯举到我们的上方,长时间地、深沉地注视着。目光久久地没有移动。风径直吹过来;烛光微微地摇曳。幽灵似的月辉泻向地面,射到墙上,交织在一起,映着那低垂的面庞;这面庞在沉思;在寻找酣睡者;在寻找他们埋葬的幸福。

"安息、安息、安息,"房子的脉搏在骄傲地跳动。"多少年了——"他叹息。"你又找到了我。""在这里,"她低诉,"我们酣睡;在花园我们阅读;在阁楼我们滚动着苹果,欢笑,是的,是在这里,我们留下了我们的财富——"他们弯下腰,手执的烛光耀得我睁不开双眼。"安息! 安息! 安息!"房子的脉搏在狂跳。我醒来,大声叫道,"哦,这就是你们所埋葬的财富? 那心中的光芒。"

最 散文
Zui Prose

[1] ponder  v. 沉思,考虑

# 哨子
# The Whistle

【美国】本杰明·富兰克林

作者简介

　　本杰明·富兰克林 (1706–1790)，十八世纪美国最伟大的科学家，著名的政治家、文学家和航海家。也是18世纪美国的实业家、社会活动家、思想家和外交家，资本主义精神最完美的代表，是美国历史上第一位享有国际声誉的发明家，美国独立战争的老战士。他一生最真实的写照是他自己所说过的一句话"诚实和勤勉，应该成为你永久的伴侣。"《哨子》吹奏的不是人生的悲歌，而是生活中取舍的艺术。

I received my dear friend's two letters, one for Wednesday and one for Saturday. This is again Wednesday. I do not deserve one for today, because I have not answered the former. But, indolent as I am, and averse to writing, the fear of having no more of your pleasing epistles, if I do not contribute to the correspondence, obliges me to take up my pen; and as Mr. B. has kindly sent me word that he sets out tomorrow to see you, instead of spending this Wednesday evening, as I have done its namesakes, in your delightful company, I sit down to spend it in thinking of you, in writing to you, and in reading over and over again your letters.

I am charmed with your description of Paradise, and with your plan of living there; and I approve much of your conclusion, that, in the meantime, we should draw all the good we can from this world. In my opinion we might all draw more good from it than we do, and suffer less evil, if we would take care not to give too much for whistles. For to me it seems that most of the unhappy people we meet with are becoming so by neglect of that caution.

You may ask what I mean? You love stories, and will excuse my telling one of myself.

When I was a child of seven years old, my friends, on a holiday, filled my pocket with coppers. I went directly to a shop where they sold toys for children; and being charmed with the sound of a whistle, that I met by the way in the hands of another boy, I voluntarily offered and gave all my money for one. I then came home, and went whistling all over the house, much pleased with my whistle, but disturbing all the family. My brothers, and sisters, and cousins, understanding the bargain I had made, told me I had given four times as much for it as it was worth; put me in mind what good things I might have bought with the rest of the money; and laughed at me so much for my folly, that I cried with vexation; and the reflection gave me more chagrin than the whistle gave me pleasure.

This, however, was afterwards of use to me, the impression continuing on my mind; so that often, when I was tempted to buy some unnecessary thing, I said to myself, don't give too much for the whistle; and I saved my money.

As I grew up, came into the world, and observed the actions of men, I thought I met with many, very many, who gave too much for the whistle.

When I saw one too ambitious of court favor, sacrificing his time in attendance on levees, his repose, his liberty, his virtue, and perhaps his friends, to attain it, I have said to myself, this man gives too much for his whistle.

When I saw another fond of popularity, constantly employing himself in political bustles, neglecting his own affairs, and ruining them by that neglect, "He pays, indeed," said I, "too much for his whistle."

If I knew a miser, who gave up every kind of comfortable living, all the pleasure of doing good to others, all the esteem of his fellow-citizens, and the joys of benevolent friendship, for the sake of accumulating wealth, "Poor man," said I, "you pay too much for your whistle."

When I met with a man of pleasure, sacrificing every laudable improvement of the mind, or of his fortune, to mere corporeal sensations, and ruining his health in their pursuit, "Mistaken man," said I, "you are providing pain for yourself, instead of pleasure; you give too much for your whistle."

If I see one fond of appearance, or fine clothes, fine houses, fine furniture, fine equipages[1], all above his fortune, for which he contracts debts, and ends his career in a prison, "Alas!" say I, "he has paid dear, very dear, for his whistle."

When I see a beautiful sweet-tempered girl married to an ill-natured brute of a husband, "What a pity," say I, "that she should pay so much for a whistle!"

In short, I conceive that great part of the miseries of mankind are brought upon them by the false estimates they have made of the value of things, and by their giving too much for their whistles.

Yet I ought to have charity for these unhappy people, when I consider that, with all this wisdom of which I am boasting, there are certain things in the world so tempting, for example, the apples of King John, which happily are not to be bought; for if they were put to sale by auction, I might very easily be led to ruin myself in the purchase, and find that I had once more given too much for the whistle.

Adieu, my dear friend, and believe me ever yours very sincerely and with unalterable affection.

我敬爱的朋友,我已经收到你的两封来信,周三、周六各一封。时光飞逝,一眨眼,又到了周三。我今天不祈求收到你的来信,因为以前的信,我还没来得及回复。我承认自己懒惰,又不爱写信,可是如果不回信的话,我又怕自己再也收不到你那令人开心的来信。想到这里,我便不得不拿起笔来了。B先生好心地告诉我,他想明日去你的家中拜访,而不是在今天晚上。坐在桌前心里想着与你快乐的接触,我整个晚上都在想念你,给你写回信,并反复阅读你的来信。

我着迷于你对天堂的描述,羡慕你去那里生活的计划,并认可你的大部分观点,在这样的基础上,我们同时一定要最大限度地从这个世界中吸取所有的善。在我看来,如果我们注意不在哨子上付出太大的代价,我们很有可能从这个世界吸取更多的善,遭受更少的恶。因为对我来说,我们所见过的闷闷不乐的人中,大部分是由于对这一警示不予理睬酿成了大祸。

你或许会问,我说的是什么意思? 你喜欢听故事,那么请允许我讲一个发生在我身上的故事。

故事发生在我7岁那年。在一个假日,我的口袋被几位朋友塞满了铜币。我赶忙直奔一家儿童玩具店跑去。在去往商店的路上,我看到一个小男孩手中有只哨子。他吹出的哨音委婉动听,我情不自禁地着迷了。于是,我来到商店,掏出所有的钱换了一只哨子。然后,回到家后,我便吹着哨子四处游荡。我对自己的哨子爱不释手,而全家人却因为哨声痛苦不堪。我的哥哥、姐姐、堂兄、堂姐、表兄、表姐得知我买哨子的价钱后,告诉我,我买这只哨子多花了3倍的价钱,还告诉我原本用那些剩下的钱可以买到哪些好东西,并肆意地嘲笑我的愚蠢。我懊恼地哭了起来。这件事带给我的苦恼远多于哨子带给我的快乐。

不过,这件事一直留在我的记忆中,给我日后的人生带来了很多益处。从那以后，每当我想去买一些不必要的东西时，就对自己说，不要为哨子支付太多金钱，于是我便能省下钱。

长大后，步入社会，遇到了很多人，观察了人们的行为，最后我发现，他们都为自己的哨子付出了过高的代价。

当我看见一个过分热衷于趋炎附势，为寻求会见而不惜牺牲自己的睡眠、自由、德行甚至朋友的人时，我便对自己说，这个人为了他的哨子付出了昂贵的代价。

当我看见另一个醉心于名望，一次又一次投身于政界的纷扰之中，忽视了自己的份内之事，最后因这种忽视而毁了自己的人生时，我会说，他确实为哨子付出了昂贵的代价。

当我得知一个守财奴，为了积累财富，宁愿放弃舒适的生活、行善的乐趣、同胞的尊重和友爱带来的欢愉时，我会说，可怜的人啊，为了哨子你付出了昂贵的代价。

当我遇到一个沉湎于享乐，为了追求肉体上的享受，牺牲一切精神或物质上值得称道的改进，甚至不惜毁掉自己健康的人时，我会说，误入歧途的人啊，你是有福不享，自讨苦吃，为了哨子，你付出了昂贵的代价。

当我看到一个人追求外在，或沉迷于精致的服装、豪华的住宅、富丽的家具、漂亮的马车，入不敷出，债台高筑，最后被投进监狱时，我会说，天啊！为了哨子他付出了如此昂贵的代价。

当我看到一个美丽动人、性情温顺的女孩，嫁给一个粗野、残忍的丈夫时，我会说，真是可惜，为了哨子她付出了昂贵的代价。

总之，我认为，人类所遭受的大部分的不幸，都是因为他们对事物的价值做出了错误的评估，是因为他们为哨子付出了过高的代价。

但是我应当对这些不幸的人们抱有同情恻隐之心。因为我觉得，尽管我有着这一切我自认可以引以为豪的智慧，可在这个世界上确实有些东西相当诱惑人。比如约翰王的苹果，幸好那是买不到的；因为如果这些苹果被拍卖着出售，我有可能很容易就被引导着在购买过程中倾家荡产，然后发现自己又一次为了那个哨子付出了过高的代价。

再见，我亲爱的朋友。请相信，我永远是你真诚的朋友，对你的情感持久不变。

[1] equipage  n. 装备；马车及侍从；用具

# 蝴蝶
# Butterflies

【美国】罗杰·迪恩·基泽

作者简介

罗杰·迪恩·基泽是美国善写孤儿故事、研究孤儿问题的著名作家，文笔细腻感人。他本人四岁成为孤儿，在孤儿院呆过，没受多少正规教育。《蝴蝶》一文中蝴蝶那被撕碎的翅膀就是一个善良孤独的孩子被撕碎的心。

There was a time in my life when beauty meant something special to me. I guess that would have been when I was about six or seven years old, just several weeks or maybe a month before the orphanage turned me into an old man.

I would get up every morning at the orphanage, make my bed just like the little soldier that I had become and then I would get into one of the two straight lines and march to breakfast with the other twenty or thirty boys who also lived in my dormitory.

After breakfast one Saturday morning I returned to the dormitory and saw the house parent chasing the beautiful monarch butterflies who lived by the hundreds in the azalea bushes strewn around the orphanage.

I carefully watched as he caught these beautiful creatures, one after the other, and then took them from the net and then stuck straight pins through their head and wings, pinning them onto a heavy cardboard sheet.

How cruel it was to kill something of such beauty. I had walked many times out into the bushes, all by myself, just so the butterflies could land on my head, face and hands so I could look at them up close.

When the telephone rang the house parent laid the large cardboard paper down on the back cement step and went inside to answer the phone. I walked up to the cardboard and looked at the one butterfly who he had just pinned to the large paper. It was still moving about so I reached down and touched it on the wing causing one of the pins to fall out. It started flying around and around trying to get away but it was still pinned by the one wing with the other straight pin. Finally its wing broke off and the butterfly fell to the ground and just quivered.

I picked up the torn wing and the butterfly and I spat on its wing and tried to get it to stick back on so it could fly away and be free before the house parent came back. But it would not stay on him.

The next thing I knew the house parent came walking back out of the back door by the garbage room and started yelling at me. I told him that I did not do anything but he did not believe me. He picked up the cardboard paper and started hitting me on the top of the head. There were all kinds of butterfly pieces going everywhere. He threw the cardboard down on the ground and told me to pick it up and put it in the garbage can inside the back room of the dormitory and then he left.

I sat there in the dirt, by that big old tree, for the longest time trying to fit all the butterfly pieces back together so I could bury them whole, but it was too hard to do. So I prayed for them and then I put them in an old torn up shoe box and I buried them in the bottom of the fort that I had built in the ground, out by the large bamboos, near the blackberry bushes.

Every year when the butterflies would return to the orphanage and try to land on me I would try and shoo them away because they did not know that the orphanage was a bad place to live and a very bad place to die.

在我生命里曾有段时间,美对我来说意味着某种特别的东西,我想那时我大概六七岁吧,可仅几周或个把月后,孤儿院就把我变成个老人。

在孤儿院,我每早起来,像我日后当的那种兵蛋子似地整理好床,然后和住在我寝室的二三十个男孩子一道归列入队,排成笔直的两行,行军向早饭挺进。

一个周六的早晨,我吃完饭回到宿舍,见到那位保育员正在追扑一群美丽的橙褐色大蝴蝶,这种蝴蝶成百上千,就生活在散播于孤儿院周围的杜鹃花丛里。

我仔细地观察着,他一个一个捕捉着这些美丽的生灵,然后从网中取出,用大头针儿插透头和双翅,把它们钉在厚重的纸盒板上。

把这么美的活物杀死真是太残忍了。多少回,我都独自一人走到院外的花丛中,就为了让蝴蝶停落在我的头上、脸上和手上,我好凑近了注视它们。

电话铃响了,保育员就把这块大纸盒板放到后面的水泥台阶上,然后到屋里接电话去了。我走到这块纸盒板跟前,看着他刚别上去的那只蝴蝶。见它还在扑腾抖动,我就伸手碰它的一只翅膀,把一枚大头针儿弄掉了。这蝴蝶开始一转一转地飞着想逃掉,可一侧翅膀仍被另一枚大头针儿别着。最终它的翅膀碎裂了,蝴蝶掉到了地上,只能颤抖了。

我拾起那张扯碎的翅膀和那蝴蝶,往那片断膀上吐了点唾沫,想把它沾回到蝴蝶身上,好让蝴蝶在保育员回来之前飞走,获得自由。可翅膀怎么也沾不上。

再就记得保育员从垃圾房旁的后门走了回来,开始冲着我嚷。我告诉他我什么也没做,可他不信。他操起那张硬纸板,就朝我的脑袋瓜上一通敲打,各色蝴蝶碎片四散飘洒。他把硬纸板往地上一摔,然后命我捡起来,投进宿舍内后屋的垃圾桶里,说完他走了。

我坐在那棵老树旁的残污里,许久许久地试着把所有的蝴蝶碎片重新拼合起来,也好让我把它们完整地埋葬,可是太难了,没法拼。于是我就为它们祈祷,并把它们安放在一只破旧的鞋盒里,然后到院外,丛丛黑刺莓附近,高大的竹子旁,那座我原先在地上垒起的要塞的最底层,把它们安葬。

每年,当蝶群返回孤儿院要停落在我身上时,我就竭力用嘘声把它们轰走,因为蝶儿们不知道——活在孤儿院这种地方很糟糕,死在这儿更糟糕。

# 送行
# Seeing People Off

【英国】马克斯·比尔伯姆

## 作者简介

　　马克斯·比尔伯姆 (1872-1956)，英国作家兼演员。擅长模仿知名作家的风格，并且也是著名的讽刺画家。他因刊登在《黄皮书》上的讽刺短文和漫画而出名。代表作有《朱莱卡·多卜森》、《二十五位绅士》等。可以说他是 20 世纪最具破坏性的模仿嘲弄者之一。《送行》把以真诚为主的不列颠民族的面子问题探讨得有滋有味。

I am not good at it. To do it well seems to me one of the most difficult things in the world, and probably seems so to you, too.

To see a friend off from Waterloo to Vauxhall was easy enough. But we are never called on to perform that small feat. It is only when a friend is going on a longish journey, and will be absent for a longish time, that we turn up at the railway station. The dearer the friend, and the longer the journey, and the longer the likely absence, the earlier do we turn up, and the more lamentably do we fail. Our failure is in exact ratio to the seriousness of the occasion, and to the depth of our feeling.

In a room, or even on a door-step, we can make the farewell quite worthily. We can express in our faces the genuine sorrow we feel. Nor do words fail us. There is no awkwardness, no restraint, on either side. The thread of our intimacy has not been snapped. The leave-taking is an ideal one. Why not, then, leave the leave-taking at that? Always, departing friends implore us not to bother to come to the railway station next morning. Always, we are deaf to these entreaties, knowing them to be not quite sincere. The departing friends would think it very odd of us if we took them at their word. Besides, they really do want to see us again. And that wish is heartily reciprocated. We duly turn up. And then, oh then, what a gulf yawns! We stretch our arms vainly across it. We have utterly lost touch. We have nothing at all to say. We gaze at each other as dumb animals gaze at human beings. We "make conversation"—and such conversation! We know that these are the friends from whom we parted overnight. They know that we have not altered. Yet, on the surface, everything is different; and the tension is such that we only long for the guard to blow his whistle and put an end to the farce.

On a cold grey morning of last week I duly turned up at Euston, to see off an old friend who was starting for America.

Overnight, we had given him a farewell dinner, in which sadness was well mingled with festivity. Years probably would elapse before his return. Some of us might never see him again. Not ignoring the shadow of the future, we gaily celebrated the past. We were as thankful to have known our guest as we were grieved to lose him; and both these emotions were made evident. It was a perfect farewell.

And now, here we were, stiff and self-conscious on the platform; and, framed in the window of the railway-carriage, was the face of our friend; but it was as the face of a stranger—a stranger anxious to please, an appealing stranger, an awkward stranger. "Have you got everything?" asked one of us, breaking a silence. "Yes, everything," said our friend, with a pleasant nod. "Everything," he repeated, with the emphasis of an empty brain. "You'll be able to lunch on the train," said I, though this prophecy had already been made more than once. "Oh yes," he said with conviction. He added that the train went straight through to Liverpool. This fact seemed to strike us as rather odd. We exchanged glances. "Doesn't it stop at Crewe?" asked one of us. "No," said our friend, briefly. He seemed almost disagreeable. There was a long pause. One of us, with a nod and a forced smile at the traveller, said "Well!" The nod, the smile, and the unmeaning monosyllable, were returned conscientiously. Another pause was broken by one of us with a fit of coughing. It was an obviously assumed fit, but it served to pass the time. The bustle of the platform was unabated. There was no sign of the train's departure. Release—ours, and our friend's—was not yet.

My wandering eye alighted on a rather portly middle-aged man who was talking earnestly from the platform to a young lady at the next window but one to ours. His fine profile was vaguely familiar to me. The young lady was evidently American, and he was evidently English; otherwise I should have guessed from his impressive air that he was her father. I wished I could hear what he was saying. I was sure he was giving the very best advice; and the strong tenderness of his gaze was really beautiful. He seemed magnetic, as he poured out his final injunctions. I could feel something of his magnetism even where I stood. And the magnetism, like the profile, was vaguely familiar to me. Where had I experienced it?

In a flash I remembered. The man was Hubert le Ros. But how changed since last I saw him! That was seven or eight years ago, in the Strand. He was then (as usual) out of an engagement, and borrowed half-a-crown. It seemed a privilege to lend anything to him. He was always magnetic. And why his magnetism had never made him successful on the London stage was always a mystery to me. He was an excellent actor, and a man of sober habit. But, like many others of his kind, Hubert le Ros (I do not, of course, give the actual name by which he was known) drifted seedily away into the provinces; and I, like every one else, ceased to remember him.

It was strange to see him, after all these years, here on the platform of Euston, looking so prosperous and solid. It was not only the flesh that he had put on, but also the clothes, that made him hard to recognise. In the old days, an imitation fur coat had seemed to be as integral a part of him as were his ill-shorn lantern jaws. But now his costume was a model of rich and sombre moderation, drawing, not calling, attention to itself. He looked like a banker. Any one would have been proud to be seen off by him.

"Stand back, please." The train was about to start, and I waved farewell to my friend. Le Ros did not stand back. He stood clasping in both hands the hands of the young American. "Stand back, sir, please!" He obeyed, but quickly darted forward again to whisper some final word. I think there were tears in her eyes. There certainly were tears in his when, at length, having watched the train out of sight, he turned round. He seemed, nevertheless, delighted to see me. He asked me where I had been hiding all these years; and simultaneously repaid me the half-crown as though it had been borrowed yesterday. He linked his arm in mine, and walked me slowly along the platform, saying with what pleasure he read my dramatic criticisms every Saturday.

I told him, in return, how much he was missed on the stage. "Ah, yes," he said, "I never act on the stage nowadays." He laid some emphasis on the word "stage," and I asked him where, then, he did act. "On the platform," he answered. "You mean," said I, "that you recite at concerts?" He smiled. "This," he whispered, striking his stick on the ground, "is the platform I mean." Had his mysterious prosperity unhinged him? He looked quite sane. I begged him to be more explicit.

"I suppose," he said presently, giving me a light for the cigar which he had offered me, "you have been seeing a friend off?" I assented. He asked me what I supposed he had been doing. I said that I had watched him doing the same thing. "No," he said gravely. "That lady was not a friend of mine. I met her for the first time this morning, less than half an hour ago, here," and again he struck the platform with his stick.

I confessed that I was bewildered. He smiled. "You may," he said, "have heard of the Anglo-American Social Bureau?" I had not. He explained to me that of the thousands of Americans who annually pass through England there are many hundreds who have no English friends. In the old days they used to bring letters of introduction. But the English are so inhospitable that these letters are hardly worth the paper they are written on. "Thus," said Le Ros, "the A.A.S.B. supplies a long-felt want. Americans are a sociable people, and most of them have plenty of money to spend. The A.A.S.B. supplies them with English friends. Fifty percent of the fees is paid over to the friends. The other fifty is retained by the A.A.S.B. I am not, alas, a director. If I were, I should be a very rich man indeed. I am only an employee. But even so I do very well. I am one of the seers-off."

Again I asked for enlightenment. "Many Americans," he said, "cannot afford to keep friends in England. But they can all afford to be seen off. The fee is only five pounds (twenty-five dollars) for a single traveller; and eight pounds (forty dollars) for a party of two or more. They send that in to the Bureau, giving the date of their departure, and a description by which the seer-off can identify them on the platform. And then—well, then they are seen off."

"But is it worth it?" I exclaimed. "Of course it is worth it," said Le Ros. "It prevents them from feeling 'out of it'. It earns them the respect of the guard. It saves them from being despised by their fellow-passengers—the people who are going to be on the boat. It gives them a footing for the whole voyage. Besides, it is a great pleasure in itself. You saw me seeing that young lady off. Didn't you think I did it beautifully?" "Beautifully," I admitted. "I envied you. There was I—" "Yes, I can imagine. There were you, shuffling from foot to foot, staring blankly at your friend, trying to make conversation. I know. That's how I used to be myself, before I studied, and went into the thing professionally. I don't say I'm perfect yet. I'm still a martyr to platform fright. A railway station is the most difficult of all places to act in, as you have discovered for yourself." "But," I said with resentment, "I wasn't trying to act. I really felt." "So did I, my boy," said Le Ros. "You can't act without feeling. What's his name, the Frenchman—Diderot, yes—said you could; but what did he know about it? Didn't you see those tears in my eyes when the train started? I hadn't forced them. I tell you I was moved. So were you, I dare say. But you couldn't have pumped up a tear to prove it. You can't express your feelings. In other words, you can't act. At any rate," he added kindly, "not in a railway station." "Teach me!" I cried. He looked thoughtfully at me. "Well," he said at length, "the seeing-off season is practically over. Yes, I'll give you a course. I have a good many pupils on hand already; but yes," he said, consulting an ornate note-book, "I could give you an hour on Tuesdays and Fridays."

His terms, I confess, are rather high. But I don't grudge the investment.

我不善于送行。在我看来，办好这桩事要算世上最棘手的难题之一；也许你多半有同感吧。

送朋友从滑铁卢车站到沃克索车站，倒是轻而易举的，但此举绝无劳神的必要。只有当朋友即将踏上较远的旅程，会离开较长的一段岁月，我们才会出现在车站的月台上。朋友愈是亲密，旅途愈是遥远，离别的岁月愈有可能长久，我们出现在站台的时间便愈早，我们也愈加可悲地陷入失望。我们的失望完全与这个场合的严肃程度和我们的感情深度成正比。

在房间里，或者就在门口，我们本来可以把送行这桩事儿办得妥妥帖帖。我们的面部可以表达出发自内心的离愁别恨，口头上也绝不乏言辞，双方都不会有任何窘困和拘束的感觉，彼此完全心照不宣，情丝相连。这样的辞别真可谓尽善尽美。那为什么又不如此告别呢？离别的友人总是恳求我们，次日早晨别再劳神去车站。我们总是对这些恳求充耳不闻，因为心里明白那不过是客气话而已；如果我们信以为真，朋友反会感到奇怪。更何况，他们真想再次见到我们。届时我们去了。可是到了车站，啊，那时才发现事与愿违，我们之间隔着一道鸿沟，无论我们怎样伸出双臂都无法横过对岸，完全不可能相互接触。彼此凝目相望，却无话可说，就像不会说话的动物呆呆望着游人那样。我们"无话找话说"——这哪算得上交谈！明明知道这些就是我们昨晚分手的朋友，他们也知道我们丝毫没有改变。然而，乍看起来，一切都不同了。在那样的紧张气氛里，我们巴不得列车员吹响口哨，早些结束这幕笑剧。

在上周的一个清冷的早晨，我准时到了尤斯顿车站，去送一位赴美的老朋友。

就在前一天晚上，我们还专门为他饯行，那时的离愁交融着欢乐的气氛。也许要过好几年他才会回来，我们中间有的人说不定再也见不到他了。尽管笼罩着这层有关未来的阴影，我们仍能愉快地缅怀往昔。庆幸相识，感伤离别，这两种情怀均充分表露出来了。那真是一次完美无缺的饯别。

可是现在到了站台，我们却感到这样僵，这样窘。朋友的面孔映在车厢的破璃窗前，竟然像是一个陌生人——急于取悦于人，投人所好，却又十分尴尬。"东西都带齐了吗？"我们之中有人打破沉默问道。"喔，带齐了。"我们的朋友点了点头回答。接着又茫然地重复强调一遍："都带齐了。"尽管已经不止一次地预告过了，我仍然说道："你可以在车上用午餐。""哦，当然。"他表示毫无疑问，并补充说，这趟车直达利物浦。在我们听来，点明这一事实颇有些奇怪。我们交换了一个眼色，又有人问道："难道不在克鲁停车吗？"我们的朋友简单地答道："不。"他似乎显出有些不快活的样子。于是大家陷入一阵长时间的沉默。我们终于有人点点头，朝即将远行的人勉强一笑，说道："好哇！"这一点头，这一强笑，以及这一声无意义的话语，立即会心地回报了。又陷入一阵沉默，直到我们有人咳嗽起来才给打破了。那显然是一阵假咳，但却有助于消磨时间。然而，站台上的喧嚣还没有止息，列车没有开动的迹象，还不到我们和我们的朋友获得解放的时候呢。

我四下张望的目光落在一个略为发胖的中年人身上，他站在月台上，正同我们近邻的一个窗口前的少妇亲切交谈。那清晰的侧面仿佛很有些眼熟。一望便

99
最散文
Zui Prose

知,少妇是美国人,而他则是英国人;要不然,他那诚挚感人的神情真会使我们把他当做她的父亲的。但愿我能听清他在讲些什么。我相信他正在给她进行贤明的忠告,他那热情慈祥的目光实在动人。当他不放过最后时刻千叮咛万嘱咐之际,他仿佛具有某种磁力似的,即使在我站立的地方也能感受到。正像他的侧面一样,这股魅力也给我似曾相识的感觉。我是在什么地方体验过的呢?

我忽然记起来了,这人名叫休伯特·勒洛斯。但自上次见面以来,他的变化多大呀!我是七八年前在斯特兰德大街见过他的。他当时(和往常一样)正失业,向我借了半块银币。能借给他点什么仿佛是件荣耀的事,他总是那样富有魅力,而这种魅力为什么没有在伦敦舞台上获得成功,一直令我大惑不解。他是一个优秀的演员,又无贪杯的嗜好。但同别的许多人一样,休伯特·勒洛斯(自然我不便说出他为人所知的姓名)穷愁潦倒,只好从京都漂泊到乡下;我同大家一样也就把他忘了。

隔了这许多年,突然见他如此阔气而富态地出现在尤斯顿站的月台上,真令人感到奇怪。使他难于被辨认的,不仅是他发胖的身体,而且还有衣着。往日他老是一副尖瘦脸,身上总不离那件假皮大衣。如今,他的衣着考究,富丽而又雅致,不只是醒目而已,简直招惹众人的注意。看上去他像个银行家,谁都会为有他这样的人来送行感到骄傲。

"请往后站!"火车就要开了,于是我向友人挥手。勒洛斯却不往后站,他仍站在那儿,双手紧紧握着那位美国少妇的手。"先生,请往后站!"他这才听从了,但立即又冲上前去,低声地叮嘱最后几句话。我想她的眼里一定噙着热泪了。不用说,他已眼泪盈眶,目送火车远去之后,他才转过身来。然而,他见到我似乎感到很愉快。他问我这些年都躲藏到哪儿去了,同时把那半块银币还与我,像是昨天刚借去似的。他挽起我的胳膊,沿着月台一道漫步,告诉我每个周六他带着何等兴致在读我写的戏剧评论。

我反过来对他说,他离开舞台后多么令人想念。"噢,是吗,"他说,"现在我从不上舞台表演了。"他特别强调了"舞台"两个字,于是我问他,那么在何处表演呢。"在站台上,"他回答道。"你的意思是说,"我问,"在音乐会的站台上朗诵吗?"他微微一笑,用手杖拄了一下地面,轻声地说:"我指的就是这个站台。"难道神秘的走运使他神经失常了吗?看上去他却神志清醒,我请他把话说明白些。

"我想,"他马上说,一边为他刚递给我的雪茄点燃火。"你刚送走一位朋友吧?"我说是的,他要我猜猜他干什么来着。我说看见他也在送行。"不,"他严肃地说,"那位少妇并不是我的朋友,今天早上才第一次见面,不到半小时之前,就在这儿。"说着又用拐杖拄了一下地面。

我承认自己给弄糊涂了。他微笑着说："你或许听说过英美交际局吧?"我没听说过。他向我解释说,每年成千上万来英游历的美国人中,总有几千人在英国是没有朋友的。过去,他们常常持介绍信而来,但英国人的反应冷淡,那些信的价值竟连写信的纸都不如。"因此,"勒洛斯说,"英美交际局便应运而生。美国人是好交际的民族,而且他们大都很阔绰。于是英美交际局为他们提供英国朋友。他们的付款的半数支给那些朋友,另一半留存在局里。遗憾的是,我并非局长,要是的话,一定成了大富翁了。我只是一名雇员。即使如此,我也混得挺不错,作为一个送行人。"

我又一次请求他明示。"许多美国人,"他说,"没有财力在英国结交朋友,但他们都付得起雇人送行的费用。单人送行只需花五镑(二十五美元)就行;送两人或两人以上的团体则需八镑(四十美元)。他们把款送到局里,同时告知启程日期,附上一个描述性的说明,以便送行者在站台上辨认他们。于是——对啦,他们便被送走了。"

"但这值得吗?"我不禁叫了一声。"当然值得,"勒洛斯说,"这使他们不至有孤苦伶仃之感,会为他们赢得列车员的尊敬,使他们免受同行旅客的蔑视——那些旅客还将与他们共舟呢。这为他们整个的旅程奠定了基础。而且,这本身就是一大乐事。刚才你看见我送那位少妇的吧。难道你不认为我干得十分出色吗?""真是出色,"我承认,"我羡慕你,可我却——""是的,我想像得到。当时你局促不安地站在那儿,茫然地望着朋友,挖空心思地无话找话说。我明白。在我做过一番研究并跻身这个行业之前,我同你一个样。我不能说自己已经达到炉火纯青的地步了,现在我仍有怯场的时候;火车站台是最难进行表演的地方,这你已经亲身体会到了。""但是,"我愤愤不平地说,"我并没有想表演的意思,那是我真实的感受。""老兄,我也一样。"勒洛斯说,"没有感情不可能表演。那个法国人叫什么名字呀——对,狄德罗——他说能够办到。但他对此懂得什么? 火车开动时,你没有见我热泪盈眶吗? 我并没有勉强挤泪。告诉你,我确实感动了。我敢说,你也一样,但你就是挤不出一滴泪水来。你不能表达自己的感情,换句话说,你缺乏表演的才能。""至少,"他体谅地补充一句,"不能在火车站台上表演。"我叫道:"教教我吧!"他沉思地望着我,最后说道:"唉,送行的季节快要完了。好吧,我给你开一门课。目前我手下的学生可不少哩。不过,"说着,他翻了翻精美的笔记簿,"每周星期二和星期五,我可以教你一个钟头。"

我得承认,他的收费相当高,但我并不吝惜这项投资。

# 拯救
# Salvation

【美国】兰斯顿·休斯

## 作者简介

　　兰斯顿·休斯(1902—1967)在美国文坛,尤其在黑人文学方面,是一个举足轻重的人物。他写过小说、戏剧、散文、历史、传记等各种文体的作品,还把西班牙文和法文的诗歌翻译成英文,甚至编辑过其他黑人作家的文选,但他主要以诗歌著称,被誉为"黑人民族的桂冠诗人"。他的诗也被列入"先锋"流派之内,但是贯穿他全部作品内容的主线却始终是鲜明的现实主义精神。《拯救》以近乎残忍的真实道出了天真的孩童对宗教的迷茫。

I was saved from sin when I was going on thirteen. But not really saved. It happened like this. There was a big revival at my Auntie Reed's church. Every night for weeks there had been much preaching, singing, praying, and shouting, and some very hardened sinners had been brought to Christ, and the membership of the church had grown by leaps and bounds. Then just before the revival ended, they held a special meeting for children, "to bring the young lambs to the fold." My aunt spoke of it for days ahead. That night I was escorted to the front row and placed on the mourners' bench with all the other young sinners, who had not yet been brought to Jesus.

My aunt told me that when you were saved you saw a light, and something happened to you inside! And Jesus came into your life! And God was with you from then on! She said you could see and hear and feel Jesus in your soul. I believed her. I had heard a great many old people say the same thing and it seemed to me they ought to know. So I sat there calmly in the hot, crowded church, waiting for Jesus to come to me.

The preacher preached a wonderful rhythmical sermon, all moans and shouts and lonely cries and dire pictures of hell, and then he sang a song about the ninety and nine safe in the fold, but one little lamb was left out in the cold. Then he said: "Won't you come? Won't you come to Jesus? Young lambs, won't you come?" And he held out his arms to all of us young sinners there on the mourners' bench. And the little girls cried. And some of them jumped up and went to Jesus right away. But most of us just sat there.

A great many old people came and knelt around us and prayed, old women with jet-black faces and braided hair, old men with work-gnarled hands. And the church sang a song about the lower lights are burning, some poor sinners to be saved. And the whole building rocked with prayer and song.

Still I kept waiting to see Jesus.

Finally all the young people had gone to the altar and were saved, but one boy and me. He was a rounder's son named Westley. Westley and I were surrounded by sisters and deacons[1] praying. It was very hot in the church, and getting late now. Finally Westley said to me in a whisper: "God damn! I'm tired o' sitting here. Let's get up and be saved." So he got up and was saved.

Then I was left all alone on the mourners' bench. My aunt came and knelt at my knees and cried, while prayers and song swirled all around me in the little church. The whole congregation prayed for me alone, in a mighty wail of moans and voices.

And I kept waiting serenely for Jesus, waiting, waiting – but he didn't come. I wanted to see him, but nothing happened to me. Nothing! I wanted something to happen to me, but nothing happened.

I heard the songs and the minister saying: "Why don't you come? My dear child, why don't you come to Jesus? Jesus is waiting for you. He wants you. Why don't you come? Sister Reed, what is this child's name?"

"Langston," my aunt sobbed.

"Langston, why don't you come? Why don't you come and be saved? Oh, Lamb of God! Why don't you come?"

Now it was really getting late. I began to be ashamed of myself, holding everything up so long. I began to wonder what God thought about Westley, who certainly hadn't seen Jesus either, but who was now sitting proudly on the platform, swinging his knickerbockered legs and grinning down at me, surrounded by deacons and old women on their knees praying. God had not struck Westley dead for taking his name in vain or for lying in the temple. So I decided that maybe to save further trouble, I'd better lie, too, and say that Jesus had come, and get up and be saved.

So I got up.

Suddenly the whole room broke into a sea of shouting, as they saw me rise. Waves of rejoicing swept the place. Women leaped in the air. My aunt threw her arms around me. The minister took me by the hand and led me to the platform.

When things quieted down, in a hushed silence, punctuated by a few ecstatic "Amens," all the new young lambs were blessed in the name of God. Then joyous singing filled the room.

That night, for the first time in my life but one for I was a big boy twelve years old—I cried. I cried, in bed alone, and couldn't stop. I buried my head under the quilts, but my aunt heard me. She woke up and told my uncle I was crying because the Holy Ghost had come into my life, and because I had seen Jesus. But I was really crying because I couldn't bear to tell her that I had lied, that I had deceived everybody in the church, that I hadn't seen Jesus, and that now I didn't believe there was a Jesus anymore, since he didn't come to help me.

　　我快要十三岁时得到了救赎。其实哪里是真的救赎。事情的经过是这样的。那时,吕德婶婶的教堂正经历巨大的复兴。几个星期的晚上连着布道、唱赞歌、祈祷,还有嘶喊,连不少顽固不化的罪人都皈依到基督的身边,于是,教堂的信徒激增。就在这次复兴活动结束前夕,他们专为孩子们举行一次特别的祈祷,"把这些迷途的小羔羊带回羊群"。婶婶谈论这件事已好几天了。到了那天晚上,我被护送到前排送葬者坐的长凳上,与所有尚未被召唤到基督跟前的小罪人挤在一起。

　　婶婶说过,得救时能看得见一缕光芒,接着内心就发生了变化！这是耶稣进入了你的生命呢！从此上帝将与你同在！她说,你看得见、听得到,能感觉出耶稣就在你的灵魂里。我相信了她。我早就听许多老年人——这档子事应该他们知道——讲过同样的事。于是,我不紧不慢地坐在又热又挤的教堂里,等待着耶稣向我走来。

　　牧师的布道抑扬顿挫,其间充满了呻吟、呼叫、孤零零的哭诉,一幅幅地狱的可怖图景。接着,他唱了一支歌,歌中说九十九只羊会在羊栏里得到庇护,还会有一只小羊羔留在外面挨冻。他接着说:"难道你们不过来吗？难道你们不想来耶稣身边吗？小羊羔们,难道你们不想过来吗？"他向我们这些坐在送葬人的长凳上的小罪人们敞开了胸怀。这时,小女孩们哭了起来；有的跳将起来,径直奔向耶稣。可我们大多数还死坐在那儿。

　　老人蜂拥而至,跪在我们四周祈祷起来,有漆黑的脸、编着辫子的老太太,有干活干得指节弯扭的老头儿。全体教徒唱起一首歌,大意是,微弱的灯儿燃着,可怜的人儿将赎去罪孽。整幢房子就在祈祷和歌声中震荡。

　　然而我还在等着见耶稣。

　　最后,所有的孩子都登上了祭坛,得到了拯救,只剩我和另外一个。他是酒鬼的儿子,名叫韦斯特里。他和我被淹没在姐妹们和执事的祈祷声中。这时教堂里很闷热，天也很晚了。终于，韦斯特里对我悄悄地说："见他妈个鬼！我可坐腻了。我们上前去被救算了。"他站起来，就赎了罪。

我就这样一个人留在了送葬人的长凳上。婶婶走过来，跪在我的膝下，哭着，而祷告声和歌声如凶猛的波涛把我卷在这小小的教堂里。全体教徒为我一人祈祷呻吟，呼喊声呼天抢地。

我安详地等待耶稣的到来，等呀，等呀——可他没来！我要见他，可什么也没发生。什么也没发生！我想要让自己身上发生点什么变化，可什么都没发生。

我听到歌声，听到牧师说："你为啥不过来？宝贝儿你为啥不过来？耶稣等着你呢。他想要救你呢。你为啥不过来？吕德姐妹，这孩子叫啥？"

"兰斯顿。"婶婶呜咽道。

"兰斯顿，你干嘛不过来？不过来，不想得到救赎吗？噢，上帝的羔羊！干嘛不过来？"

这时，天的确很晚了。我开始为自己羞愧了，都是我，让大伙儿耽搁这么久。我想弄明白上帝会对韦斯特里怎么想了，他准没看见耶稣，可瞧他现在在祭坛上那个得意劲儿，一边晃荡着穿灯笼裤的双脚，一边和我扮着鬼脸，还有执事和老太太们团团地跪在周围为他祈祷。上帝并没有因他玩弄自己的名义、在教堂里撒谎而将他用轰雷劈死呀。于是，我明白，要避免进一步的麻烦，我最好也撒个慌，说看到耶稣来了，站起来，去得救。

于是，我站了起来。

霎时，整个大厅成了欢呼的海洋。欢腾的声浪席卷着小教堂。女人们向空中雀跃。婶婶双臂围住了我。牧师拉住我的手，领我上了祭坛。

等平静下来，四周一片静默，不时听得几声狂喜的"阿门"，在这种气氛中，所有的小羊羔都以上帝的名义得到了祝福。接着，欢乐的歌声响彻大厅。

那天夜里，我哭了——这是倒数第二次哭，我毕竟已是十二岁的大孩子了。我哭着，床上一个人，哭得不能自已。我把头埋进了被窝，婶婶还是听见了。她醒来告诉叔叔，说圣灵来到了我心中，说我看见了耶稣，所以我哭了。可其实我哭是因为我不忍心告诉她我撒了谎，我骗了教堂里所有的人，而且我实在没有看见耶稣，而现在我再也不相信有耶稣，不然，他总得来帮我一把呀。

[1] deacon  n. (教会的)执事

# 第三卷

人生路漫漫
Long Life Road

# 人生的节奏
# The Rhythm of Life

【英国】艾丽斯·梅内尔

作者简介

　　艾丽斯·梅内尔(1847-1922),英国诗人和散文家。颇为王尔德赏识。她的第一部诗集名为《序曲》。青年时代主要在意大利度过,晚年积极参与女性投票权的活动。《人生的节奏》道出的是不是只是:人生沧桑起伏,潮涨潮落呢?

人生的节奏
The Rhythm of Life

If life is not always poetical, it is at least metrical. Periodicity rules over the mental experience of man, according to the path of the orbit of his thoughts. Distances are not gauged, ellipses not measured, velocities not ascertained, times not known. Nevertheless, the recurrence is sure. What the mind suffered last week, or last year, it does not suffer now; but it will suffer again next week or next year. Happiness is not a matter of events; it depends upon the tides of the mind. Disease is metrical, closing in at shorter and shorter periods towards death, sweeping abroad at longer and longer intervals towards recovery. Sorrow for one cause was intolerable yesterday, and will be intolerable tomorrow; today it is easy to bear, but the cause has not passed. Even the burden of a spiritual distress unsolved is bound to leave the heart to a temporary peace; and remorse itself does not remain—it returns. Gaiety takes us by a dear surprise. If we had made a course of notes of its visits, we might have been on the watch, and would have had an expectation instead of a discovery. No one makes such observations; in all the diaries of students of the interior world, there have never come to light the records of the Kepler of such cycles. But Thomas à Kempis knew of the recurrences[1], if he did not measure them. In his cell alone with the elements—'What wouldst thou more than these? for out of these were all things made' —he learnt the stay to be found in the depth of the hour of bitterness, and the remembrance that restrains the soul at the coming of the moment of delight, giving it a more conscious welcome, but presaging for it an inexorable flight. And 'rarely, rarely comest thou,' sighed Shelley, not to Delight merely, but to the Spirit of Delight. Delight can be compelled beforehand, called, and constrained to our service—Ariel can be bound to a daily task; but such artificial violence throws life out of metre, and it is not the spirit that is thus compelled. That flits upon an orbit elliptically or parabolically or hyperbolically[2] curved, keeping no man knows what trysts with Time.

It seems fit that Shelley and the author of the Imitation should both have been keen and simple enough to perceive these flights, and to guess at the

109

最散文
Zui Prose

order of this periodicity. Both souls were in close touch with the spirits of their several worlds, and no deliberate human rules, no infractions of the liberty and law of the universal movement, kept from them the knowledge of recurrences. Eppur si muove ["And yet it still moves"—Galileo]. They knew that presence does not exist without absence; they knew that what is just upon its flight of farewell is already on its long path of return. They knew that what is approaching to the very touch is hastening towards departure. 'O wind,' cried Shelley, in autumn,

*O wind,*

*If winter comes, can spring be far behind?*

They knew that the flux is equal to the reflux; that to interrupt with unlawful recurrences, out of time, is to weaken the impulse of onset and retreat; the sweep and impetus of movement.

To live in constant efforts after an equal life, whether the equality be sought in mental production, or in spiritual sweetness, or in the joy of the senses, is to live without either rest or full activity. The souls of certain of the saints, being singularly simple and single, have been in the most complete subjection to the law of periodicity.

Ecstasy and desolation visited them by seasons. They endured, during spaces of vacant time, the interior loss of all for which they had sacrificed the world. They rejoiced in the uncovenanted beatitude of sweetness alighting in their hearts. Like them are the poets whom, three times or ten times in the course of a long life, the Muse has approached, touched, and forsaken. And yet hardly like them; not always so docile, nor so wholly prepared for the departure, the brevity, of the golden and irrevocable hour. Few poets have fully recognised the metrical absence of their Muse. For full recognition is expressed in only one way—silence.

It has been found that several tribes in Africa and in America worship the moon, and not the sun; a great number worship both; but no tribes are known to adore the sun, and not the moon. For the periodicity of the sun is still in part a secret; but that of the moon is modestly apparent, perpetually influential. On her depend the tides; and she is Selene, mother of Herse, bringer of the dews that recurrently irrigate lands where rain is rare. More than any other companion of earth is she the Measurer. Early Indo–Germanic languages knew her by that name.

Her metrical phases are the symbol of the order of recurrence. Constancy in approach and in departure is the reason of her inconstancies. Juliet will not receive a vow spoken in invocation of the moon; but Juliet did not live to know that love itself has tidal times—lapses and ebbs which are due to the metrical rule of the interior heart, but which the lover vainly and unkindly attributes to some outward alteration in the beloved. For man— except those elect already named—is hardly aware of periodicity. The individual man either never learns it fully, or learns it late. And he learns it so late, because it is a matter of cumulative experience upon which cumulative evidence is lacking. It is in the after–part of each life that the law is learnt so definitely as to do away with the hope or fear of continuance. That young sorrow comes so near to despair is a result of this young ignorance. So is the early hope of great achievement. Life seems so long, and its capacity so great, to one who knows nothing of all the intervals it needs must hold— intervals between aspirations, between actions, pauses as inevitable as the pauses of sleep. And life looks impossible to the young unfortunate, unaware of the inevitable and unfailing refreshment.

It would be for their peace to learn that there is a tide in the affairs of men, in a sense more subtle—if it is not too audacious to add a meaning to Shakespeare—than the phrase was meant to contain. Their joy is flying away from them on its way home; their life will wax and wane; and if they would be wise, they must wake and rest in its phases, knowing that they are ruled by the law that commands all things—a sun's revolutions and the rhythmic pangs of maternity.

111

最散文
Zui Prose

　　假如生活不总是充满诗情画意，它至少是富有悠扬韵律的。从思想轨道的路径来看，人的内心体验呈现周期性。不知彼此距离有多远，不知椭圆轨道有多长，不知运行速度有多快，不知循环周期有多久。但是，周而复始的循环往复确定无疑。上周或去年内心曾经遭受的痛苦，现在烟消云散了；但下周或来年痛苦仍然会卷土重来。快乐不在于我们经历的是是非非，而取决于心灵的潮起潮落。疾病是带有节奏规律的，行将就木之际疾病来袭的周期愈来愈短，身体复原时疾病的发作周期愈来愈长。因为某事，痛不欲生，这种痛楚昨日曾不堪承受，明日也将不堪承受；今日却不难忍受，尽管伤心事并未过去。甚至未解的精神上的痛苦负担，也定能让内心得到片刻的宁静；悔恨本身并非驻足不去，它只不过是再度光临。快乐令人又惊又喜。倘若觉察到快乐来临的路线，我们可能会翘首以待，因此快乐如期而至，而非突如其来。实际上，无人做过这种观察；在人们关于内心世界的所有日记中，尚未出现开普勒式的人物记录过这种循环往复。但是坎普滕的托马斯对这种周而复始略有觉察，尽管他并未测量它的循环周期。"除此之外，夫复何求?万事万物皆由此构成"——他发现在痛苦至深时反能找到快乐的逗留，快乐时刻来临时，人的心灵受到记忆的抑制，迎接快乐之情更强烈，但是预感快乐将无情地转瞬即逝。"你甚少，甚少光临"，雪莱长吁短叹，伤感的并非快乐本身，而是快乐的精灵。我们可以事先强迫快乐听候我们随意调遣，伺候我们——每日分派埃里厄尔任务；但是这种人为的勉强破坏了生活的节奏韵律，何况如此强迫的并非快乐的精灵。快乐的精灵在椭圆形、抛物线形或双曲线形的轨道上飞来飞去，无人知晓与时间有怎样的约会。

　　雪莱与《效法基督》的作者可以敏锐而简单地察觉到快乐精灵的飞翔往来，并猜测其周期性，这并非巧合。这两个人的灵魂与他们生活的多个世界中的精灵密切接触，因此任何人类的繁文缛节，任何对普遍运动的自由和规则的背道而驰，都不能阻止他们发现周而复始这一规律。"它仍然在转动。——伽利略"他们知道无往不复，没有暂离便没有来临；他们知道飘然离去意味着漫长的回程；他们知道姗姗来迟的、似乎触手可及的东西却又正急忙转身匆匆而去。"啊!西风，"雪莱在秋季感慨万端，"啊!西风，冬天来了，春天还会远吗?"

　　他们知道潮涨意味着潮落，不合时宜的、人为的周期干扰将使潮流的进退失据，削弱运动的气势和原动力。

　　如果一生矢志追求平等的生活，无论是在智力产出上的平等、在精神惬意上的平等、抑或是在感官享受上的平等，生活都将毫无安宁，也了无生气。一些圣人生活单纯专一，与众不同，他们的灵魂完全符合周期性的规律。

欣喜若狂与孤寂凄苦交替拜访他们。他们放弃了凡尘俗世,却四顾茫然,忍受种种内心痛苦。他们为心中偶然闪烁的非同凡响的甜美而欣喜万分。与圣人相仿的还有诗人骚客,在漫漫人生旅途上,缪斯女神三次或十次降临他们身边,点拨他们,最后抛弃他们。但是与圣人又截然不同,诗人不总是驯服的,对无可挽回的黄金时光的短暂与离去并无完全的心理准备。极少有诗人彻底承认他们的缪斯女神常常离开,因为只有一种方式表达这种彻底承认,那就是搁笔沉默。

人们发现非洲和美洲的一些部落崇拜月亮而不崇拜太阳;大多数部落则两者都顶礼膜拜;但是单崇拜太阳而不崇拜月亮的部落尚未有所闻。因为太阳的周期律仍然不完全为人所知,而月亮的周期律则较为明显,影响四季。月亮决定了潮汐的涨落起伏,她是塞勒涅,月之女神,赫斯之母,她带来露水,在雨水稀少的地方,露水不断滋润着大地。与地球的其他任何伴星相比,她是度量者。早期的印欧语系中的语言对她便如此相称。

月亮的盈亏圆缺象征着周而复始的秩序。常中有变,月亮的定期而至、按期而返正是她反复多变的原因。朱丽叶不愿接受指月盟誓,但是她红颜薄命,至死不明白爱情本身也如潮汐一样起伏消涨,由炽而衰——爱的衰退消逝全由内心的反复无常所致,但是恋人却徒劳无情地将其归之于他所爱的人外表的某些变化。因为除了刚才已讲的非同一般的人之外,人们甚少了解世事的沧桑变化。一个人要么自始至终对此浑然不觉,要么感觉到了却又失之过迟。他要到很晚才能知道这一点,因为这需要经验的不断累积,但是累积的证据却又不见于人。一直要到一个人的后半生,这一规律才为人所彻底认识,并因此才放弃对至死不渝、永不变心的期望和担忧。年轻人的悲痛几近绝望正是由于年轻人对这一规律毫不知晓。希望早日建功立业的想法亦是如此。对人生当中必需的间歇停顿——愿望之间的间歇、行动之间的间歇,这些间歇如同睡眠的间歇一样无可避免——一无所知的人,人生似乎特别漫长,潜力无穷。另一方面,因为全然不解时来运转亦是命中注定、必然而至的,所以对时运不济的年轻人来说,人生似乎不可思议,难以对付。

他们如若知道,在更为高深莫测的微妙意义上,人间世事有起有伏,如同潮汐的涨落——如果对莎翁的原句意义加以引申,不至于被认为胆大妄为的话——心里一定会如释重负。快乐弃他们而去,赶在回家的路上;他们的人生会有甘有苦,亦喜亦悲;如果了解人情世态,他们就须与时偕行,时行则行,时止则止,因为他们知道人受制于天地万物的法则——太阳的旋转与产妇的阵痛。

---

[1] recurrence  n. 再现,再发生,反复
[2] hyperbolically  adv. 双曲线地;夸张地

# 两条路
# The Two Roads

【英国】约翰·鲁斯金

### 作者简介

约翰·鲁斯金(1819－1900)英国作家、批评家。在英国被人称为"美的使者"达50年之久。他一生为"美"而战斗。代表作有《时至今日》(1862)、《芝麻与百合》(1865)、《野橄榄花冠》(1866)、《劳动者的力量》(1871)和《经济学释义》(1872)等。他的文字也非常优美,色彩绚丽,音调铿锵。如《现代画家》和《往昔》,都是散文中的佳作。《两条路》用直白而有张力的文字表现了对易逝光阴的思索。

It was New Year's night. An aged man was standing at a window. He raised his mournful eyes towards the deep blue sky, where the stars were floating like white lilies on the surface of a clear calm lake. Then he cast them on the earth, where few more hopeless people than himself now moved towards their certain goal—the tomb. He had already passed sixty of the stages leading to it, and he had brought from his journey nothing but errors and remorse. Now his health was poor, his mind vacant, his heart sorrowful, and his old age short of comforts.

The days of his youth appeared like dreams before him, and he recalled the serious moment when his father placed him at the entrance of the two roads—one leading to a peaceful, sunny place, covered with flowers, fruits and resounding with soft, sweet songs; the other leading to a deep, dark cave, which was endless, where poison flowed instead of water and where devils and poisonous snakes hissed and crawled.

He looked towards the sky and cried painfully, "O youth, return! O my father, place me once more at the entrance to life, and I'll choose the better way!" But both his father and the days of his youth had passed away.

He saw the lights flowing away in the darkness. These were the days of his wasted life; he saw a star fall from the sky and disappear, and this was the symbol of himself. His remorse, which was like a sharp arrow, struck deeply into his heart. Then he remembered his friends in his childhood, who entered on life together with him. But they had made their way to success and were now honoured and happy on this New Year's night.

The clock in the high church tower struck and the sound made him remember his parents' early love for him. They had taught him and prayed to God for his good. But he chose the wrong way. With shame and grief he dared no longer to look towards that heaven where his father lived. His darkened eyes were full of tears, and with a despairing effort, he burst out a cry: "Come back, my early days! Come back!"

And his youth did return, for all this was only a dream which he had on New Year's night. He was still young though his faults were real; he had not yet entered the deep, dark cave, and he was still free to walk on the road which leads to the peaceful and sunny land.

Those who still linger on the entrance of life, hesitating to choose the bright road, remember that when years are passed and your feet stumble on the dark mountains, you will cry bitterly, but in vain: "O youth, return! Oh give me back my early days!"

除夕之夜，一位老人伫立窗前。他满眼哀伤，仰望着深蓝色的天空，那儿，星星如清澈平静的湖面上的朵朵白莲在漂移着；后来，他将目光投向地面，几个比他更加绝望的人正在走向人生的终点——坟墓。在通往人生终点的道路上，他已走过了60多个驿站，除了过失和悔恨，他一无所获。现在，他健康欠佳，精神空虚，心情忧郁，缺少晚年应有的舒适和安逸。

青春的岁月如梦幻般浮现在他眼前，他回想起父亲将他放在人生岔路口上的关键时刻，当时，他面前有两条路：一条通向和平宁静、阳光灿烂的地方，那里到处是花果，到处回荡着柔和甜美的歌声；另一条则通向黑暗无底的深渊，那里流淌着毒液而不是清水，恶魔肆虐，毒蛇嘶嘶爬动。

他仰望天空，痛苦地哭喊："哦，青春，你回来吧！哦，爸爸，请把我重新放到人生的路口上吧，我会做出更好的选择。"然而他的父亲和他的青春年华皆离他远去。

他看见灯消逝在黑暗中，那便是他虚度的时光；他看见一颗星星从空中陨落、消失，那是他自身的象征。悔恨如同一支利箭，深深地刺进他的心。接着，他想起童年时代的朋友，他们曾与他一同踏上人生的旅程，现已获得成功，受到人们的尊敬，此刻正在幸福中欢度除夕。

教堂塔顶的钟声响了，使他回忆起父母早年对他的爱，他们曾给予他谆谆教诲，曾为他的幸福祈祷上帝。可他偏偏选择人生的歧途。羞愧和忧伤使他再也不敢正视他父亲所在的天堂。他双眼黯然无光，饱噙着泪水，在绝望中，他拼力高喊："回来吧，我那逝去的年华！回来吧！"

青春真的回来了，因为以上所发生的一切只是他在除夕所做的一场梦。他仍旧年轻，当然他真的犯有过失；但还未堕入深渊；他仍然可以自由地走上通向宁静和光明的道路。

在人生路口徘徊，不知该不该选择光明大道的年轻人啊，你们千万要记住：当你青春已逝，双足在黑暗的群山中举步维艰，跌跌撞撞之时，你才痛心疾首地呼唤："哦，回来吧、青春！哦，把我的美好年华还给我！"但这只是徒劳无益的。

# 享受此刻
# Relish the Moment

【美国】罗伯特·杰·哈斯丁斯

**作者简介**

罗伯特·杰·哈斯丁斯(1924-1997)，美国作家，名著为《车站》(The Station)。《享受此刻》一文以劝说的语气娓娓道来，格言警句点缀其中，语言精到，说明时不我待的永恒真理。

Tucked away in our subconscious is an idyllic vision. We see ourselves on a long trip that spans the continent. We are traveling by train. Out the windows, we drink in the passing scene of cars on nearby highways, of children waving at a crossing, of cattle grazing on a distant hillside, of smoke pouring from a power plant, of row upon row of corn and wheat, of flatlands and valleys, of mountains and rolling hillsides, of city skylines and village halls.

But uppermost in our minds is the final destination. On a certain day at a certain hour, we will pull into the station. Bands will be playing and flags waving. Once we get there, so many wonderful dreams will come true and the pieces of our lives will fit together like a completed jigsaw puzzle. How restlessly we pace the aisles, damning the minutes for loitering—waiting, waiting, waiting for the station.

"When we reach the station, that will be it!" we cry. "When I'm 18. " "When I buy a new 450SL Mercedes Benz! " "When I put the last kid through college. " "When I have paid off the mortgage!" "When I get a promotion." "When I reach the age of retirement, I shall live happily ever after!"

Sooner or later, we must realize there is no station, no one place to arrive at once and for all. The true joy of life is the trip. The station is only a dream. It constantly outdistances[1] us.

"Relish the moment" is a good motto, especially when coupled with Psalm 118:24: "This is the day which the Lord hath made; we will rejoice and be glad in it." It isn't the burdens of today that drive men mad. It is the regrets over yesterday and the fear of tomorrow. Regret and fear are twin thieves who rob us of today.

So stop pacing the aisles and counting the miles. In stead, climb more mountains, eat more ice cream, go barefoot more often, swim more rivers, watch more sunsets, laugh more, cry less. Life must be lived as we go along. The station will come soon enough.

　　我们的潜意识里藏着一派田园诗般的风光！我们仿佛身处一次横贯大陆的漫漫旅程之中！乘着火车，我们领略着窗外流动的景色：附近高速公路上奔驰的汽车、十字路口处招手的孩童、远山上吃草的牛群、源源不断地从电厂排放出的烟尘、一片片的玉米和小麦、平原与山谷、群山与绵延的丘陵、天空映衬下城市的轮廓，以及乡间的庄园宅第！

　　然而我们心里想得最多的却是最终的目的地！在某一天的某一时刻，我们将会抵达进站！迎接我们的将是乐队和飘舞的彩旗！一旦到了那儿，多少美梦将成为现实，我们的生活也将变得完整，如同一块理好了的拼图！可是我们现在在过道里不耐烦地踱来踱去，咒骂火车的拖拖拉拉！我们期待着，期待着，期待着火车进站的那一刻！

　　"当我们到站的时候，一切就都好了！"我们呼喊着！"当我18岁的时候！""当我有了一辆新450SL奔驰的时候！""当我供最小的孩子念完大学的时候！""当我偿清贷款的时候！""当我官升高任的时候！""当我到了退休的时候，就可以从此过上幸福的生活啦！"

　　可是我们终究会认识到人生的旅途中并没有车站，也没有能够"一劳永逸"的地方！生活的真正乐趣在于旅行的过程，而车站不过是个梦，它始终遥遥领先于我们！

　　"享受现在"是句很好的箴言，尤其是当它与《圣经·诗篇》中第118页24行的一段话相映衬的时候，更是如此："今日乃主所创造；生活在今日我们将欢欣、高兴！"真正令人发疯的不是今日的负担，而是对昨日的悔恨及对明日的恐惧！悔恨与恐惧是一对孪生窃贼，将今天从你我身边偷走！

　　那么就不要在过道里徘徊吧，别老惦记着你离车站还有多远！何不换一种活法，将更多的高山攀爬，多吃点儿冰淇淋甜甜嘴巴，经常光着脚板儿溜达溜达，在更多的河流里畅游，多看看夕阳西下，多点欢笑哈哈，少让泪水滴答！生活得一边过一边瞧！车站就会很快到达！

---

[1] outdistance  v. 把……抛在后头；大大超过

# 无知之乐
# The Pleasures of Ignorance

【美国】罗伯特·林德

作者简介

罗伯特·林德(1879－1949)英国批评家,散文家。他与E·V·卢卡斯都是复兴查尔斯·兰姆散文体传统的先驱。他是以小品文著称的作家。其最负盛名的著作是为《新政治家》等报刊写的随笔、小品文。另有著作《爱尔兰漫游散记》、《探照灯和夜莺》等。《无知之乐》一文形散而神不散,表明无知的真正乐趣在于永远保持一颗求知的心。

# 无知之乐
## The Pleasures of Ignorance

It is impossible to take a walk in the country with an average townsman—especially, perhaps, in April or May—without being amazed at the vast continent of his ignorance. It is impossible to take a walk in the country oneself without being amazed at the vast continent of one's own ignorance. Thousands of men and women live and die without knowing the difference between a beech and an elm, between the song of a thrush and the song of a blackbird. Probably in a modern city the man who can distinguish between a thrush's and a blackbird's song is the exception. It is not that we have not seen the birds. It is simply that we have not noticed them. We have been surrounded by birds all our lives, yet so feeble is our observation that many of us could not tell whether or not the chaffinch[1] sings, or the colour of the cuckoo. We argue like small boys as to whether the cuckoo always sings as he flies or sometimes in the branches of a tree—whether Chapman[2] drew on his fancy or his knowledge of nature in the lines:

*When in the oak's green arms the cuckoo sings,*
*And first delights men in the lovely springs.*

This ignorance, however, is not altogether miserable. Out of it we get the constant pleasure of discovery. Every fact of nature comes to us each spring, if only we are sufficiently ignorant, with the dew still on it. If we have lived half a lifetime without having ever even seen a cuckoo, and know it only as a wandering voice, we are all the more delighted at the spectacle of its runaway flight as it hurries from wood to wood conscious of its crimes, and at the way in which it halts hawk-like in the wind, its long tail quivering, before it dares descend on a hill-side of fir-trees where avenging presences may lurk. It would be absurd to pretend that the naturalist does not also find pleasure in observing the life of the birds, but his is a steady pleasure, almost a sober and plodding[3] occupation, compared to the morning enthusiasm of the man who sees a cuckoo for the first time, and, behold, the world is made new.

And, as to that, the happiness even of the naturalist depends in some measure upon his ignorance, which still leaves him new worlds of this kind to conquer. He may have reached the very Z of knowledge in the books, but he still feels half ignorant until he has confirmed each bright particular with his eyes. He wishes with his own eyes to see the female cuckoo—rare spectacle!—

121

最 散文
Zui Prose

as she lays her egg on the ground and takes it in her bill to the nest in which it is destined to breed infanticide. He would sit day after day with a field-glass against his eyes in order personally to endorse or refute the evidence suggesting that the cuckoo does lay on the ground and not in a nest. And, if he is so far fortunate as to discover this most secretive of birds in the very act of laying, there still remain for him other fields to conquer in a multitude of such disputed questions as whether the cuckoo's egg is always of the same colour as the other eggs in the nest in which she abandons it. Assuredly the men of science have no reason as yet to weep over their lost ignorance. If they seem to know everything, it is only because you and I know almost nothing. There will always be a fortune of ignorance waiting for them under every fact they turn up. They will never know what song the Sirens sang to Ulysses any more than Sir Thomas Browne did.

If I have called in the cuckoo to illustrate the ordinary man's ignorance, it is not because I can speak with authority on that bird. It is simply because, passing the spring in a parish that seemed to have been invaded by all the cuckoos of Africa, I realised how exceedingly little I, or anybody else I met, knew about them. But your and my ignorance is not confined to cuckoos. It dabbles in all created things, from the sun and moon down to the names of the flowers. I once heard a clever lady asking whether the new moon always appears on the same day of the week. She added that perhaps it is better not to know, because, if one does not know when or in what part of the sky to expect it, its appearance is always a pleasant surprise. I fancy, however, the new moon always comes as a surprise even to those who are familiar with her time-tables. And it is the same with the coming in of spring and the waves of the flowers. We are not the less delighted to find an early primrose because we are sufficiently learned in the services of the year to look for it in March or April rather than in October. We know, again, that the blossom precedes and not succeeds the fruit of the apple-tree, but this does not lessen our amazement at the beautiful holiday of a May orchard.

At the same time there is, perhaps, a special pleasure in re-learning the names of many of the flowers every spring. It is like re-reading a book that one has almost forgotten. Montaigne tells us that he had so bad a memory that he could always read an old book as though he had never read it before. I have myself a capricious and leaking memory. I can read *Hamlet* itself and *The Pickwick Papers* as though they were the works of new authors and had come wet from the press, so much of them fades between one reading and another. There are occasions on which a memory of this kind is an affliction, especially if one has a passion for accuracy. But this is only when life has an object beyond entertainment. In respect of mere luxury, it may be doubted whether there is not as much to be said for a bad memory as for a good one. With a bad memory one can go on reading Plutarch and *The Arabian Nights* all one's life. Little shreds and tags, it is probable, will stick even in the worst memory, just as a succession of sheep cannot leap through a gap in a hedge without leaving a few wisps of wool on the thorns. But the sheep themselves escape, and the great authors leap in the same way out of an idle memory and leave little enough behind.

And, if we can forget books, it is as easy to forget the months and what they showed us, when once they are gone. Just for the moment I tell myself that I know May like the multiplication table and could pass an examination on its flowers, their appearance and their order. Today I can affirm confidently that the buttercup has five petals. (Or is it six? I knew for certain last week.) But next year I shall probably have forgotten my arithmetic, and may have to learn once more not to confuse the buttercup with the celandine. Once more I shall see the world as a garden through the eyes of a stranger, my breath taken away with surprise by the painted fields. I shall find myself wondering whether it is science or ignorance which affirms that the swift (that black exaggeration of the swallow and yet a kinsman of the humming-bird) never settles even on a nest, but disappears at night into the heights of the air. I shall learn with fresh astonishment that it is the male, and not the female, cuckoo that sings. I may have to learn again not to call the campion a wild geranium, and to rediscover whether the ash comes early or late in the etiquette of the trees. A contemporary English novelist was once asked by a foreigner what was the most important crop in England. He answered without a moment's hesitation: "Rye." Ignorance so complete as this seems to me to be touched with magnificence; but the ignorance even of illiterate persons is enormous. The average man who uses a telephone could not explain how a telephone works. He takes for granted the telephone, the railway train, the linotype, the aeroplane, as our grandfathers took for granted the miracles of the gospels. He neither questions nor understands them. It is as though each of us investigated and made his own only a tiny circle of facts. Knowledge outside the day's work is regarded by most men as a gewgaw. Still we are constantly in reaction against our ignorance. We rouse ourselves at intervals and speculate. We revel in speculations about anything at all—about life after death or about such questions as that which is said to have puzzled Aristotle, "Why sneezing from noon to midnight was good, but from night to noon unlucky." One of the greatest joys known to man is to take such a flight into ignorance in search of knowledge. The great pleasure of ignorance is, after all, the pleasure of asking questions. The man who has lost this pleasure or exchanged it for the pleasure of dogma, which is the pleasure of answering, is already beginning to stiffen. One envies so inquisitive a man as Jowett[4], who sat down to the study of physiology in his sixties. Most of us have lost the sense of our ignorance long before that age. We even become vain of our squirrel's hoard of knowledge and regard increasing age itself as a school of omniscience. We forget that Socrates was famed for wisdom not because he was omniscient but because he realised at the age of seventy that he still knew nothing.

同一个普通城里人在乡下散步——也许,特别是在四月份或五月份——而不对他的无知的领域像大陆那样辽阔感到震惊是不可能的。一个人在乡下散步而不对自己的无知的领域像大陆般宽阔感到惊讶是不可能的。成千上万的男女活着然后死去,一辈子也不知道山毛榉和榆树之间有什么区别,不知道乌鸫和画眉的啼鸣有什么不同。很可能,在一座现代化的城市里,能够辨别乌鸫和画眉的啼鸣的人是例外。这并不是因为我们没有见过这些鸟,而仅仅是因为我们没有注意到它们。我们整整一生都有鸟生活在我们的周围,然而我们的观察力是如此微弱,以致我们中间许多人弄不清楚苍头燕雀是否会唱歌,说不出布谷鸟是什么颜色。我们像孩子似地争论布谷鸟是否飞的时候总是唱歌还是仅仅有时候在树枝上唱歌，争论查普曼的下面两行诗是根据他的想象呢，还是根据他对大自然的认识写的：

*当布谷鸟在翠绿的橡树怀中歌唱，*

*初次使人们在明媚春天心花怒放。*

然而，这种无知并不完全是可悲的。从这种无知我们可以得到有所发现的乐趣。只要我们足够无知，那么每年春天，大自然的每一个事实就会来到我们面前，而每个事实的上面还带着露水。如果我们活了半辈子还从来没有见过布谷鸟，而且只知道它是一个流浪者的声音，那么当我们看到它因为深知自己的罪过而从一座树林匆匆忙忙地飞逃到另一座树林时，我们是特别地高兴的；我们对布谷鸟在敢于降落到枞树山坡上（那里可能有复仇者潜伏着）之前，像鹰那样在风中停住，长长的尾巴颤抖着的样子，也特别高兴。假装说博物学家在观察鸟类生活中并无乐趣将是荒谬的，但他的乐趣是稳定的，同生平第一次看见布谷鸟的人的最初兴奋心情相比，几乎是一种理智的、缓慢沉重的消遣；而且瞧吧，世界给变成新的啦。

博物学家的幸福在某种程度上也取决于他的无知，无知给他留下这类新天地让他去征服。他可能在书本上已经达到了知识的顶峰，但在他用自己的眼睛证实每一个光辉的细节之前，他仍然感到是半无知的。他希望亲眼看见雌布谷鸟的一种罕见的情景——在地上卜蛋然后用嘴把蛋叼到窝里去（在这窝里注定要发生杀害幼鸟的事件）。他将一天又一天地坐在那里，望远镜紧贴着眼睛，为的是亲自确认或驳斥这样的说法，说布谷鸟确实是在地上而不是在窝里下蛋的。如果他十分有幸竟然发现了这种最遮遮掩掩的鸟在下蛋，那么也仍然有其他领域在等待他去征服，有一大堆有争论的问题等待他去解答。无疑，科学家们迄今没有理由为他们错过的无知而哭泣。要是他们似乎什么都懂，那么这仅仅是因为你我几乎什么都不懂。在他们发掘出的每一个事实下面总是有一笔无知的财富在等待着他们。他们将永远不会比托马斯·布朗爵士更多地知道塞壬唱给尤利塞斯听的是什么歌。

我把布谷鸟请了进来作为例子来说明普通人的无知，这并不是因为我可以就这种鸟作权威性的发言。理由仅仅是因为我曾经在一个似乎受到过非洲所有布谷鸟的侵袭的教区里度过春天，我从而认识到，对它们，或者任何一个我遇见过的人，是了解得十分十分少的。但你我的无知并不局限于布谷鸟。它涉及所有上帝创造出来的东西，从太阳和月亮一直到花卉的名字。我曾经有一次听到一位聪明的太太问，新月是否总是在相同的星期几出现。她补充说也许最好是不要知道，因为，如果人们事先不知道什么时候在天上的哪个地方能够看见新月，那么它的出现总会给人带来意外的愉快。然而，我想，即使对那些熟悉新月活动时间表的人们，新月也总是出乎意料地来到的。我们并不会因为我们对一年四季的职司有足够的知识，知道要在三月或四月，而不是在十月里，去找报春花，而在发现一株早开的报春花时就不那么高兴。我们也知道苹果树是在结果子之前而不是在结果子之后开花的，但当五月份我们到一家果园去度假日时，这并不会减少我们对假日之美妙所感到的惊讶。

也许，与此同时，每年春天重新温习许多花卉的名字会有一种特殊的愉悦。这就像重读一本人们几乎已经忘了的书一样。蒙田告诉我们说，他的记忆力非常糟糕，糟糕到每次读一本旧书就好像以前从来没有读过这本书一样。我自己就有一个不可捉摸的、有漏洞的记忆力。我甚至能够读起《哈姆雷特》和《匹克威克外传》来好像是在读新作家油墨未干的作品一样，因为在一次阅读和另一次阅读的间隔中间，这些书的内容有那么多都消失了。有些时候，这样一种记忆力是一种苦恼，特别是如果你热爱准确性的话。但这种情况只会发生在当生活（除娱乐之外）另有其目的的时候。就纯粹给人以享受这方面来说，坏的记忆值得一提的地方也并不见得比好的记忆力少。一个记忆力坏的人可以一辈子继续不断地阅读普鲁塔克的作品和《天方夜谭》。就像一群羊一个接一个地从树篱的缺口跳过去，不可能不在荆棘上留下撮毛一样，很可能，即使在记忆力最坏的脑子里也会留下零星片段的东西。但是羊本身逃出去了，那些大作家也以同样的方式从一个懒惰的脑子里跳出去了，留下来的东西真够少的。

而如果我们能够把书忘掉的话，那么当一年十二个月一旦过去之后，要把这些月份和它们向我们说明的问题忘掉是同样容易的。仅仅在刹那间我告诉我自己，我熟悉五月就像熟悉乘法口诀表一样，并且我能够通过一场关于五月的花卉、这些花卉的样子和它们的先后顺序方面的考试。今天我能够满怀信心地断言：金凤花有五个花瓣（或许是六个？上个星期我是知道得很肯定的）。但明年我将很可能忘记了我的算术，并且可能得再学习一次以免把金凤花同白屈莱混淆起来。我将再一次通过一个陌生人的眼睛把世界看作是一个花园，美丽如画的田野将出乎意料地使我大吃一惊。我将发现自己在问自己，宣称雨燕（那种黑色的被夸大了的燕子；然而又是蜂鸟的亲属）永远不落下来栖息，哪怕是在一个鸟窝上也不落下,而是在夜间消逝在高空的是科学呢还是无知？我将带着新的惊讶了解到唱歌的布谷鸟是雄的而不是雌的。我也许要再学习一遍以免把狗筋曼叫做野天竺葵，也许要再学习一遍去重新发现白蜡树在树木的成规中是来得早的还是来得晚的。一位当代的英国小说家曾经有一次被外国人问到：在英国，最重要的庄稼是什么？他毫不犹豫地回答："黑麦"。像这样完全的无知，在我看来似乎带有豪言壮语的味道；但是，即使是不识字的人的无知也是巨大的。使用电话机的普通人解释不了电话机是怎样工作的。他把电话、火车、铸造排字机、飞机视为理所当然的东西，正象我们的祖先把福音书中的奇迹视作理所当然的东西一样。对这些东西，他既不质疑也不理解。我们每一个人好像只是调查了一个小圈子里面的事实并把这些事实变成了自己的。日常工作以外的知识被大多数人看作是华而不实的东西。然而我们还是经常对我们的无知作出反应，加以反对的。我们不时地唤起自己去思考。我们喜欢对什么事情都思考——思考死后的生活或思考那些像据说曾经使亚里士多德感到困惑的问题——"为什么从中午到子夜打喷嚏是好的，但从半夜到中午打喷嚏则是不吉利的？"——人类感受过的最大欢乐之一是：迅速逃到无知中去追求知识。无知的巨大乐趣，归根结底，是提问题的乐趣。已经失去了这种乐趣的人或已经用这种乐趣去换取教条的乐趣（这就是回答问题的乐趣）的人，已经在开始僵化。人们羡慕像乔伊特那样爱一问到底的人，他在六十岁之后还坐下来学习生理学。我们中间的大多数人在到达他这个年龄以前早就已经失去了无知感。我们甚至对我们像松鼠那样积攒的一点知识感到自负，并把不断增长的年龄本身看作是无所不知的源泉。我们忘记了苏格拉底之所以以智慧闻名于世并不是因为他无所不知而是因为他在七十岁的时候认识到他还什么都不知道。

[1] chaffinch n. 花鸡, 苍头燕雀

[2] Chapman, 英国作家和翻译家

[3] plodding adj. 沉重缓慢的

[4] Jowett, 1817—1893, 英国古典学者

# 我的世界观
# The World As I See It

【美国】阿尔伯特·爱因斯坦

### 作者简介

阿尔伯特·爱因斯坦(1879-1955),举世闻名的德裔美国科学家,犹太人,现代物理学的开创者和奠基人,相对论、"质能关系"的提出者,"决定论量子力学诠释"的捍卫者。被称为不掷骰子的上帝。曾被美国《时代》周刊评选为"世纪伟人"。《我的世界观》率真而深刻地表现了作者的爱与憎,把一个人不同于兽的基本点尽皆展现。

How strange is the lot of us mortals! Each of us is here for a brief sojourn; for what purpose he knows not, though he sometimes thinks he senses it. But without deeper reflection one knows from daily life that one exists for other people—first of all for those upon whose smiles and well-being our own happiness is wholly dependent, and then for the many, unknown to us, to whose destinies we are bound by the ties of sympathy. A hundred times every day I remind myself that my inner and outer life are based on the labors of other men, living and dead, and that I must exert myself in order to give in the same measure as I have received and am still receiving. I am strongly drawn to the simple life and am often oppressed by the feeling that I am engrossing an unnecessary amount of the labor of my fellowmen. I regard class differences as contrary to justice and, in the last resort, based on force. I also consider that plain living is good for everybody, physically and mentally.

In human freedom in the philosophical sense I am definitely a disbeliever. Everybody acts not only under external compulsion but also in accordance with inner necessity. Schopenhauer's saying, that "a man can do as he will, but not will as he will," has been an inspiration to me since my youth up, and a continual consolation and unfailing well-spring of patience in the face of the hardships of life, my own and others. This feeling mercifully mitigates the sense of responsibility which so easily becomes paralyzing, and it prevents us from taking ourselves and other people too seriously; it conduces to a view of life in which humor, above all, has its due place.

To inquire after the meaning or object of one's own existence or of creation generally has always seemed to me absurd from an objective point of view. And yet everybody has certain ideals which determine the direction of his endeavors and his judgments. I have never looked upon ease and happiness as ends in themselves—this critical basis I call the ideal of a pigsty. The ideals that have lighted my way, and time after time have given me new courage to face life cheerfully, have been Kindness, Beauty, and Truth. Without the sense of kinship with men of like mind, without the occupation with the objective world, the eternally unattainable in the field of art and scientific endeavors, life would have seemed empty to me. The trite objects of human efforts—possessions, outward success, luxury—have always seemed to me contemptible.

My passionate sense of social justice and social responsibility has always contrasted oddly with my pronounced lack of need for direct contact with other human beings and human communities. I am truly a 'lone traveler' and have never belonged to my country, my home, my friends, or even my immediate family, with my whole heart; in the face of all these ties, I have never lost a sense of distance and a need for solitude—a feeling which increases with the years. One is sharply conscious, yet without regret, of the limits to the possibility of mutual understanding and sympathy with one's fellow-creatures. Such a person no doubt loses something in the way of geniality and light-heartedness; on the other hand, he is largely independent of the opinions, habits, and judgments of his fellows and avoids the temptation to take his stand on such insecure foundations.

My political ideal is democracy. Let every man be respected as an individual and no man idolized. It is an irony of fate that I myself have been the recipient of excessive admiration and reverence from my fellow-beings, through no fault, and no merit, of my own. The cause of this may well be the desire, unattainable for many, to understand the few ideas to which I have with my feeble powers attained through ceaseless struggle. I am quite aware that for any organization to reach its goals, one man must do the thinking and directing and generally bear the responsibility. But the led must not be coerced, they must be able to choose their leader. In my opinion, an autocratic system of coercion soon degenerates; force attracts men of low morality, and I believe it to be an invariable rule that tyrants of genius are succeeded by scoundrels. For this reason I have always been passionately opposed to systems such as we see in Italy and Russia today. The thing that has brought discredit upon the form of democracy as it exists in Europe today is not to be laid to the door of the democratic principle as such, but to the lack of stability of governments and to the impersonal character of the electoral system. I believe that in this respect the United States of America have found the right way. They have a President powers really to exercise his responsibility. What I value, on the other hand, in the German political system is the more extensive provision that it makes for the individual in case of illness or need. The really valuable thing in the pageant of human life seems to me not the political state, but the creative, sentient[1] individual, the personality; it alone creates the noble and the sublime, while the herd as such remains dull in thought and dull in feeling.

This topic brings me to that worst outcrop of herd life, the military system, which I abhor. That a man can take pleasure in marching in formation to the strains of a band is enough to make me despise him. He has only been given his big brain by mistake; a backbone was all he needed. This plague-spot of civilization ought to be abolished with all possible speed. Heroism on command, senseless violence, and all the loathsome nonsense that goes by the name of patriotism—how passionately I hate them! War seems to me a mean, contemptible thing: I would rather be hacked in pieces than take part in such an abominable business. And yet so high, in spite of everything, is my opinion of the human race that I believe this bogey would have disappeared long ago, had the sound sense of the nations not been systematically corrupted by commercial and political interests acting through the schools and the press.

The most beautiful experience we can have is the mysterious. It is the fundamental emotion that stands at the cradle of true art and true science. Whoever does not know it and can no longer wonder, no longer marvel, is as good as dead, and his eyes are dimmed. It was the experience of mystery— even if mixed with fear—that engendered religion. A knowledge of the existence of something we cannot penetrate, our perceptions of the profoundest reason and the most radiant beauty, which only in their most primitive forms are accessible to our minds: it is this knowledge and this emotion that constitute true religiosity. In this sense, and only this sense, I am a deeply religious man. I cannot conceive of a God who rewards and punishes his creatures, or has a will of the type of which we are conscious in ourselves. And individual who should survive his physical death is also beyond my comprehension, nor do I wish it otherwise; such notions are for the fears or absurd egoism of feeble souls. I am satisfied with the mystery of life's eternity and with a knowledge, a sense, of the marvelous structure of existence—as well as the humble attempt to understand even a tiny portion of the Reason that manifests itself in nature.

131

最散文
Zui Prose

我们这些总有一死的人的命运多么奇特！我们每个人在这个世界上都只作一个短暂的逗留；目的何在却无从知道，尽管有时自以为对此若有所感。但是，不必深思，只要从日常生活就可以明白：人是为别人而生存的——首先是为那样一些人，我们的幸福全部依赖于他们的喜悦和健康；其次是为许多我们所不认识的人，他们的命运通过同情的纽带同我们密切结合在一起。我每天上百次的提醒自己：我的精神生活和物质生活都是以别人（包括生者和死者）的劳动为基础的，我必须尽力以同样的分量来报偿我所领受了的和至今还在领受着的东西。我强烈地向往着俭朴的生活。并且时常发觉自己占用了同胞的过多劳动而难以忍受。我认为阶级的区分是不合理的，它最后所凭借的是以暴力为根据。我也相信，简单淳朴的生活，无论在身体上还是在精神上，对每个人都是有益的。

我完全不相信人类会有那种在哲学意义上的自由。每一个人的行为不仅受着外界的强制，而且要适应内在的必然。叔本华说："人虽然能够做他所想做的，但不能要他所想要的。"这句格言从我青年时代起就给了我真正的启示；在我自己和别人的生活面临困难的时候，它总是使我们得到安慰，并且是宽容的持续不断的源泉。这种体会可以宽大为怀地减轻那种容易使人气馁的责任感，也可以防止我们过于严肃地对待自己和别人；它导致一种特别给幽默以应有地位的人生观。

要追究一个人自己或一切生物生存的意义或目的，从客观的观点看来，我总觉得是愚蠢可笑的。可是每个人都有一些理想，这些理想决定着他的努力和判断的方向。就在这个意义上，我从来不把安逸和享乐看作生活目的本身——我把这种伦理基础叫做猪栏的理想。照亮我道路的是善、美和真。它们经常给我积极乐观面对生活的新的勇气。要是没有志同道合者之间的亲切感情，要不是全神贯注于客观世界——那个在艺术和科学工作领域里永远达不到的对象，那么在我看来，生活就会是空虚的。我总觉得，人们所努力追求的庸俗目标——财产、虚荣、奢侈的生活——都是可鄙的。

我有强烈的社会正义感和社会责任感，但我又明显地缺乏与别人和社会直接接触的要求，这两者总是形成古怪的对照。我实在是一个"孤独的旅客"，我未曾全心全意地属于我的国家、我的家庭、我的朋友，甚至我最为接近的亲人；在所有这些关系面前,我总是感觉到一定距离而且需要保持孤独——而这种感受正与年俱增。人们会清楚地发觉,同别人的相互了解和协调一致是有限度的,但这不值得惋惜。无疑,这样的人在某种程度上会失去他的天真无邪和无忧无虑的心境;但另一方面,他却能够在很大程度上不为别人的意见、习惯和判断所左右,并且能够避免那种把他的内心平衡建立在这样一些不可靠的基础之上的诱惑。

我的政治理想是民主政体。让每一个人都作为个人而受到尊重,而不让任何人成为被崇拜的偶像。我自己一直受到同代人的过分的赞扬和尊敬,这不是由于我自己的过错,也不是由于我自己的功劳,而实在是一种命运的嘲弄。其原因大概在于人们有一种愿望,想理解我以自已微薄的绵力,通过不断的斗争所获得的少数几个观念,而这种愿望有很多人却未能实现。我完全明白,一个组织要实现它的目的,就必须有一个人去思考,去指挥,并且全面担负起责任来。但是被领导的人不应当受到强迫,他们必须能够选择自己的领袖。在我看来,强迫的专制制度很快就会腐化堕落。因为暴力所招引来的总是一些品德低劣的人,而且我相信,天才的暴君总是由无赖来继承的,这是一条千古不易的规律。就是由于这个缘故,我总强烈地反对今天在意大利和俄国所见到的那种制度。像欧洲今天所存在的情况,已使得民主形式受到怀疑,这不能归咎于民主原则本身,而是由于政府的不稳定和选举制度中与个人无关的特征。我相信美国在这方面已经找到了正确的道路。他们选出了一个任期足够长的总统,他有充分的权力来真正履行他的职责。另一方面,在德国政治制度中,为我所看重的是它为救济患病或贫困的人作出了可贵的广泛的规定。在人生的丰富多彩的表演中,我觉得真正可贵的,不是政治上的国家,而是有创造性的、有感情的个人,是人格;只有个人才能创造出高尚的和卓越的东西,而群众本身在思想上总是迟钝的,在感觉上也总是迟钝的。

讲到这里,我想起了群众生活中最坏的一种表现,那就是使我厌恶的军事制度。一个人能够洋洋得意的随着军乐队在四列纵队里行进,单凭这一点就足以使我对他鄙夷不屑。他所以长了一个大脑,只是个错误;光有脊椎就可满足他的全部需要了。文明的这种罪恶的渊薮,应当尽快加以消灭。任人支配的英雄主义、冷酷无情的暴行,以及在爱国主义名义下的一切可恶的胡闹,所有这些都使我深恶痛绝! 在我看来,战争是多么卑鄙、下流:我宁愿被千刀万剐,也不愿参与这种可憎的勾当。尽管如此,我对人类的评价还是十分高的,我相信,要是人民的健康感情没有遭到那些通过学校和报纸而起作用的商业利益和政治利益的蓄意败坏,那么战争这个妖魔早就该绝迹了。

我们所能有的最美好的经验是奥秘的经验。它是坚守在真正艺术和真正科学发源地上的基本感情。谁要体验不到它,谁要是不再有好奇心,也不再有惊讶的感觉,谁就无异于行尸走肉,他的眼睛便是模糊不清的。就是这样奥秘的经验——虽然掺杂着恐惧——产生了宗教。我们认识到有某种为我们所不能洞察的东西存在,感觉到那种只能以其最原始的形式接近我们心灵的最深奥的理性和最灿烂的美——正是这种认识和这种情感构成了真正的宗教感情。在这个意义上,而且也只是在这个意义上,我才是一个具有深挚宗教感情的人。我无法想象存在这样一个上帝,它会对自己的创造物加以赏罚,会具有我们在自己身上所体验到的那种意志。我不能也不愿去想象一个人在肉体死亡以后还会继续活着;让那些脆弱的灵魂,由于恐惧或者由于可笑的唯我论,去拿这种思想当宝贝吧! 我自己只求满足于生命永恒的奥秘,满足于觉察现存世界的神奇结构,窥见它的一鳞半爪,并且以诚挚的努力去领悟在自然界中显示出来的理性的那一部分,倘若真能如此,即使只领悟其极小的一部分,我也就心满意足了。

---

[1] sentient adj. 有知觉的,知悉的

# 第四卷

---

## 品味乾坤
## Tasting the Universe

我上班的公司
The Company in Which I Work

【美国】约瑟夫·海勒

· · · · · · · · · · · · · · · · · · · · · · · · · · · · · · · · · · · · · · · · ·

作者简介

　　约瑟夫·海勒(1923-1999)美国著名作家,被誉为"黑色幽默"的巨星。其代表作《第二十二条军规》以荒诞的形式、多角度、多层次地展示了生活,已成为讽刺文学的经典之作。除小说外,他还创作过一些舞台剧、电影剧本、短篇小说和评论。《我上班的公司》表现了一个在大公司工作的员工因制度和环境而造成的内心扭曲与心理灰暗。

In the company in which I work, each of us is afraid of at least one person. The lower your position is, the more people you are afraid of. And all the people are afraid of the twelve men at the top who helped found and build the company and now own and direct it.

All these twelve men are elderly now and drained by time and success of energy and ambition. Many have spent their whole lives here. They seem friendly, slow, and content when I come upon them in the halls and always courteous and mute when they ride with others in the public elevators. They no longer work hard. They hold meetings, make promotions, and allow their names to be used on announcements that are prepared and issued by somebody else. Nobody is sure anymore who really runs the company (not even the people who are credited with running it), but the company does run.

In the normal course of a business day... I am afraid of Jack Green because my department is part of his department and Jack Green is my boss; Green is afraid of me because most of the work in my department is done for the Sales Department, which is more important than his department, and I am much closer to Andy Kagle and the other people in the Sales Department than he is.

Green distrusts me fitfully. He makes it clear to me every now and then that he wishes to see everything coming out of my department before it is shown to other departments. I know he does not really mean this: he is too busy with his own work to pay that much attention to all of mine, and I will by pass him on most of our assignments rather than take up his time and delay their delivery to people who have an immediate need for them. Most of the work we do in my department is, in the long run, trivial. But Green always grows alarmed when someone from another department praises something that has come from my department. He turns scarlet with rage and embarrassment if he has not seen or heard of it.

In my department, there are six people who are afraid of me, and one small secretary who is afraid of all of us. I have one other person working for me who is not afraid of anyone, not even me, and I would fire him quickly, but I'm afraid of him...

The people in the company who are most afraid of most people are the salesmen. They live and work under pressure that is extraordinary. When things are bad, they are worse for the salesmen; when things are good, they are not much better.

They are always on trial, always on the verge of failure, collectively and individually. They strain, even the most secure and self-assured of them, to look good on paper; and there is much paper for them to look good on. Each week, for example, a record of the sales results of the preceding week for each sales office and for the Sales Department as a whole for each division of the company is kept and compared to the sales results for the corresponding week of the year before. The figures are photocopied and distributed throughout the company to all the people and departments whose work is related to selling. The result of this photocopying and distributing is that there is almost continuous public scrutiny and discussion throughout the company of how well or poorly the salesmen in each sales office of each division of the company are doing at any given time.

When salesmen are doing well, there is pressure upon them to begin doing better, for fear they may start doing worse. When they are doing poorly, they are doing terribly. When a salesman lands a large order or brings in an important new account, his elation is brief, for there is danger he might lose that large order or important new account to a salesman from a competing company the next time around. It might even be canceled before it is filled, in which case no one is certain anything was gained or lost. So there is crisis and alarm even in their triumphs.

Nevertheless, the salesmen love their work and would not choose any other kind. They are a vigorous, fun-loving bunch when they are not suffering abdominal cramps or brooding miserably about the future; on the other hand, they often turn cranky without warning and complain a lot. Each of them can name at least one superior in the company who he feels has a grudge against him and is determined to wreck his career.

The salesmen work hard and earn big salaries, with large personal expense accounts that they squander generously on other people in and out of the company, including me. They own good houses in good communities and play good games of golf on good private golf courses. The company encourages this. The company, in fact, will pay for their country club membership and all charges they incur there, and rewards salesmen who make a good impression on the golf course.

Unmarried men are not wanted in the Sales Department, not even widowers, for the company has learned from experience that it is difficult and dangerous for unmarried salesmen to mix socially with prominent executives and their wives or participate with them in responsible civic affairs. If a salesman's wife dies and he is not ready to remarry, he is usually moved into an administrative position after several months of mourning. Bachelors are never hired for the sales force, and salesmen who get divorced, or whose wives die, know they had better remarry or begin looking ahead toward a different job.

Strangely enough, the salesmen react very well to the constant pressure and rigid supervision to which they are subjected. They are stimulated and motivated by discipline and direction. They thrive on explicit guidance toward clear objectives. For the most part, they are cheerful, confident, and gregarious when they are not irritable, anxious, and depressed. There must be something in the makeup of a man that enables him not only to be a salesman, but to want to be one.

The salesmen are proud of their position and of the status and importance they enjoy within the company, for the function of my department, and of most other departments, is to help the salesmen sell. The company exists to sell. That's the reason we were hired, and the reason we are paid.

The people in the company who are least afraid are the few in our small Market Research Department, who believe in nothing and are concerned

139

最散文
Zui Prose

with collecting, organizing, interpreting, and reorganizing statistical information about the public, the market, the country, and the world. For one thing, their salaries are small, and they know they will not have much trouble finding jobs paying just as little in other companies if they lose their jobs here. Their budget, too, is small, for they are no longer permitted to undertake large projects.

Most of the information we use now is obtained free from trade associations and some governmental organizations, and there is no way of knowing anymore whether the information on which we base our own information for distribution is true or false. But that doesn't seem to matter; all that does matter is that the information comes from a reputable source. People in the Market Research Department are never held to blame for conditions they discover outside the company that place us at a competitive disadvantage. They are not expected to change reality, but merely to find it if they can and suggest ingenious ways of disguising it. To a great extent, that is the nature of my own work, and all of us under Green work closely with the Sales Department and the Public Relations Department in converting whole truths into half truths and half truths into whole ones.

I am very good at these techniques of deception although I am not always able anymore to deceive myself. In fact, I am continuously astonished by people in the company who fall victim to their own propaganda. There are so many now who actually believe that what we do is really important. This happens not only to salesmen, but to the shrewd, capable executives in top management. It happens to people on my own level and lower. It happens to just about everybody in the company who graduated from a good business school with honors. Every time we launch a new advertising campaign, for example, people inside the company are the first ones to be taken in by it. Every time we introduce a new product, or an old product with a different cover, color, and name that we present as new, people inside the company are the first to rush to buy it—even when it's no good.

It's a wise person, I guess, who knows he's dumb, and an honest person who knows he's a liar. And it's a dumb person who's convinced he is wise. We wise grownups here at the company go sliding in and out all day long, scaring each other at our desks and trying to evade the people who frighten us. We come to work, have lunch, and go home. We goose-step in and goose-step out, change our partners and wander all about, and go back home till we all drop dead. Really, I ask myself every now and then, depending on how well or poorly things are going at the office or at home with my wife, or with my retarded son, or with my other son, or my daughter, or the colored maid, or the nurse for my retarded son, is this all there is for me to do? Is this really the most I can get from the few years left in this one life of mine?

And the answer I get, of course, is always—Yes! ...

I am bored with my work very often now. Everything routine that comes in I pass along to somebody else. This makes my boredom worse. It's a real problem to decide whether it's more boring to do something boring than to pass along everything boring that comes in to somebody else and then have nothing to do at all.

Actually, I enjoy my work when the assignments are large and urgent and somewhat frightening and will come to the attention of many people. I get scared, and am unable to sleep at night, but I usually perform at my best under this stimulating kind of pressure and enjoy my job the most. I handle all of these important projects myself, and I rejoice with tremendous pride and vanity in the compliments I receive when I do them well. But between such peaks of challenge and elation there is monotony and despair. (And I find, too, that once I've succeeded in impressing somebody, I'm not much excited about impressing that same person again; there is a large, emotional letdown after I survive each crisis, a kind of empty, tragic disappointment, and last year's threat, opportunity, and inspiration are often this year's inescapable tedium. I frequently feel I'm being taken advantage of merely because I'm asked to do the work I'm paid to do.)

On days when I'm especially melancholy, I began constructing tables of organization... classifying people in the company on the basis of envy, hope, fear, ambition, frustration, rivalry, hatred, or disappointment. I call these charts my Happiness Charts. These exercises in malice never fail to boost my spirits—but only for a while. I rank pretty high when the company is analyzed this way, because I'm not envious or disappointed, and I have no expectations. At the very top, of course, are those people, mostly young and without dependents, to whom the company is not yet an institution of any sacred merit but still only a place to work, and who regard their present association with it as something temporary. I put these people at the top because if you asked any one of them if he would choose to spend the rest of his life working for the company, he would give you a resounding No!, regardless of what inducements were offered. I was that high once. If you asked me that same question today, I would also give you a resounding No! and add:

"I think I'd rather die now."

But I am making no plans to leave.

I have the feeling now that there is no place left for me to go.

在我上班的公司里,我们每一个人至少害怕一个人。你的职位越低,你所畏惧的人就越多。所有的员工都害怕领导层的12个成员,他们组建了并正在拥有和经营着这家公司。

现在所有这12个人都已经老了,而且由于长年努力为成功而奋斗已耗尽精力。他们中许多人在公司度过了一生。当我在大厅里碰上他们,他们显得友善、稳重而且自得。当他们和他人共乘公共电梯时,他们总是彬彬有礼而且保持沉默。他们不再努力工作。他们召开会议,研究该提升谁,别人准备并发布的声明上也要署上他们的名字。没有人能真正肯定谁在经营这家公司(甚至连被认为是在经营这家公司的人也不知道),但公司确实在运转。

在平常的工作中,我害怕杰克·格林,因为我的部门隶属于他的部门,他是我的老板。格林害怕我,因为我的部门大部分的工作是为销售部做的,而销售部要比格林的部门更重要。我与安迪·凯格和销售部其他成员的关系要比格林与他们之间的关系更亲密。

格林一阵阵地不信任我。他不时地让我清楚一个事实,即他希望我的部门所出的成果在显示给其他部门之前先给他看看。我知道这并非他本意。他忙于他的工作,没有时间来关注我的工作。在我大多数的工作中,我都绕过他,不占用他的时间,不耽搁送货给那些急需我们货物的人。我的部门所做的大部分工作最终都是琐碎的,但当别的部门的人表扬我部门的成果时,格林总是很不安。如果这些成果是他闻所未闻、见所未见的,他会因愤怒和尴尬而恼羞成怒。

在我的部门里,害怕我的有6个人,还有一个怕每个人的小秘书。在我手下还有一个员工,他不怕任何人,甚至连我都不怕,我想很快解雇他,但我害怕他……

在我的公司里,畏惧大多数人的是推销员,他们生活、工作在巨大的压力之下。当一切进展不顺利时,推销员的日子更难过,而一切进展顺利时,他们的日子也好不到哪去。

推销员总是处于接受检查的状态之中,处于失败的边缘,集体地或是个人地。即便是最有把握、最自信的推销员,为了在文件中把自己的业绩编写得很出色,也在努力地工作着。这样的文件有许多需要他们填写。比如说,每个星期都记载下本周公司的每个销售办公室和每个销售部门的销售结果,然后和前一年的相应星期的销售结果作比较,这些统计数字被复印下来,发给整个公司所有与销售相关的部门与人员。这种做法的结果是公司每个部门的每个销售办公室的推销员在任何规定的时期内业绩的好坏都不断地处于公众的审查和评论之中。

当推销员干得好时,他们会承受压力以便干得更好,惟恐自己会开始走下坡路。当他们干得不好时,他们的日子就更不好过了。当一个推销员获得一张大订单或得到一笔新账款,他只有短暂的兴奋,因为他会面临下一次这笔订单和账款被与本公司竞争的公司的推销员夺走的危险。在没人确保是否会赢利还是赔钱的情况下,订单可能会在没填之前就被取消。所以即便在推销员的辉煌时期也存在危机。

然而,推销员喜欢自己的工作,不愿选择其他工作。当他们不腹痛、不为自己的未来忧虑时,他们是一群精力充沛、好开玩笑的人。另一方面,他们经常毫无

143

预警地变得古怪并且牢骚满腹。每个推销员至少能说出一个公司上层人物，他认为这个上层人物对他有恶意，而且有意破坏他的事业。

推销员工作努力，工资高，他们还有公司负担的个人费用账户，用这个账户里的钱他们很大方地宴请包括我在内的公司内外的人。他们在好的住宅区拥有好房子，在上等的私家高尔夫球场打精彩的高尔夫球。公司鼓励他们这样做。事实上，公司将支付他们的乡村俱乐部会员费以及他们在俱乐部的一切开销，并奖赏那些在高尔夫球场上给人留下好印象的推销员。

销售部不要未婚男子，哪怕是鳏夫也不要，因为公司从以往的经验中了解到，对未婚的推销员来说，在社交场合与著名的上层管理人员和他们的妻子聚会或与这些人一起参加重大活动是很困难和危险的。如果推销员的妻子死了而他又不准备再婚，通常在经过几个月的哀悼期之后，他会被调到行政部门。推销员的队伍从不雇佣单身汉，那些离了婚或死了妻子的推销员知道自己最好再婚或寻找另一份工作。

特别奇怪的是，推销员们对持续不断的压力和不得不服从的严格监督反应良好。纪律和监督激励着他们。他们在明确的目标、明确的指导下获得成功。大体上，当他们不烦躁、不忧虑、不沮丧时，他们是快活、自信、合群的。在其身上肯定有某种气质使他们不仅成为推销员，而且想当推销员。

推销员以他们的职位及在公司的地位和重要性而感到自豪，因为我的部门和大多数部门的职责是帮助推销员卖货。公司靠卖货为生。这就是我们被雇佣、被发薪水的原因。

公司里最不怕别人的是那几个市场调研部的成员。他们什么也不担心，任务就是对公众、市场、国家和世界的统计数字进行收集、组织、解释、重新组织。一方面，他们的工资低，而且他们知道如果在这儿丢了工作，到其他公司找一份同样低工资的工作不会有什么困难。他们的经费也很少，因为公司不再允许他们承担大的项目。

我们现在所使用的大部分信息是从商贸协会和一些政府机构免费得来的，我们无法知道我们经销所依据的信息是真是假。但这似乎不重要；重要的是信息来源于信誉好的源头。市场调研部的人从未因他们所发现的公司外部的情况使我们处于竞争的不利地位而受责备。没人指望他们改变事实，而只是看他们是否能有创造性的意见来掩盖事实。在很大程度上，这也是我的工作本质。格林所有的下属密切地和销售部以及公关部合作，来把整个事实转变成一半事实，把一半事实转变成整个事实。

我十分擅长这些骗术,虽然我已不能再欺骗自己。事实上,我总是感到震惊,公司的一些人竟然被自己的宣传所欺骗。有许多人真的相信我们所做的是重要的,不仅推销员这样认为,而且那些精明的、能力强的高级管理层的人员也这样认为。还有那些与我职位相当或比我职位低的人,以及以优异成绩毕业于名牌商业学校的人也都这样认为。比如说,每次我们发动一场广告大战,公司内部的人是最先被广告吸引的。每次我们推出一种新产品,或把以前的产品换上不同的包装、颜色、名字,并按新产品推出,公司内部的人最先踊跃购买——即便产品没什么用。

我认为,知道自己笨的人是明智的,知道自己是说谎的人才是诚实的。认为自己是明智的人是愚笨的。公司聪明的成年人整天悄悄地潜入办公室监督工作,又不知何时悄悄地离开,使工作人员相互害怕,而同时他们又躲避令他们自己感到害怕的人。我们上班、吃午饭、回家。我们出入公司走姿规矩,下班后和其他伙伴(而不是本部门的同事)去闲荡消遣直到精疲力尽才回家。根据我办公室工作的进展情况,或在家中和我妻子、我那智障儿子,或其他儿女,或那个黑人女仆,或照料我傻儿子的护士关系进展情况,我真的不时地问自己,这就是我所要做的一切吗? 这就是我从余生中能获得的最多的吗?

我所得到的答案总是——是的! ……

我现在时常对我的工作感到厌烦。日常的常规工作我都交给别人去做。而这样却使我感到更加无聊。做令人厌烦的事情是否比把令人厌烦的事情交给别人去做而自己无所事事更令人厌烦呢? 这真是一个要做出决定的问题。

事实上,我喜欢我的工作,当工作量大、紧急而且还有点令人害怕,并且能引起许多人关注的时候。我害怕,而且晚上睡不着,但是在这种刺激性压力下我却能表现得最好而且最喜欢做这份工作。我亲自处理所有的重要计划,当我把一切处理妥当,我会很高兴地接受别人的恭维,这些恭维之辞极大地满足了我的虚荣心,使我感到特自豪。但是在这种挑战和兴奋的高峰之间还有乏味和绝望。(我也发觉一旦我成功地给某人留下印象,那么给同一个人再一次留下印象时,我就不会再那么兴奋了。每次成功地渡过危机之后,我会有一种情感上的失落。一种空空的、悲伤的失望感。去年的威胁、机遇、鼓励常常成为今年无法躲开的乏味。我时常感到我被利用只是因为我被要求去做能付我工资的工作。)

在我特别忧郁的日子里,我编一个表把公司的人按嫉妒、希望、害怕、野心、挫折、竞争、仇恨或失望排在表内。我把这表叫"幸福之表"。这种恶意游戏总能振奋我的精神——但仅仅是短时间的。通过把公司里的人进行上述分析,我可以排得靠前,因为我不爱嫉妒、不沮丧,没有奢望。排在表的最前列的当然是那些年轻人,他们不需要供养谁,对于他们来说公司不是有着神圣业绩的单位而仅仅是一个工作的地方,而且他们认为自己与公司的关系是暂时的。我把这些人排在前列,因为如果你问他们中的任何一个人他是否愿意把自己的余生贡献给公司,他会声音洪亮地回答:不!不管给他什么样的诱惑。我也曾经排得靠前。如果你今天问我同样的问题,我也会高声地回答:不!而且加上一句:

"我想我宁愿现在死掉。"

但目前我不打算离开公司。

我觉得没有我能去的地方。

# 论老之将至
# How to Grow Old

【英国】波特兰·罗素

## 作者简介

　　波特兰·罗素(1872－1970)是二十世纪最有影响力的哲学家、数学家和逻辑学家之一,也是活跃的政治活动家,并致力于哲学的大众化、普及化。虽政治立场频惹争议,但无数人将罗素视为这个时代的先知。1950年,罗素获得诺贝尔文学奖,以表彰其"多样且重要的作品,持续不断的追求人道主义理想和思想自由"。

In spite of the title, this article will really be on how not to grow old, which, at my time of life, is a much more important subject. My first advice would be to choose your ancestors carefully. Although both my parents died young, I have done well in this respect as regards my other ancestors. My maternal grandfather, it is true, was cut off in the flower of his youth at the age of sixty-seven, but my other three grandparents all lived to be over eighty. Of remoter ancestors I can only discover one who did not live to a great age, and he died of a disease which is now rare, namely, having his head cut off. A great-grandmother of mine, who was a friend of Gibbon[1], lived to the age of ninety-two, and to her last day remained a terror to all her descendants. My maternal grandmother, after having nine children who survived, one who died in infancy, and many miscarriages, as soon as she became a widow devoted herself to women's higher education. She was one of the founders of Girton College[2], and worked hard at opening the medical profession to women. She used to tell of how she met in Italy an elderly gentleman who was looking very sad. She asked him why he was so melancholy and he said that he had just parted from his two grandchildren. "Good gracious," she exclaimed, "I have seventy-two grandchildren, and if I were sad each time I parted from one of them, I should have a miserable existence!" "Madre snaturale!" [3] he replied. But speaking as one of the seventy-two, I prefer her recipe. After the age of eighty she found she had some difficulty in getting to sleep, so she habitually spent the hours from midnight to 3 a.m. in reading popular science. I do not believe that she ever had time to notice that she was growing old. This, I think, is the proper recipe for remaining young. If you have wide and keen interests and activities in which you can still be effective, you will have no reason to think about the merely statistical fact of the number of years you have already lived, still less of the probable shortness of your future.

As regards health, I have nothing useful to say as I have little experience of illness. I eat and drink whatever I like, and sleep when I cannot keep awake. I never do anything whatever on the ground that it is good for health, though in actual fact the things I like doing are mostly wholesome.

Psychologically there are two dangers to be guarded against in old age. One of these is undue absorption in the past. It does not do to live in memories, in regrets for the good old days, or in sadness about friends who are dead. One's thoughts must be directed to the future, and to things about which there is something to be done. This is not always easy; one's own past is a gradually increasing weight. It is easy to think to oneself that one's emotions used to be more vivid than they are, and one's mind more keen. If this is true it should be forgotten, and if it is forgotten it will probably not be true.

The other thing to be avoided is clinging to youth in the hope of sucking vigour from its vitality. When your children are grown up they want to live their own lives, and if you continue to be as interested in them as you were when they were young, you are likely to become a burden to them, unless they are unusually callous. I do not mean that one should be without interest in them, but one's interest should be contemplative and, if possible, philanthropic, but not unduly emotional. Animals become indifferent to their young as soon as their young can look after themselves, but human beings, owing to the length of infancy, find this difficult.

I think that a successful old age is easiest for those who have strong impersonal interests involving appropriate activities. It is in this sphere that long experience is really fruitful, and it is in this sphere that the wisdom born of experience can be exercised without being oppressive. It is no use telling grownup children not to make mistakes, both because they will not believe you, and because mistakes are an essential part of education. But if you are one of those who are incapable of impersonal interests, you may find that your life will be empty unless you concern yourself with your children and grandchildren. In that case you must realise that while you can still render them material services, such as making them an allowance or knitting them jumpers, you must not expect that they will enjoy your company.

最 散文
Zui Prose

Some old people are oppressed by the fear of death. In the young there is a justification for this feeling. Young men who have reason to fear that they will be killed in battle may justifiably feel bitter in the thought that they have been cheated of the best things that life has to offer. But in an old man who has known human joys and sorrows, and has achieved whatever work it was in him to do, the fear of death is somewhat abject and ignoble. The best way to overcome it –so at least it seems to me–is to make your interests gradually wider and more impersonal, until bit by bit the walls of the ego recede, and your life becomes increasingly merged in the universal life. An individual human existence should be like a river: small at first, narrowly contained within its banks, and rushing passionately past rocks and over waterfalls. Gradually the river grows wider, the banks recede, the waters flow more quietly, and in the end, without any visible break, they become merged in the sea, and painlessly lose their individual being. The man who, in old age, can see his life in this way, will not suffer from the fear of death, since the things he cares for will continue. And if, with the decay of vitality, weariness increases, the thought of rest will not be unwelcome. I should wish to die while still at work, knowing that others will carry on what I can no longer do and content in the thought that what was possible has been done.

虽然有这样一个标题，这篇文章真正要谈的却是怎样才能不老。在我这个年纪，这实在是一个至关重要的问题。我的第一个忠告是，要仔细选择你的祖先。尽管我的双亲皆属早逝，但是考虑到我的其他祖先，我的选择还是很不错的。是的，我的外祖父六十七岁时去世，正值盛年，可是另外三位祖父（母）辈的亲人都活到八十岁以上。至于稍远些的亲戚，我只发现一位没能长寿的，他死于一种已罕见的病症：被杀头。我的一位曾祖母是吉本的朋友，她活到九十二岁高龄，一直到死，她始终是让子孙们全都感到敬畏的人。我的外祖母，一辈子生了十个孩子,活了九个,还有一个早年夭折,此外还有过多次流产。守寡之后,她马上就致力于妇女的高等教育事业。她是格顿学院的创办人之一,力图使妇女进入医疗行业。她总是讲起她在意大利遇到过的一位面容悲哀的老年绅士,她询问他忧郁的缘故,他说他刚刚失去了两个孙子。"天哪!"她叫道:"我有七十二个孙儿孙女,如果我每失去一个就要悲伤不止,那我就没法活了!""奇怪的母亲!"他回答说。但是,作为她的七十二个孙儿孙女中的一员,我却要说我更喜欢她的见地。上了八十岁,她开始感到有些难以入睡,她便经常在午夜时分至凌晨三时这段时间里阅读科普方面的书籍。我想她根本就没有工夫去留意她在衰老。我认为,这就是保持年轻的最佳方法。如果你的兴趣和活动既广泛又浓烈,而且你又能从中感到自己仍然精力旺盛,那么你就不必去考虑你已经活了多少年这种纯粹的统计学情况,更不必去考虑你那也许不很长久的未来。

至于健康,由于我这一生几乎从未患过病,也就没有什么有益的忠告。我吃喝皆随心所欲,困了的时候就睡觉。我做事情从不以它是否有益健康为依据,尽管实际上我喜欢做的事情通常是有益健康的。

从心理角度讲,老年需防止两种危险。一是过分沉湎于往事。人不能生活在回忆当中,不能生活在对美好往昔的怀念或对逝去友人的哀念之中。一个人应当把心思放在未来,放到需要自己去做点什么的事情上,要做到这一点并非轻而易举,往事的影响总是在不断地增加。人们总认为自己过去的情感要比现在强烈得多,头脑也比现在敏锐。假如真的如此,就该忘掉它;而如果可以忘掉它,那你自以为是的情况就可能并不是真的。

另一件应当避免的事是依恋年轻人,期望从他们的勃勃生气中获取力量。子女们长大成人之后,都想按照自己的意愿生活。如果你还像他们年幼时那样关心他们,你就会成为他们的包袱,除非他们是异常迟钝的人。我不是说不应该关心子女,而是说这种关心应该是含蓄的,假如可能的话,还应是宽厚的,而不应该过分地感情用事。动物的幼崽一旦自立,大动物就不再关心它们了。人类则因其幼年时期较长而难于做到这一点。

我认为,对于那些具有强烈的爱好,其活动又都恰当适宜,并且不受个人情感影响的人们,成功地度过老年绝非难事。只有在这个范围里,长寿才真正有益;只有在这个范围里,源于经验的智慧才能不受压制地得到运用。告诫已经成人的孩子别犯错误是没有用处的,因为一来他们不会相信你,二来错误原本就是教育必不可少的要素之一。但是,如果你是那种受个人情感支配的人,你就会感到,不把心思都放在子女和孙儿女身上,你就会觉得生活很空虚。假如事实确实如此,那么当你还能为他们提供物质上的帮助,譬如支援他们一笔钱或者为他们编织毛线外套的时候,你就必须明白,绝不要期望他们会因为你的陪伴而感到快活。

有些老人因害怕死亡而苦恼。年轻人害怕死亡是可以理解的。有些年轻人担心他们会在战斗中丧生。一想到会失去生活能够给予他们的种种美好事物,他们就感到痛苦。这种担心也是情有可原的。但是,对于一位经历了人世的悲欢、履行了个人职责的老人,害怕死亡就有些可怜且可耻了。克服这种恐惧的最好办法是——至少我是这样看的——逐渐扩大你的兴趣范围并使其不受个人情感的影响,直至包围自我的围墙一点一点地离开你,而你的生活则越来越融合于大家的生活之中。每一个人的生活都应该像河水一样——开始是细小的,被限制在狭窄的两岸之间,然后热情地冲过巨石、滑下瀑布。渐渐地,河道变宽了,河岸扩展了,河水流得更平缓了。最后,河水汇入了海洋,不再有明显的间断和停顿,而后便毫无痛苦地摆脱了自身的存在。能够这样理解自己的一生的老人,将不会因害怕死亡而痛苦,因为他所珍爱的一切都将继续存在下去。而且,如果随着精力的衰退,疲倦之感日渐增加,长眠非是不受欢迎的念头。我渴望死于尚能劳作之时,同时知道他人将继续我未尽的事业,我大可因为已经尽了自己之所能而感到安慰。

---

[1] Gibbon 吉本(1737–1794),英国历史学家,著有《罗马帝国衰亡史》等著作。

[2] Girton College 格顿学院,剑桥大学的第一所女子学院,建于1869年。

[3] Madre snaturale 奇怪的母亲,原文为拉丁文

# 给年轻人的忠告
## Advice to Youth

【美国】马克·吐温

### 作者简介

　　马克·吐温(1835～1910)是美国批判现实主义文学的奠基人,世界著名的短篇小说大师。其写作风格融幽默与讽刺于一体,既富于独特的个人机智与妙语,又不乏深刻的社会洞察与剖析,既是幽默辛辣的小说杰作,又有悲天悯人的严肃!威廉·福克纳称马克·吐温为"第一位真正的美国作家,我们都是继承他而来"。《给年轻人的忠告》幽默而又符合年轻人心理地忠告了年轻人,童稚中透着犀利。

Being told I would be expected to talk here, I inquired what sort of talk I ought to make. They said it should be something suitable to youth—something didactic, instructive, or something in the nature of good advice. Very well. I have a few things in my mind which I have often longed to say for the instruction of the young; for it is in one's tender early years that such things will best take root and be most enduring and most valuable. First, then, I will say to you my young friends—and I say it beseechingly[1], urgingly—

Always obey your parents, when they are present. This is the best policy in the long run, because if you don't, they will make you. Most parents think they know better than you do, and you can generally make more by humoring that superstition than you can by acting on your own better judgment.

Be respectful to your superiors, if you have any, also to strangers, and sometimes to others. If a person offended you, and you are in doubt as to whether it was intentional or not, do not resort to extreme measures; simply watch your chance and hit him with a brick. That will be sufficient. If you shall find that he had not intended any offense, come out frankly and confess yourself in the wrong when you struck him; acknowledge it like a man and say you didn't mean to. Yes, always avoid violence; in this age of charity and kindliness, the time has gone by for such things. Leave dynamite to the low and unrefined.

Go to bed early, get up early—this is wise. Some authorities say get up with the sun; some say get up with one thing, others with another. But a lark is really the best thing to get up with. It gives you a splendid reputation with everybody to know that you get up with the lark; and if you get the right kind of lark, and work at him right, you can easily train him to get up at half past nine, every time—it's no trick at all.

Now as to the matter of lying. You want to be very careful about lying; otherwise you are nearly sure to get caught. Once caught, you can never again be in the eyes to the good and the pure, what you were before. Many a young person has injured himself permanently through a single clumsy and ill finished lie, the result of carelessness born of incomplete training. Some authorities hold that the young ought not to lie at all. That of course, is putting it rather stronger than necessary; still while I cannot go quite so far as that, I do maintain, and I believe I am right, that the young ought to be temperate in the use of this great art until practice and experience shall give them that confidence, elegance, and precision which alone can make the accomplishment graceful and profitable. Patience, diligence, painstaking attention to detail—these are requirements; these in time, will make the student perfect; upon these only, may he rely as the sure foundation for future eminence. Think what tedious years of study, thought, practice, experience, went to the equipment of that peerless old master who was able to impose upon the whole world the lofty and sounding maxim that "Truth is mighty and will prevail"—the most majestic compound fracture of fact which any of woman born has yet achieved. For the history of our race, and each individual's experience, are sewn thick with evidences that a truth is not hard to kill, and that a lie well told is immortal. There is in Boston a monument of the man who discovered anesthesia; many people are aware, in these latter days, that that man didn't discover it at all, but stole the discovery from another man. Is this truth mighty, and will it prevail? Ah no, my hearers, the monument is made of hardy material, but the lie it tells will outlast it a million years. An awkward, feeble, leaky lie is a thing which you ought to make it your unceasing study to avoid; such a lie as that has no more real permanence than an average truth. Why, you might as well tell the truth at once and be done with it. A feeble, stupid, preposterous lie will not live two years—except it be a slander upon somebody. It is indestructible, then of course, but that is no merit of yours. A final word: begin your practice of this gracious and beautiful art early—begin now. If I had begun earlier, I could have learned how.

Never handle firearms carelessly. The sorrow and suffering that have been caused through the innocent but heedless handling of firearms by the young! Only four days ago, right in the next farm house to the one where I am spending the summer, a grandmother, old and gray and sweet, one of the loveliest spirits in the land, was sitting at her work, when her young grandson crept in and got down an old, battered, rusty gun which had not been touched for many years and was supposed not to be loaded, and pointed it at her, laughing and threatening to shoot. In her fright she ran screaming and pleading toward the door on the other side of the room; but as she passed him he placed the gun almost against her very breast and pulled the trigger! He had supposed it was not loaded. And he was right—it wasn't. So there wasn't any harm done. It is the only case of that kind I ever heard of. Therefore, just the same, don't you meddle with old unloaded firearms; they are the most deadly and unerring things that have ever been created by man. You don't have to take any pains at all with them; you don't have to have a rest; you don't have to have any sights on the gun; you don't have to take aim, even. No, you just pick out a relative and bang away, and you are sure to get him. A youth who can't hit a cathedral at thirty yards with a Gatling gun in three quarters of an hour, can take up an old empty musket and bag his grandmother every time, at a hundred. Think what Waterloo would have been if one of the armies had been boys armed with old muskets supposed not to be loaded, and the other army had been composed of their female relations. The very thought of it makes one shudder.

There are many sorts of books; but good ones are the sort for the young to read. Remember that. They are a great, an inestimable, and unspeakable means of improvement. Therefore be careful in your selection, my young friends; be very careful; confine yourselves exclusively to Robertson's *Sermons*, Baxter's *Saint's Rest*, *The Innocents Abroad*, and works of that kind.

But I have said enough. I hope you will treasure up the instructions which I have given you, and make them a guide to your feet and a light to your understanding. Build your character thoughtfully and painstakingly upon these precepts, and by and by, when you have got it built, you will be surprised and gratified to see how nicely and sharply it resembles everybody else's.

听说期望我来谈谈，我便询问应该发表什么样的谈话。他们说应当适宜于青年的话题——教诲性的、启发性的话题，或者实质上是良言忠告之类的话题。好吧。关于开导青年人，我心里倒是有几件事是时常想说的；因为正是在人幼小时，这些事最适合扎根，而且最持久、最有价值。那么，首先呢，我要对你们，我的年轻朋友们说的是——我恳切地、迫切地要说的是——

永远服从你们的父母，只要他们在场的时候。长远看来这是上策，因为你们要是不服从的话，他们也非要你们服从。大多数家长认为比你们懂得多，一般说来你们迁就那种迷信的话，比起你们根据自以为是的判断行事，你们会建树大些。

要是你们有了上司，对待上司要尊重；对待陌生人，有时还有别人，也要尊重。如果有人得罪了你们，你们要犹豫一番，看看是存心的还是无意的，不要采取极端的做法；只要看好机会用砖块打他一下，那就足够了。如果你们发现他并非故意冒犯，那就坦然走出来，承认自己打他个不对；像个男子汉认个错，说声不是故意的。况且，永远要避免动武；处于这个仁慈和睦的时代，此类举动的年代已经过去了。"炸药"留给卑下而无教养的人吧。

早睡早起——这是聪明的。有的权威讲，跟着太阳起床；还有的讲，跟着这样东西起床；又有的讲，跟着那样东西起床。其实跟着云雀起床才是再好不过的。这样你就落个好名声，人人都知道你跟着云雀起床；如果弄到一只那种适当的云雀，在它身上花些功夫，你就很容易把它调教到九点半起来，每次都是——这可决不是欺人之谈。

接着来谈谈说谎的问题。你们可要非常谨慎地对待说谎；否则十有八九会被揭穿。一旦揭穿，在善良和纯洁的眼光看来，你就再也不可能是过去的你了。多少年轻人，因为一次拙劣难圆的谎言，那是由于不完整的教育而导致的轻率的结果，使得自己永远蒙受损害。有些权威认为，年轻人根本不该说谎。当然，这种说法言之过甚，其实未必如此；不过，虽然我可不能把话讲得太过分，我却认定而且相信自己看法正确,那就是,在实践和经验使人获得信心、文雅、严谨之前,年轻人运用这门了不起的艺术时要有分寸,只有这三点才能使得说谎的本领无伤大雅,带来好处。耐性、勤奋、细致入微——这些是必要素质;这些素质日久天长便会使学生变得完善起来;凭借这些,只有凭借这些,他才可能为将来的出类拔萃打下稳固的基础。试想一下,要付出多么漫长的岁月,通过学习、思考、实践、经验,那位盖世无双的前辈大师才具有如此的素养,他迫使全世界接受了"真理是强大的而且终将取胜"这句崇高而掷地有声的格言——这是关于事实的复杂层面道出的最豪迈的话,迄今任何出自娘胎的人都未获得。因为我们人类的历史,还有每个个人的经验,都深深地埋下了这样的证据:一个真理不难扼杀,一个说得巧妙的谎言则历久不衰。波士顿有座发现麻醉法的人的纪念碑;许多人到后来才明白,那个人根本没有发现麻醉法,而是剽窃了另一个人的发现。这个真理强大吗? 它终将取胜吗? 唉,错哉,听众们,纪念碑是用坚硬材料建造的,而它所晓示的谎言却将比它持久百万年。一个笨拙脆弱而有破绽的谎言是你们应该不断学会避免的东西;诸如此类的谎言比起一个普通事实来,决不具有更加真实的永恒性。嗨,你们倒不如既讲真话又和真理打交道。一个脆弱愚蠢而又荒谬的谎言持续不了两年——除非是对什么人物的诽谤。当然,那种谎言是牢不可破的,不过那可不是你们的光彩。最后说一句:早些开始实践这门优雅美妙的艺术——从现在做起。要是我早些做起,我就能学会门道儿了。

切莫随便摆弄枪支。年轻人无知而又冒失地摆弄枪支,造成了多少悲伤痛苦。就在四天前,就在我度夏的农庄住家的隔壁人家,一位祖母,年老花发一团和气,是当地最可爱的一个人物,坐着在干活,这时她的小孙儿悄悄进屋,取下一把破烂生锈的旧枪,多年无人碰过,以为没装子弹,把枪对准了她,哈哈笑了吓唬着要开枪。她惊骇得边跑边叫边求饶,朝屋子对面的门口跑去;可是经过他身边的时候,小孙儿几乎把枪贴在她的胸口上,扣动了扳机! 他以为枪里没有子弹。他猜对了——没装子弹。所以没有造成什么伤害。这是我听到的同类情况中绝无仅有的。因此呢,同样的,你们可不要乱动没装子弹的旧枪支;它们是人所创造的最致命的每发必中的家伙。你们不必在这些东西上花什么功夫;你们不必搞个枪架;你们不必在枪上装什么准星;你们连瞄准都没有必要。用不着,你就随便挑个亲属,一枪崩过去,肯定一打一个准儿。三刻钟内用加特林机枪在三十码处不能击中一个教堂的年轻人,却可以站在百码开外,举起一把空膛的旧火枪,趄趄把祖母当靶子击倒。再试想一下,倘若有一支旧火枪武装起来的童子军,大概没有装上子弹,而另一支部队是由他们的女亲戚组成的,那么滑铁卢战役会是什么结局。只要一想到此,就会令人不寒而栗。

图书有许多种类;但好书才是年轻人该读的一类。记住这一点。好书是一种伟大、无价、无言的完善自我的工具。因此,要小心选择,年轻的朋友们;罗伯逊的《布道书》、巴克斯特的《圣者的安息》以及《傻瓜出国记》这一类的作品,你们应该只读这些书。

我可是说得不少了。我希望大家会铭记我给你们的言教,让它成为你们脚下的指南和悟性的明灯。用心刻苦地根据这些规矩培养自己的品格,天长日久,培养好了品格,你们将会惊喜地看到,这种品格多么准确而鲜明地类似其他每个人的品格。

159

最
散文
Zui Prose

[1] beseechingly adv. 恳求地; 乞求地

# 梦中的孩子
# Dream–Children

【英国】查尔斯·兰姆

作者简介

　　查尔斯·兰姆(1775-1834)，英国散文家。作品追求个性和感情的解放。兰姆在他的随笔中使用了一种特殊的文风，个性毕露、披肝沥胆。他的文章写得文白交错、迂回曲折而又跌宕多姿、妙趣横生——这是由他那不幸遭遇所形成的性格，以及他那博览群书所养成的"杂学"决定的。《梦中的孩子》探讨的是个宗教的话题：生命是否是种虚无？红尘中的情愫牵缠是否只是一场场梦？

Children love to listen to stories about their elders, when they were children; to stretch their imagination to the conception of a traditional great-uncle or grandame[1], whom they never saw. It was in this spirit that my little ones crept about me the other evening to hear about their great-grandmother Field, who lived in a great house in Norfolk (a hundred times bigger than that in which they and papa lived) which had been the scene—so at least it was generally believed in that part of the country—of the tragic incidents which they had lately become familiar with from the ballad of the *Children in the Wood*. Certain it is that the whole story of the children and their cruel uncle was to be seen fairly carved out in wood upon the chimney-piece of the great hall, the whole story down to the Robin Redbreasts, till a foolish rich person pulled it down to set up a marble one of modern invention in its stead, with no story upon it. Here Alice put out one of her dear mother's looks, too tender to be called upbraiding. Then I went on to say, how religious and how good their great-grandmother Field was, how beloved and respected by everybody, though she was not indeed the mistress of this great house, but had only the charge of it (and yet in some respects she might be said to be the mistress of it too) committed to her by the owner, who preferred living in a newer and more fashionable mansion which he had purchased somewhere in the adjoining county; but still she lived in it in a manner as if it had been her own, and kept up the dignity of the great house in a sort while she lived, which afterward came to decay, and was nearly pulled down, and all its old ornaments stripped and carried away to the owner's other house, where they were set up, and looked as awkward as if someone were to carry away the old tombs they had seen lately at the Abbey, and stick them up in Lady C's tawdry gilt drawing-room. Here John smiled, as much as to say, "that would be foolish indeed." And then I told how, when she came to die, her funeral was attended by a concourse of all the poor, and some of the gentry too, of the neighborhood for many miles round, to show their respect for her memory, because she

161

had been such a good and religious woman; so good indeed that she knew all the Psaltery by heart, aye, and a great part of the Testament besides. Here little Alice spread her hands. Then I told what a tall, upright, graceful person their great—grandmother Field once was; and how in her youth she was esteemed the best dancer—here Alice's little right foot played an involuntary movement, till upon my looking grave, it desisted—the best dancer, I was saying, in the county, till a cruel disease, called a cancer, came, and bowed her down with pain; but it could never bend her good spirits, or make them stoop, but they were still upright, because she was so good and religious. Then I told how she was used to sleeping by herself in a lone chamber of the great lone house; and how she believed that an apparition of two infants was to be seen at midnight gliding up and down the great staircase near where she slept, but she said "those innocents would do her no harm"; and how frightened I used to be, though in those days I had my maid to sleep with me, because I was never half so good or religious as she—and yet I never saw the infants. Here John expanded all his eyebrows and tried to look courageous. Then I told how good she was to all her grand—children, having us to the great house in the holidays, where I in particular used to spend many hours by myself, in gazing upon the old busts of the Twelve Caesar, that had been Emperors of Rome, till the old marble heads would seem to live again, or I would seem to be turned into marble with them; how I never could be tired with roaming about that huge mansion, with its vast empty rooms, with their worn—out hangings, fluttering tapestry, and carved oaken panels, with the gilding almost rubbed out—sometimes in the spacious old-fashioned gardens, which I had almost to myself, unless when now and then a solitary gardening man would cross me—and how the nectarines and peaches hung upon the walls, without my ever offering to pluck them, because they were forbidden fruit, unless now and then,—and because I had more pleasure in strolling about among the old melancholy-looking yew trees, or the firs, and picking up the red berries, and the fir apples, which were good for nothing but to look at—or in lying about upon the fresh grass, with all the fine garden smells around me—or basking in the orangery, till I could almost fancy myself ripening, too, along with the oranges and the limes in that grateful warmth—or in watching the dace that darted to and fro in the fish pond, at the bottom of the garden, with here and there a great sulky pike hanging midway down the water in silent state, as if it mocked at their impertinent friskings,—I had more pleasure in these busy-idle diversions than in all the sweet flavors of peaches, nectarines, oranges, and such like common baits of children. Here John slyly deposited back upon the plate a bunch of grapes, which, not unobserved by Alice, he had mediated dividing with her, and both seemed to be willing to relinquish them for the present as irrelevant. Then, in somewhat a more heightened tone, I told how, though their great-grandmother Field loved all her grand-children, yet in an especial manner she might be said to love their uncle, John L, because he was so handsome and spirited a youth, and a king to the rest of us; and, instead of moping about in solitary corners, like some of us, he would mount the most mettlesome horse he could get, when but an imp no bigger than themselves, and make it carry him half over the county in a morning, and join the hunters when there were any out—and yet he loved the old great house and gardens too, but had too much spirit to be always pent up within their boundaries — and how their uncle grew up to man's estate as brave as he was handsome, to the admiration of everybody, but of their great-grandmother Field most especially; and how he used to carry me upon his back when I was a lame-footed boy—for he was a good bit older than me—many a mile when I could not walk for pain; and how in after life he became lame-footed too, and I did not always (I fear) make allowances enough for him when he was impatient, and in pain, nor remember sufficiently how considerate he had been to me when I was lame-footed; and how when he died, though he had not been dead an hour, it seemed as if he had died a great while ago, such a

163

最散文
Zui Prose

distance there is between life and death; and how I bore his death as I thought pretty well at first, but afterward it haunted and haunted me; and though I did not cry or take it to heart as some do, and as I think he would have done if I had died, yet I missed him all day long, and knew not till then how much I had loved him. I missed his kindness, and I missed his crossness, and wished him to be alive again, to be quarreling with him (for we quarreled sometimes), rather than not have him again, and was as uneasy without him, as he their poor uncle must have been when the doctor took off his limb. Here the children fell a crying, and asked if their little mourning which they had on was for uncle John, and they looked up and prayed me not to go on about their uncle, but to tell them some stories about their pretty dead mother. Then I told them how for seven long years, in hope sometimes, sometimes in despair, yet persisting ever, I courted the fair Alice W——n; and, as much as children could understand, I explained to them what coyness, and difficulty, and denial meant in maidens—when suddenly, turning to Alice, the soul of the first Alice looked out at her eyes with such a reality of re-presentment, that I became in doubt which of them stood there before me, or whose that bright hair was; and while I stood gazing, both the children gradually grew fainter to my view, receding, and still receding till nothing at last but two mournful features were seen in the uttermost distance, which, without speech, strangely impressed upon me the effects of speech: "We are not of Alice, nor of thee, nor are we children at all. The children of Alice call Bartrum father. We are nothing; less than nothing, and dreams. We are only what might have been, and must wait upon the tedious shores of Lethe millions of ages before we have existence, and a name" —and immediately awaking, I found myself quietly seated in my bachelor armchair, where I had fallen asleep, with the faithful Bridget unchanged by my side—but John L. (or James Elia) was gone forever.

孩子们总是爱听关于他们长辈童年的故事的:他们总是极力驰骋他们的想象,以便对某个传说般的老舅爷或老祖母多少得点印象,而这些人他们是从来不曾见过的。正是由于这个缘故,前几天的一个夜晚,我那几个小东西便都跑到了我的身边,要听他们曾祖母费尔得的故事。这位曾祖母的住地为诺福克的一家巨宅(那里比他们爸爸的住处要大上百倍),而那里便曾——至少据当地的传闻是如此——他们最近从《林中的孩子》歌谣里听的那个悲惨故事的发生地。其实,关于那些儿童及其残酷的叔叔的一段传说,甚至一直到后面红胸知更鸟的全部故事,在那座大厅的壁炉台上原就有过精美的木雕,只是后来一个愚蠢的富人把它拆了下来,另换了一块现代式的大理石面,因而上面便不再有那故事了。听到这里,爱丽丝不觉微含嗔容,完全是她妈妈的一副神气,只是温柔有余,愠怒不足。接着我又继续讲道,他们的曾祖母费尔得是一位多么虔敬而善良的人,是多么受人敬重与爱戴,尽管她并不是(虽然在某些方面也不妨说就是)那座巨宅的女主人,而只是受了房主之托代为管理,而说起那房主,他已在附近另置房产,喜欢住在那更入时的新居里;但尽管这样,她住在那里却好像那房子便是她自己的一般,她在生前始终非常注意维持它的体面与观瞻,但到后来这座宅院就日渐倾圮,而且拆毁严重,房中一切古老摆设家具都被拆卸一空,运往房主的新宅,然后胡乱地堆在那里,那刺目的情形正像有谁把威斯敏斯特教堂中的古墓盗出,生硬地安插到一位贵妇俗艳的客厅里去。听到这里,约翰不禁笑了,仿佛是在批评,"这实在是件蠢事"。接着我又讲道,她下世葬礼是如何隆重,附近几里的一切穷人以及部分乡绅都曾前来吊唁,以示哀悼,因为这位老人素来便以善良和虔敬闻名;这点的一个证明便是全部赞美诗她都能熟记成诵,另外还能背得新约的大部分内容。听到这里,爱丽丝不觉伸出大拇指,表示叹服。然后我又说道,他们的曾祖母当年是怎样一个个子高高,模样挺好的美人:年轻时候是最会跳舞的人——这时爱丽丝的小巧右脚不自觉地舞动起来,但是看到我神情严肃,便又止住——是的,她一直是全郡之中最会跳舞的人,可是后来得了一种叫癌症的重病,才使她受尽痛苦,跳不成了;但是疾病并没有摧折她的精神,或使她萎靡不振,她依旧心气健旺,这主要因为她虔诚善良。接着我又讲道,她晚上是如何一个人单独睡在那座空荡宅院零乱的房间里;以及她又如何仿佛瞥见那两个婴孩的鬼魂半夜时候在靠近她床榻的楼梯地方往上滑下,但是她却心中坚信,那天真的幽灵不会加害于她;而我自己

童稚的时候却是多么地害怕哟，虽然那时我身边还有女佣人和我同睡，这主要因为我没有她那么虔诚善良——不过我倒没有见着那婴儿们的鬼魂。听到这里，约翰马上睁大眼睛，露出一副英勇气概。接着我又讲道，她对她的孙子孙女曾是多么关心爱护，每逢节日总是把我们接到那巨宅去玩，而我在那里常常一个人独自玩上半天，常常目不转睛地凝注着那十二个古老的凯撒头像出神（那些罗马皇帝），最后那些古老的大理石像仿佛又都栩栩然活了一般，甚至连我自己也和他们一起化成了石像；另外我自己在那座庞大的宅邸之中是如何兴致勃勃，流连忘返，那里有许多高大空荡的房间，到处张挂着古旧的帘幕和飘动的绣帏，四壁都是橡木护板，只是板面的敷金已剥落殆尽——有时我也常常跑到那敞阔的古老花园里去游玩，那里几乎成了我一个人的天地，只是偶尔才遇上一名园丁从我面前经过——再有那里的油桃与蜜桃又是怎样嘉实累累地垂满墙头，但是我却连手都不伸一伸，因为它们一般乃是禁果，除非是偶一为之——另一方面也是因为我自己意不在此，我的乐趣是到那些容貌惝郁的古老水松或冷杉间去遨游，随处撷拾几枚绛红的浆果或枞果，而其实这些都是中看而不中吃的——不然便是全身仰卧在葱翠的草地上面，默默地吮吸着满园的清香——或者长时间曝浴在桔林里面，慢慢地在那暖人的温煦之下，我仿佛觉得自己也和那满林橙桔一道烂熟起来——或者便是到园中低处去观鱼，那是一种鲦鱼，在塘中倏往倏来，动作疾迅，不过时而也瞥见一条个子大大但性情执拗的狗鱼竟一动不动地悬浮在水面，仿佛其意在嘲笑那胡乱跳跃的轻浮举止，——总之，我对这类说闲也闲说忙又忙的消遣玩乐要比对蜜桃柑桔等那些只能吸引一般儿童的甜蜜东西的兴趣更浓厚得多。听到这里，约翰不禁把一串葡萄悄悄地又放回到盘子里去，而这串葡萄（按：并没有能瞒过爱丽丝的眼睛）他原是准备同她分享的，但是，至少目前，他们两人都宁愿忍痛割舍。接着我又以一种更加高昂的语调讲道，虽然他们的曾祖母费尔得非常疼爱她的每个孙子，她却尤其疼爱他们的伯伯约翰·兰，因为他是一个非常俊美和非常精神的少年，而且是我们大家的共同领袖；当他还是个比我们大不了许多的小东西时，他绝不像我们那样，常常绕着个荒凉的角落呆呆发愁，而是要骑马外出，特别能骑那些烈性的马，往往不消一个上午，早已跑遍大半个郡，而且每次必与猎户们一起——不过他对这古邸与花园倒也同样喜爱，只是他的性情过于跅弛奔放，受不了那里的约束——另外待到伯伯长大成人之后，他又是怎样既极英俊又极勇武，结果不仅人人称羡，尤其深得那曾祖母的赞赏；加上他比我们又大许多，所以我小时候因为腿瘸不便走时，他总是背着我，而且一背就是几里；以及后来他自己又怎样也变跛足，而有时（我担心）我对他的急躁情绪与痛苦程度却往往体谅不够，或者忘记过去我跛足时他对自己曾是如何体贴；但是当他真的故去，虽然刚刚一霎工夫，在我已经恍如隔世，生死之间竟是这样判若霄壤；对于他的夭亡起初我总以为早已不再置念，谁知这事却愈来愈萦回于我的胸臆；虽然我并没有像一些人那样为此而痛哭失声或久久不能释怀（真的，如果那次死的是我，他定然会是这样的），但是我对他确实是昼夜思念不已，而且只是到了这时我才真正了解我们之间的手足深情。我不仅怀念他对我的好处，我甚至怀念他对我的粗暴，我一心只盼他能再复活过来，能再和他争争吵吵（因为我们兄弟平时也难免阋墙），即使这样也总比他不在要好，但是现在没有了他，心里那种凄惶不安的情形正像当年你们那伯伯被医生截去了腿脚时那样。听到这里，孩子们不禁泫然泪下，于是问道，如此说来，那么目前他们身上的丧服便是为的这位伯伯，说罢，仰面叹息，祈求我再别叙说伯伯的遭遇，而给他们讲点关于他们那（已故的）美丽的妈妈的故事。于是我又向他们讲了，过去在悠悠七载的一段时光中——这期间真是忽而兴奋，忽而绝望，但却始终诚挚不渝——我曾如何向那美丽的爱丽丝·温——登表示过殷勤；然后，按着一般儿童所能理解的程度，尽量把一位少女身上所独具的那种娇羞、迟疑与回绝等等，试着说给他们——说时，目光不觉扫了一下爱丽丝，殊不料蓦然间那位原先的爱丽丝的芳魂竟透过这小爱丽丝的明眸而形容宛肖地毕现眼前，一时简直说不清这伫立在眼前的形体竟是哪位，或者那一头的秀发竟是属于谁个；而正当我定睛审视时，那两个儿童已经从我的眼前慢慢逝去，而且愈退愈远，最后朦胧之中，只剩得两张哀愁的面孔而已；他们一言不发，但说也奇怪，却把要说的意思传给了我："我们并不属于爱丽丝，也不属于你，实际上我们并不是什么孩子。那爱丽丝的孩子是管巴尔图姆叫爸爸的。我们只是虚无；甚至不够虚无；我们只是梦幻。我们只是一种可能，或者将来在忘河的苦水边上修炼千年万年方能转个人形，取个名义"——这时我蘧然而觉，发现自己仍然安稳地坐在我那个单身汉的安乐椅上，而适才的种种不过是一场梦，这时忠诚的布里吉特仍然厮守在我的身边——但是约翰·兰——（亦即詹姆斯·伊里亚）却已杳不可见了。

---

[1]grandame: grandmother  n. 祖母

# 写作的乐趣
# The Joys of Writing

【英国】温斯顿·丘吉尔

## 作者简介

  温斯顿·丘吉尔(1874-1965),政治家、画家、演说家、作家以及记者,1953年诺贝尔文学奖得主,曾两度任英国首相,被认为是20世纪最重要的政治领袖之一,带领英国获得第二次世界大战的胜利。被公认为世界上掌握单词词汇量最多的人(5万多)。《写作的乐趣》以细致准确的文字表现了才华横溢的作者淡定的生活态度,更体现了作者对祖国与英语的自豪。

写作的乐趣
The Joys of Writing

The fortunate people in the world—the only really fortunate people in the world, in my mind,—are those whose work is also their pleasure. The class is not a large one, not nearly so large as it is often represented to be; and authors are perhaps one of the most important elements in its composition. They enjoy in this respect at least a real harmony of life. To my mind, to be able to make your work your pleasure is the one class distinction in the world worth striving for; and I do not wonder that others are inclined to envy those happy human beings who find their livelihood in the gay effusions of their fancy, to whom every hour of labour is an hour of enjoyment, to whom repose—however necessary—is a tiresome interlude, and even a holiday is almost deprivation. Whether a man writes well or ill, has much to say or little, if he cares about writing at all, he will appreciate the pleasures of composition. To sit at one's table on a sunny morning, with four clear hours of uninterruptible security, plenty of nice white paper, and a Squeezer pen—that is true happiness. The complete absorption of the mind upon an agreeable occupation—what more is there than that to desire? What does it matter what happens outside? The House of Commons may do what it likes, and so may the House of Lords. The heathen may rage furiously in every part of the globe. The bottom may be knocked clean out of the American market. Consols[1] may fall and suffragettes may rise. Never mind, for four hours, at any rate, we will withdraw ourselves from a common, ill-governed, and disorderly world, and with the key of fancy unlock that cupboard where all the good things of the infinite are put away.

And speaking of freedom, is not the author free, as few men are free? Is he not secure, as few men are secure? The tools of his industry are so common and so cheap that they have almost ceased to have commercial value. He needs no bulky pile of raw material, no elaborate apparatus, no service of men or animals. He is dependent for his occupation upon no one but himself, and nothing outside him that matters. He is the sovereign of an empire, self-supporting, self-contained. No one can sequestrate his estates. No one can deprive him of his stock in trade; no one can force him to exercise his faculty against his will; no one can prevent him exercising it as he chooses. The pen is the great liberator of men and nations. No chains can bind, no poverty can choke, no tariff can restrict the free play of his mind, and even the "Times" Book Club can only exert a moderately depressing influence upon his rewards. Whether his work is good or bad, so long as he does his best he is happy. I often fortify myself amid the uncertainties and vexations of political life by believing that I possess a line of retreat into a peaceful and fertile country where no rascal can pursue and where one needs never be dull or idle or even wholly without power. It is then, indeed, that I feel devoutly thankful to have been born fond of writing. It is then, indeed, that I feel grateful to all the brave and generous spirits who, in every age and in every land, have fought to establish the now unquestioned freedom of the pen.

And what a noble medium the English language is! It is not possible to write a page without experiencing positive pleasure at the richness and variety, the flexibility and the profoundness of our mother-tongue. If an English writer cannot say what he has to say in English, and in simple English, depend upon it, it is probably not worth saying. What a pity it is that English is not more generally studied! I am not going to attack classical education. No one who has the slightest pretension to literary tastes can be insensible to the attraction of Greece and Rome. But I confess our present educational system excites in my mind grave misgivings. I cannot believe that a system is good, or even reasonable, which thrusts upon reluctant and uncomprehending multitudes treasures which can only be appreciated by the privileged and gifted few. To the vast majority of boys who attend our public schools a classical education is from beginning to end one long useless, meaningless rigmarole. If I am told that classes are the best preparation for the study of English, I reply that by far the greater number of students finish their education while this preparatory stage is still incomplete and without deriving any of the benefits which are promised as its result.

And even of those who, without being great scholars, attain a certain general acquaintance with the ancient writers, can it really be said that they have also obtained the mastery of English? How many young gentlemen there are from the universities and public schools who can turn a Latin verse with a facility which would make the old Romans squirm in their tombs. How few there are who can construct a few good sentences, or still less a few good paragraphs of plain, correct, and straightforward English. Now, I am a great admirer of the Greeks, although, of course, I have to depend upon what others tell me about them, —and I would like to see our educationists imitate in one respect, at least, the Greek example. How is it that the Greeks made their language the most graceful and compendious mode of expression ever known among men? Did they spend all their time studying the languages which had preceded theirs? Did they explore with tireless persistency the ancient root dialects of the vanished world? Not at all. They studied Greek. They studied their own language. They loved it, they cherished it, they adorned it, they expanded it, and that is why it survives a model and delight to all posterity. Surely we, whose mother-tongue has already won for itself such an unequalled empire over the modern world, can learn this lesson at least from the ancient Greeks and bestow a little care and some proportion of the years of education to the study of a language which is perhaps to play a predominant part in the future progress of mankind.

Let us remember the author can always do his best. There is no excuse for him. The great cricketer may be out of form. The general may on the day of decisive battle have a bad toothache or a bad army. The admiral may be seasick—as a sufferer I reflect with satisfaction upon that contingency. Caruso may be afflicted with catarrh, or Hacken-schmidt with influenza. As for an orator, it is not enough for him to be able to think well and truly. He must think quickly. Speed is vital to him. Spontaneity is more than ever the hallmark of good speaking. All these varied forces of activity require from the performer the command of the best that is in him at a particular moment which may be fixed by circumstances utterly beyond his control. It is not so

171

最 散文
Zui Prose

with the author. He need never appear in public until he is ready. He can always realise the best that is in him. He is not dependent upon his best moment in any one day. He may group together the best moments of twenty days. There is no excuse for him if he does not do his best. Great is his opportunity; great also his responsibility. Someone—I forget who—has said: "Words are the only things which last for ever." That is, to my mind, always a wonderful thought. The most durable structures raised in stone by the strength of man, the mightiest monuments of his power, crumble into dust, while the words spoken with fleeting breath, the passing expression of the unstable fancies of his mind, endure not as echoes of the past, not as mere archaeological curiosities or venerable relics, but with a force and life as new and strong, and sometimes far stronger than when they were first spoken, and leaping across the gulf of three thousand years, they light the world for us today.

最
散文
Zui Prose

　　在我看来,世上幸运的人——世上惟一真正幸运的人,是那些以工作为乐的人。这类人并不多,还没有人们常说的那样多。也许,作家是其中最重要的组成部分之一。就幸运而言,他们至少享受着生活中真正的和谐美。依我看,能使工作成为乐趣,是世人值得为之奋斗的一种崇高的荣誉;而且,我毫不怀疑别人会羡慕这些幸福的人,因为他们在快乐的喷涌的幻想中找到了生计,对他们来说,每劳动一小时,就是享受一小时,而休息——无论多么有必要——是令人讨厌的插曲,甚至度假也几乎成了一种损失。无论写得好坏,写成多少,只要在意,就可尝到谋篇布局的乐趣。在一个阳光明媚的早晨,临桌而坐,整整四个小时不受打扰,有足够数量的雪白稿纸,还有一支"挤压式"妙笔——那才叫真正的幸福。全心全意地投入一项令人愉快的职业——此愿足矣! 外面发生什么事又有何妨? 下议院想干什么就干什么吧,上议院也可如此。异教徒可以在全球各地大发作。美国市场可以彻底崩溃。证券可以下跌;女权运动可以兴起。没有关系,不管怎么说,我们有四个小时可以躲开这俗气的、治理不善的、杂乱无章的世界,并且用想象这把钥匙,去开启藏有大千世界一切宝物的小橱。

　　说到自由,既然自由自在的人为数不多,难道作家还不算自由? 既然获得安全感的人并不多,难道作家还不算安全? 作家作业的工具极为平常,极为便宜,几乎不再有商业价值。他不需要成堆的原材料,不需要精密仪器,不需要有人或动物效犬马之劳。他的职业不靠任何人,只靠自己;除了他自己以外,任何事都无关紧要。他就是一国之君,既自给,又自立。任何人都不能没收他的资产。任何人都不能剥夺他的从业资本;任何人都不能强迫他违心地施展才华;任何人都不能阻止他按自己的选择发挥天赋。他的笔就是人类和各民族的大救星。他的思想在自由驰骋,任何锁链束缚不住,任何贫困阻挡不住,任何关税限制不住,甚至"泰晤士"图书俱乐部也只能有节制地对他的收获泼一点冷水。无论作品是好是糟,只要已经尽力而为,他就会感到欢快。在变幻无常、扑朔迷离的政坛活动中,我每每以此信念自励:我有一条通向安逸富饶之地的退路,在那里,任何无赖都不能追踪,我永远不必垂头丧气或无所事事,即便没有一丁点权力。确实,在那时,我才为自己生来就爱好写作而真诚地感到欣慰不已;在那时,我才对各个时代、各个国家所有勇敢而慷慨的人充满感激之情,因为他们为确立如今无可争议的写作自由进行了斗争。

　　英语是多么崇高的工具! 我们每写下一页,都不可能不对祖国语言的丰富多采、灵巧精深产生一种实实在在的喜悦。如果一位英国作家不能用英语,不能用简单的英语说出他必须说的话,请诸位相信,那句话也许就不值得说。英语没有更广泛地得到学习是何等的憾事! 我不是要攻击古典教育。凡自命对文学有一丁点鉴赏力的人,都不可能对希腊罗马的吸引力无动于衷。但我承认,我国目前的教育制度却使我忧心忡忡。我无法相信这个制度是好的,甚至是合理的,因为它把唯有少数特权人物和天才人物才能欣赏的东西,一古脑儿摆在很不情愿又很不理解的人民大众面前。对公立学校的广大学童来说,古典教育从头至尾都是一些冗长的、毫无用处和毫无意义的废话。如果有人告诉我,古典课程是学习英语的最好准备,那我就回答说,迄今为止,大批学生已完成了学业,而这个准备阶段却仍然很不完善,未能收到它所保证的任何好处。

　　即使那些无缘成为大学者、但对古代作家有所了解的人,难道可以说他们已经掌握了英语吗? 究竟有多少从大学和公学毕业的年轻绅士,能够娴熟地写下一段拉丁诗文,使坟墓中的古罗马人闻之动情? 能写出几行佳句的人何其少也! 更不要说能用简单的、正确的和练达的英语写出几个精彩段落的人了。不过,我倒是极为仰慕古希腊人——当然我得仰仗别人把他们的情况告诉我——我想见到我们的教育专家至少能在一个方面效仿古希腊人。古希腊人是如何使自己的语言,成为人类迄今所知最典雅、最简练的表达方式的呢? 他们花费毕生时间学习希腊语以前的语言了吗? 他们无休止地坚持探索已消失的世界的原始方言了吗? 根本没有! 他们只学习希腊语。他们学习自己的语言。他们热爱它,珍惜它,点缀它,发展它,因此,它才能延续下来,成为所有后代人的楷模和乐趣。毫无疑问,对我们来说,既然英语已经为自己在现代世界赢得了如此无与伦比的疆域,我们至少能从古希腊人那里学到一条道理,在数年教育中稍微操点心而拨出一些时间,去学习一种也许将在人类未来进步中起到主导作用的语言。

让我们都记住,作家永远可以尽最大的努力,他没有任何借口不这样做。板球巨星也许会状态不佳。将军在决战之日也许会牙疼,或者他的部队很糟糕。舰队司令也许会晕船——我作为晕船者满意地想到了那种意外。卡鲁索也许会得黏膜炎,哈肯施米特也许会得流感。至于一位演说家,想得好和想得正确是不够的,他还需想得快。速度至关重要;随机应变越来越成为优秀演说家的标志。所有上述活动都需要行动者在一个特定的时刻倾其所能,而这一时刻也许决定于他完全无法控制的种种事态。作家的情况不一样。不到万事俱备,他永远不必出场。他永远可以发挥最大的能力。他并不依赖于自己在某一天的最佳一刻,他可以把20天的最佳时刻加起来。他没有理由不尽最大的努力。他的机会很多;他的责任也很重。某人说过——我忘了此君是谁——"话语乃惟一持久不灭之物"。依我看,这永远是绝妙的思想。人类力量的最伟大的杰作,即人类用石块垒起的无比坚固的大厦,也会夷为废墟,而那脱口而出的话语,那思绪起伏时转瞬即逝的表达却延续了下来,但它不是过去的回响,不是纯粹的建筑奇迹或神圣的遗址,它力量依旧,生命依旧,有时候远比初说时更坚强有力,它越过了3000年时光的峡谷,为今天的我们照亮了世界。

[1] consols n. 统一公债(由英国政府1751年开始发行的长期债券)

# 第五卷

畅言无忌
Free Speech

# 贝多芬百年祭
# Beethoven's Centenary

【英国】乔治·萧伯纳

**作者简介**

　　乔治·萧伯纳(1856-1950)，爱尔兰剧作家。他成功地使英国戏剧摆脱了19世纪60至70年代的思想、艺术绝境，使它能敏锐地反映迫切的社会问题，并使之具有出色的讽刺和离奇的形式。1925年"因为作品具有理想主义和人道主义"而获诺贝尔文学奖。他还写了许多文艺评论。《贝多芬百年祭》就是其音乐评论的名篇。文中独到而深刻的见解以及生动酣畅的表达真让人拍案叫绝。

A hundred years ago a crusty old bachelor of fifty-seven, so deaf that he could not hear his own music played by a full orchestra, yet still able to hear thunder, shook his fist at the roaring heavens for the last time, and died as he had lived, challenging God and defying the universe. He was Defiance Incarnate: he could not even meet a Grand Duke and his court in the street without jamming his hat tight down on his head and striding through the very middle of them. He had the manners of a disobliging steamroller (most steamrollers are abjectly obliging and conciliatory); and he was rather less particular about his dress than a scarecrow: in fact he was once arrested as a tramp because the police refused to believe that such a tatterdemalion could be a famous composer, much less a temple of the most turbulent spirit that ever found expression in pure sound. It was indeed a mighty spirit; but if I had written the mightiest, which would mean mightier than the spirit of Handel, Beethoven himself would have rebuked me; and what mortal man could pretend to be a spirit mightier than Bach's? But that Beethoven's spirit was the most turbulent is beyond all questions. The impetuous fury of his strength, which he could quite easily contain and control, but often would not, and the uproariousness of his fun, go beyond anything of the kind to be found in the works of other composers. Greenhorns write of syncopation now as if it were a new way of giving the utmost impetus to a musical measure; but the rowdiest jazz sounds like the Maiden's Prayer after Beethoven's third Leonora overture; and certainly no negro corobbery that I ever heard could inspire the blackest dancer with such diable au corps as the last movement of the Seventh Symphony. And no other composer has ever melted Beethoven's Centenary his hearers into complete sentimentality by the tender beauty of his music, and then suddenly turned on them and mocked them with derisive trumpet blasts for being such fools. Nobody but Beethoven could govern Beethoven; and when, as happened when the fit was on him, he deliberately refused to govern himself, he was ungovernable.

It was this turbulence, this deliberate disorder, this mockery, this reckless and triumphant disregard of conventional manners that set

177

Beethoven apart from the musical geniuses of the ceremonious seventeenth and eighteenth centuries. He was a giant wave in that storm of the human spirit which produced the French Revolution. He called no man master. Mozart, his greatest predecessor in his own department, had from his childhood been washed, combed, splendidly dressed, and beautifully behaved in the presence of royal personages and peers. His childish outburst at the Pompadour[1], "Who is this woman who does not kiss me? The Queen kisses me," would be incredible of Beethoven, who was still an unlicked cub even when he had grown into a very grizzly bear. Mozart had the refinement of convention and society as well as the refinement of nature and of the solitudes of the soul. Mozart and Gluck are refined as the court of Louis XIV was refined: Haydn is refined as the most cultivated country gentlemen of his day were refined: compared to them socially Beethoven was an obstreperous Bohemian: a man of the people. Haydn, so superior to envy that he declared his junior, Mozart, to be the greatest composer that ever lived, could not stand Beethoven. Mozart, more farseeing, listened to his playing, and said "You will hear of him some day"; but the two would never have hit it off together had Mozart lived long enough to try. Beethoven had a moral horror of Mozart, who in Don Giovanni had thrown a halo of enchantment round an aristocratic blackguard, and then, wither the unscrupulous moral versatility of a born dramatist, turned round to cast a halo of divinity round Sarastro[2], setting his words to the only music yet written that would not sound out of place in the mouth of God.

Beethoven was no dramatist: moral versatility was to him revolting cynicism. Mozart was still to him the master of masters (this is not an empty eulogistic superlative: it means literally that Mozart is a composer's composer much more than he has ever been a really popular composer); but he was a court flunkey in breeches whilst Beethoven was a Sansculotte; and Haydn also was a flunkey in the old livery: the Revolution stood between them as it stood between the eighteenth and nineteenth centuries. But to Beethoven Mozart was worse than Haydn because he trifled with morality by setting vice to music as magically as virtue. The Puritan who is in every true Sansculotte rose up against him in Beethoven, though Mozart had shewn him all the possibilities of nineteenth-century music. So Beethoven cast back for a hero to Handel, another crusty old bachelor of his own kidney, who despised Mozart's hero Gluck, though the pastoral symphony in The Messiah is the nearest thing in music to the scenes in which Gluck, in his Orfeo, opened to us the plains of Heaven.

Thanks to broadcasting, millions of musical novices will hear the music of Beethoven this anniversary year for the first time with their expectations raised to an extraordinary pitch by hundreds of newspaper articles piling up all the conventional eulogies that are applied indiscriminately to all the great composers. And like his contemporaries they will be puzzled by getting from him not merely a music that they did not expect, but often an orchestral hurlyburly that they may not recognize as what they call music at all, though they can appreciate Gluck and Haydn and Mozart quite well. The explanation is simple enough. The music of the eighteenth century is all dance music. A dance is a symmetrical pattern of steps that are pleasant to move to; and its music is a symmetrical pattern of sound that is pleasant to listen to even when you are not dancing to it. Consequently the sound patterns, though they begin by being as simple as chessboards, get lengthened and elaborated and enriched with harmonies until they are more like Persian carpets; and the composers who design these patterns no longer expect people to dance to them. Only a whirling Dervish could dance a Mozart symphony: indeed, I have reduced two young and practised dancers to exhaustion by making them dance a Mozart overture. The very names of the dances are dropped: instead of suites consisting of sarabands, pavanes, gavottes, and jigs, the designs are presented as sonatas and symphonies consisting of sections called simply movements, and labelled according to their speed (in Italian) as allegros, adagios, scherzos, and prestos. But all the time, from Bach's preludes to Mozart's Jupiter Symphony, the music makes a symmetrical sound pattern, and gives us the dancer's pleasure always as the form and foundation of the piece.

Music, however, can do more than make beautiful sounds patterns. It can express emotions. You can look at a Persian carpet and listen to a Bach prelude with a delicious admiration that goes no further than itself; but you cannot listen to the overture to Don Giovanni without being thrown into a complicated mood which prepares you for a tragedy of some terrible doom overshadowing an exquisite but Satanic gaiety. If you listen to the last movement of Mozart's Jupiter Symphony, you hear that it is as much a riotous corobbery as the last movement of Beethoven's Seventh Symphony: it is an orgy of ranting drumming tow-row-row, made poignant by an opening strain of strange and painful beauty which is woven through the pattern all through. And yet the movement is a masterpiece of pattern designing all the time.

Now what Beethoven did, and what made some of his greatest contemporaries give him up as a madman with lucid intervals of clowning and bad taste, was that he used music altogether as a means of expressing moods, and completely threw over pattern designing as an end in itself. It is true that he used the old patterns all his life with dogged conservatism (another Sansculotte characteristic, by the way); but imposed on them such an overwhelming charge of human energy and passion, including that highest passion which accompanies thought, and reduces the passion of the physical appetites to mere animalism, that he not only played Old Harry with their symmetry but often made it impossible to notice that there was any pattern at all beneath the storm of emotion. The Eroica Symphony begins by a pattern (borrowed from an overture which Mozart wrote when he was a boy), followed by a couple more very pretty patterns; but they are tremendously energized, and in the middle of the movement the patterns are torn up savagely; and Beethoven, from the point of view of the mere pattern musician, goes raving mad, hurling out terrible chords in which all the notes of the scale are sounded simultaneously, just because he feels like that, and wants you to feel like it.

And there you have the whole secret of Beethoven. He could design patterns with the best of them; he could write music whose beauty will last you all your life; he could take the driest sticks of themes and work them up so interestingly that you find something new in them at the hundredth hearing: in short, you can say of him all that you can say of the greatest pattern composers; but his diagnostic, the thing that marks him out from all the others, is his disturbing quality, his power of unsettling us and imposing his giant moods on us. Berlioz was very angry with an old French composer who expressed the discomfort Beethoven gave him by saying "J'aime la musique qui me berce," "I like music that lulls me." Beethoven's is music that wakes you up; and the one mood in which you shrink from it is the mood in which you want to be let alone.

When you understand this you will advance beyond the eighteenth century and the old-fashioned dance band (jazz, by the way, is the old dance band Beethovenized), and understand not only Beethoven's music, but what is deepest in post-Beethoven music as well.

一百年前，一位虽还听得见雷声但已聋得听不见大型交响乐队演奏自己乐曲的五十七岁的倔强的单身老人最后一次举拳向着咆哮的天空，然后逝去了，还是和他生前一直那样地唐突神灵，蔑视天地。他是反抗性的化身：他甚至在街上遇上一位大公和他的随从时也总不免把帽子向下按得紧紧地，然后从他们正中间大踏步地直穿而过。他有着不听话的蒸汽轧路机的风度（大多数轧路机还恭顺地听使唤和不那么调皮呢）；他穿衣服之不讲究尤甚于田间的稻草人；事实上有一次他竟被当做流浪汉给抓了起来，因为警察不肯相信穿得这样破破烂烂的人竟会是一位大作曲家，更不能相信这副躯体竟能容得下纯音响世界最奔腾澎湃的灵魂。他的灵魂是伟大的；但是如果我使用了最伟大的这种字眼，那就是说比韩德尔的灵魂还要伟大，贝多芬自己就会责怪我；而且谁又能自负为灵魂比巴哈的还伟大呢？但是说贝多芬的灵魂是最奔腾澎湃的那可没有一点问题。他的狂风怒涛一般的力量他自己能很容易控制住，可是常常并不愿去控制，这个和他狂呼大笑的滑稽诙谐之处是在别的作曲家作品里都找不到的。毛头小伙子们现在一提起切分音就好像是一种使音乐节奏成为最强而有力的新方法；但是在听过贝多芬的第三里昂诺拉前奏曲之后，最狂热的爵士乐听起来也像"少女的祈祷"那样温和了，可以肯定地说我听过的任何黑人的集体狂欢都不会像贝多芬的第七交响乐最后的乐章那样可以引起最黑最黑的舞蹈家拼了命地跳下去，而且也没有另外哪一个作曲家可以先以他乐曲的阴柔之美使得听众完全溶化在缠绵悱恻的境界里，而后突然以铜号的猛烈声音吹向他们，带着嘲讽似地使他们觉得自己真是傻。除了贝多芬之外谁也管不住贝多芬；而疯劲上来之后，他总有意不去管住自己，于是也就成为管不住的了。

正是由于这钟奔腾澎湃，这种有意的散乱无章，这种嘲讽，这样无顾忌的骄纵的不理睬传统的风尚——使得贝多芬不同于十七和十八世纪谨守法度的其他音乐天才。他是造成法国革命的精神风暴中的一个巨浪。他不认任何人为师，他同行里的先辈莫扎特从小起就是梳洗干净，穿着华丽，在王公贵族面前举止大方的。莫扎特小时候曾为了彭巴杜夫人发脾气说："这个女人是谁，也不来亲亲我，连皇后都亲我呢"。这种事在贝多芬看来是不可想象的，因为甚至在他已老到像一头苍熊时，他仍然是一只未经驯服的熊崽子。莫扎特天性文雅，与当时的传统和社会很合拍，但也有灵魂的孤独。莫扎特和格鲁克之文雅就犹如路易十四宫廷之文雅。海顿之文雅就犹如他同时代的最有教养的乡绅之文雅。和他们比起来，从社会地位上说贝多芬就是个不羁的艺术家，一个不穿紧腿裤的激进共和主义者。海顿从不知道什么是嫉妒，曾称呼比他年青的莫扎特是有史以来最伟大的作曲家，可他就是吃不消贝多芬。莫扎特是更有远见的，他听了贝多芬的演奏后说："有一天他是要出名的，"但是即使莫扎特活得长些，这两个人恐也难以相处下去。贝多芬对莫扎特有一种出于道德原因的恐怖。莫扎特在他的音乐中给贵族中的浪子唐璜加上了一圈迷人的圣光，然后像一个天生的戏剧家那样运用道德的灵活性又回过来给莎拉斯特罗加上了神圣的光辉，给他口中的歌词谱上了前所未有的就是出自上帝口中都不会显得不相称的乐调。

贝多芬不是戏剧家：赋予道德以灵活性对他来说就是一种可厌恶的玩世不恭。他仍然认为莫扎特是大师中的大师（这不是一顶空洞的高帽子，它的的确确就是说莫扎特是个为作曲家们欣赏的作曲家，而远远不是流行作曲家）；可是他是穿紧腿裤的官廷侍从，而贝多芬却是个穿散腿裤的激进共和主义者；同样地，海顿也是穿传统制服的侍从。在贝多芬和他们之间隔着一场法国大革命，划分开了十八世纪和十九世纪。但对贝多芬来说莫扎特可不如海顿，因为他把道德当儿戏，用迷人的音乐把罪恶谱成了像德行那样奇妙。如同每一个真正激进共和主义者都具有的，贝多芬身上的清教徒性格使他反对莫扎特，固然莫扎特曾向他启示了十九世纪音乐的各种创新的可能。因此贝多芬上溯到韩德尔，一位和贝多芬同样倔强的老单身汉，把他做为英雄。韩德尔瞧不上莫扎特崇拜的英雄格鲁克，虽然在韩德尔的《弥赛亚》里的田园乐是极为接近格鲁克在他的歌剧《奥菲欧》里那些向我们展示出天堂的原野的各个场面的。

因为有了无线电广播，成百万对音乐还接触不多的人在他百年祭的今年将第一次听到贝多芬的音乐。充满着照例不加选择地加在大音乐家身上的颂扬话的成百篇的纪念文章将使人们抱有通常少有的期望。像贝多芬同代的人一样，虽然他们可以懂得格鲁克、海顿和莫扎特，但从贝多芬那里得到的不但是一种使他们困惑不解的意想不到的音乐，而且有时候简直是听不出是音乐的由管弦乐器发出来的杂乱音响。要解释这也不难。十八世纪的音乐都是舞蹈音乐。舞蹈是由动起来令人愉快的步子组成的对称样式；舞蹈音乐是不跳舞也听起来令人愉快的由声音组成的对称的样式。因此这些乐式虽然起初不过是像棋盘那样简单，但被展开了，复杂化了，用和声丰富起来了，最后变得类似波斯地毯；而设计像波斯地毯那种乐式的作曲家也就不再期望人们跟着这种音乐跳舞了。要有神巫打旋子的本领才能跟着莫扎特的交响乐跳舞。有一回我还真请了两位训练有素的青年舞蹈家跟着莫扎特的一阕前奏曲跳了一次，结果差点没把他们累垮了。就是音乐上原来使用的有关舞蹈的名词也慢慢地不用了，人们不再使用包括萨拉班德舞、帕凡宫廷舞、加伏特舞和小步舞等等在内的组曲形式，而把自己的音乐创作表现为奏鸣曲和交响乐，里面所包含的各部分也干脆叫做乐章，每一章都按速度用意大利文标记，如快板、柔板、谐谑曲板、急板等等。但在任何时候，从巴哈的序曲到莫扎特的《天神交响乐》，音乐总呈现出一种对称的音响样式，给我们以一种舞蹈的乐趣来作为乐曲的形式和基础。

可是音乐的作用并不止于创造悦耳的乐式。它还能表达感情，你能去津津有味地欣赏一张波斯地毯或者听一曲巴哈的序曲，但乐趣只止于此；可是你听了《唐璜》前奏曲之后却不可能不产生一种复杂的心情，它使你有心理准备地去面对一场可怕的末日悲剧，这悲剧遮暗了精致的、魔鬼似的欢乐。听莫扎特的《天神交响乐》最后一章时你会觉得那和贝多芬的第七交响乐的最后乐章一样,都是狂欢的音乐:它用响亮的鼓声奏出如醉如狂的旋律,而从头到尾又交织着一开始就具有的一种不寻常的悲伤之美的乐调,因之更加沁人心脾。莫扎特的这一乐章又自始至终是乐式设计的杰作。

但是贝多芬所做到了的一点,也是使得某些与他同时代的伟人不得不把他当做一个疯人,有时清醒就出些洋相或者显示出格调不高的一点,在于他把音乐完全用作了表现心情的手段,并且完全不把设计乐式本身作为目的。不错,他一生非常保守地(顺便说一句,这也是激进共和主义者的特点)使用着旧的乐式;但是他加给它们以惊人的活力和激情,包括产生于思想高度的那种最高的激情,使得产生于感觉的激情显得仅仅是感官上的享受,于是他不仅打乱了旧乐式的对称,而且常常使人听不出在感情的风暴之下竟还有什么样式存在着了。他的《英雄交响乐》一开始使用了一个乐式(这是从莫扎特幼年时一个前奏曲里借来的),跟着又用了另外几个很漂亮的乐式;这些乐式被赋予了巨大的内在力量,所以到了乐章的中段,这些乐式就全被不客气地打散了;于是,在只追求乐式的音乐家看来,贝多芬是发了疯了,他抛出了同时使用音阶上所有单音的恐怖的和弦。他这么做只是因为他觉得非如此不可,而且还要求你也觉得非如此不可呢。

以上就是贝多芬之谜的全部。他有能力设计最好的乐式;他能写出使你终身享受不尽的美丽的乐曲;他能挑出那些最干燥无味的旋律,把它们展开得那样吸引人,使你听上一百次但每次都能发现新东西:一句话,你可以拿所有用来形容以乐式见长的作曲家的话来形容他;但是他的病症,也就是不同于别人之处在于他那激动人的品质,他能使我们激动,并用他那奔放的激情笼罩着我们。当柏辽兹听到一位法国作曲家因为贝多芬的音乐使他听了很不舒服而说"我爱听能使我入睡的音乐"时,他非常生气。贝多芬的音乐是使你清醒的音乐;而当你想独自一个人静一会儿的时候,你就怕听他的音乐。

懂了这个,你就从十八世纪前进了一步,也从旧式的跳舞乐队前进了一步(爵士乐,附带说一句,就是贝多芬化了的老式跳舞乐队),不但能懂得贝多芬的音乐而且也能懂得贝多芬以后的最有深度的音乐了。

---

[1] Pompadour 彭巴杜女侯爵(1721-1764),是法皇路易十五的情妇,权势炙手可热几乎有二十年。

[2] Sarastro 莎拉斯特罗,莫扎特的歌剧《魔笛》中的一个人物。

# 势力种种
# Selected Snobberies

【英国】阿尔多斯·赫胥黎

**作者简介**

阿尔多斯·赫胥黎(1894-1963),英国著名小说家及散文家。著有《天演论》的大生物学家托·亨·赫胥黎是他的祖父。阿尔多斯·赫胥黎是个学识渊博、思想复杂的多产作家,各类散文包罗万象,涉及现代文明各个重要方面。社会讽刺小说《旋律与对位》(1928)和"反乌托邦"幻想小说《美妙的新世界》(1932)是他最有名的代表作。主要作品还有神秘主义小说《加沙的盲人》(1936)等。《势力种种》用以小见大的方法表现了作者对社会的认识,讽刺了社会的丑态,折射出人性的光辉。

All men are snobs about something. One is almost tempted to add: There is nothing about which men cannot feel snobbish. But this would doubtless be an exaggeration. There are certain disfiguring and mortal diseases about which there has probably never been any snobbery. I cannot imagine, for example, that there are any leprosy-snobs. More picturesque diseases, even when they are dangerous, and less dangerous diseases, particularly when they are the diseases of the rich, can be and very frequently are a source of snobbish self-importance. I have met several adolescent consumption-snobs, who thought that it would be romantic to fade away in the flower of youth, like Keats or Marie Bashkirtseff. Alas, the final stages of the consumptive fading are generally a good deal less romantic than these ingenuous young tubercle-snobs seem to imagine. To anyone who has actually witnessed these final stages, the complacent poeticizings of these adolescents must seem as exasperating as they are profoundly pathetic. In the case of those commoner disease-snobs, whose claim to distinction is that they suffer from one of the maladies of the rich, exasperation is not tempered by very much sympathy. People who possess sufficient leisure, sufficient wealth, not to mention sufficient health, to go travelling from spa to spa from doctor to fashionable doctor, in search of cures from problematical diseases (which, in so far as they exist at all, probably have their source in overeating) cannot expect us to be very lavish in our solicitude and pity.

Disease-snobbery is only one out of a great multitude of snobberies, of which now some, now others take pride of place in general esteem. For snobberies ebb and flow; their empire rises, declines, and falls in the most approved historical manner. What were good snobberies a hundred years ago are now out of fashion. Thus, the snobbery of family is everywhere on the decline. The snobbery of culture, still strong, has now to wrestle with an organized and active low-browism, with a snobbery of ignorance and stupidity unique, so far as I know, in the whole of history... Hardly less characteristic of our age is that repulsive booze-snobbery, born of

American Prohibition. The malefic influences of this snobbery are rapidly spreading all over the world. Even in France, where the existence of so many varieties of delicious wine had hitherto imposed a judicious connoisseurship and has led to the branding of mere drinking as a brutish solecism, even in France the American booze-snobbery, with its odious accompaniments a taste for hard drinks in general and for cocktails in particular is making headway among the rich. Booze snobbery has now made it socially permissible, and in some circles even rather creditable, for well-brought-up men and (this is the novelty) well-brought up women of all ages, from fifteen to seventy, to be seen drunk, if not in public, at least in the very much tempered privacy of a party.

Modernity snobbery, though not exclusive to our age, has come to assume an unprecedented importance. The reasons for this are simple and of a strictly economic character. Thanks to modern machinery, production is outrunning consumption. Organized waste among consumers is the first condition of our industrial prosperity. The sooner a consumer throws away the object he has bought and buys another, the better for the producer. At the same time, of course, the producer must do his bit by producing nothing but the most perishable articles. "The man who builds a skyscraper to last more than forty years is, a traitor to the building trade." The words are those of a great American contractor. Substitute motor-car, boot, suit of clothes, etc., for skyscraper, and one year, three months, six months, and so on for forty years, and you have the gospel of any leader of any modern industry. The modernity-snob, it is obvious, is this industrialist's best friend. For modernity-snobs naturally tend to throw away their old possessions and buy new ones at a greater rate than those who are not modernity-snobs. Therefore it is in the producer's interest to encourage modernity-snobbery, which in fact he does do on an enormous scale and to the tune of millions and millions a year by means of advertising. The newspapers do their best to help those who help them; and to the flood of advertisement is added a flood of less directly paid-for propaganda in favour of modernity-snobbery.

The public is taught that up-to-dateness is one of the first duties of man. Docile, it accepts the reiterated suggestion. We are all modernity-snobs now.

Most of us are also art-snobs. There are two varieties of art-snobbery: the platonic and the unplatonic. Platonic art-snobs merely "take an interest" in art. Unplatonic art-snobs go further and actually buy art. Unplatonic art-snobbery is a hybrid or mule; for it is simultaneously a sub-species of culture-snobbery and of possession-snobbery. A collection of works of art is a collection of culture symbols, and culture-symbols still carry social prestige. It is also a collection of wealth-symbols, for an art collection can represent money more effectively than a whole fleet of motor-cars.

The value of art-snobbery, to living artists, is considerable. True most art snobs collect only the works of the dead; for an old master is both a safer investment and a holier culture-symbol than a living master. But some art-snobs are also modernity-snobs. There are enough of them, with the few eccentrics who like works of art for their own sake, to provide living artists with the means of subsistence.

The value of snobbery in general, its humanistic "point", consists in its power to stimulate activity. A society with plenty of snobberies is like a dog with plenty of fleas: it is not likely to become comatose. Every snobbery demands of its devotees unceasing efforts, a succession of sacrifices. The society-snob must be perpetually lion-hunting; the modernity-snob can never rest from trying to be up-to-date. Swiss doctors and the Best that has been thought or said must be the daily and nightly preoccupation of all the snobs respectively of disease and culture.

If we regard activity as being in itself a good, then we must count all snobberies as good; for all provoke activity. If, with the Buddhists, we regard all activities in this world of illusion as bad, then we shall condemn all snobberies out of hand. Most of us, I suppose, take up our position somewhere between the two extremes. We regard some activities as good, others as indifferent or downright bad. Our approval will be given only to such snobberies as excite what we regard as the better activities; the others we shall either tolerate or detest. For example, most professional intellectuals will approve of culture-snobbery (even while intensely, disliking most individual culture-snobs ), because it compels the philistines[1] to pay at least some slight tribute to the things of the mind and so helps to make the world less dangerously unsafe for ideas than it otherwise might have been. A manufacturer of motor-cars, on the other hand, will rank the snobbery of possessions above culture-snobbery; he will do his best to persuade people that those who have fewer possessions, particularly possessions on four wheels, are inferior to those who have more possessions. And so on. Each hierarchy culminates in its own particular Pope.

189

最 散文
Zui Prose

　　人人都有势利之处。人们几乎很想加一句：任何东西都可引起人们的势利感。不过这一点无疑是一种夸张。也许某些毁容或致命的疾病从来没有使人感到势利，例如我无法想像会有麻风病势利者。一些纵使有危险但较为别致的疾病，以及不太危险的病，特别是富人爱得的病，能够并常常是使人感到势利、自以为了不起的根源。我遇见过好几位因患肺结核而有势利感的年轻人，他们觉得像济慈或玛丽·巴什基尔采夫那样在青春妙龄时死去是一件很浪漫的事。哎呀，结核病晚期通常远远不像这些天真的年轻结核势利者想像得那么浪漫。对任何一个亲眼目睹过晚期状态的人，这些少年的自我满足的浪漫诗情必定会显得既令人恼怒又深觉可怜。至于那些较常见疾病的势利者，由于得的是有钱人易得的病而自称与众不同，对他便没有多少同情来减少恼怒了。拥有充足的闲暇，充足的财富，更别说充足的健康的人们从一个矿泉疗养地旅行到又一个矿泉疗养地，从一个医生那里到又一个时髦的医生那里去寻求对那些很难说是否存在的疾病的治疗（如果真有什么病的话，可能病因是吃得太多了），他们不可能指望我们会对他们慷慨地表示关怀和同情。

　　因疾病而生之势利仅是众多的势利中的一种，在这众多的势利中，有时有这样或那样的势利在人们心目中独尊其位，因为势利也有盛衰消长，他们的帝国也以最为公认的历史方式兴盛、衰落、消亡。一百年以前的好势利感现在已经过时了，因此，家庭出身的势利感在各地都在衰落之中，仍在盛行的文化势利感现在必须和有组织的、活跃的大老粗主义，以及就我所知在整个历史上独一无二的无知愚昧势利力量去拼搏。几乎同样反映了我们时代特征的是那令人厌恶的产生于美国禁酒时期的对狂饮的势利感。这种势利的有害影响正迅速扩散到全世界。即使在法国，由于有这样多不同种类的葡萄美酒，一直使品酒时极有鉴赏力，而把喝烈酒视为粗野的失礼行为；即使在法国，美国的狂饮势利感及其伴随而来的可憎的爱好——通常喜欢喝烈酒，特别是爱喝鸡尾酒——在有钱人中大有进展。由于这一势利感，有教养的男子和(这一点很新奇)从15岁到70岁之间的一切年龄的有教养的妇女，如果还不能在大庭广众之下，至少在相当公开的社交聚会上，在众目睽睽下喝醉酒是为社会允许的，而且在某些圈子里还是相当受赞赏的事。

新潮势利感虽然不是我们的时代所特有的，却具有了空前的重要性，理由很简单，而且完全是经济上的。由于有了现代化的机器，生产超过了消费。消费者有组织的浪费是我们工业繁荣的首要条件。消费者越快扔掉买来的东西再买新的，对生产者就越有利。当然，与此同时，生产者必须尽一己之力，只生产最易损坏的东西。"把一座摩天大楼建造得可以耐用40年以上的人是建筑行业的叛徒。"这是美国一个大承包商说的话。如果用汽车、靴子、一套衣服等等来代替摩天大楼，用1年、3个月、6个月等等来代替40年，你得出的就是任何现代工业所有领导遵从的信条。很明显，新潮势利感是这位实业家最好的朋友，因为新潮势利者自然会比无此势利感的人更快地抛弃他们所拥有的旧东西并购买新东西。因此鼓励新潮势利感是对生产者有利的，而实际上他也是这样做的，以一年成百上千万的金钱进行大规模广告宣传。报纸也尽一切力量帮助那些帮助它们的人们，在洪水般的广告之外再加上洪水般的不那么直接花钱去做的有利于新潮势利感的宣传。公众被教育说保持时尚是人类首要的职责之一，驯服的公众接受了这个一再被重申的启发。现在我们全都成了新潮势利者了。

我们中多数人也是艺术势利者，这种势利感有两类，一是纯精神的，另一类则与之相反。纯精神的艺术势利者只是对艺术"感兴趣"，非纯精神的则进一步而且真的购买艺术，这种势利感是一种杂交品种或者说是一头骡子，因为它同时是文化势利感和财产势利感的亚种，收集艺术作品就是收集文化象征，而文化象征则仍意味着社会声望。它又是财富象征的收集，因为艺术收藏比一整队汽车更能有效地代表金钱。

艺术势利感对活着的艺术家具有极大的价值。的确，多数艺术势利者只收集已故艺术家的作品，因为古代艺术大师比起活着的大师来既是安全的投资又是较神圣的文化象征。但某些艺术势利者同时也是新潮势利者，他们这些人再加上少数出于对艺术品本身的喜爱而买画的怪人，足以使活着的艺术家获得必需的生活资料。

总的来说，势利感的价值，即它与人相关的意义，在于它有能刺激行动的能力。一个有许多种势利感的社会就像一只有许多跳蚤的狗，它不太可能变得麻木倦惰。每种势利感都要求其信徒作出不懈的努力，一个接一个的牺牲。社会地位势利者必须不停地巴结社会名流，新潮势利者永远不可能停止追求时尚，疾病或文化势利者各自朝思暮想的必定是瑞士医生或人们认为被称作是最好的一切。

如果我们把行动本身看作是好事，那么我们必须把一切势利感当作好事，因为它们全都能引起行动。如果我们和佛教徒一样，认为在这个虚幻的世界上一切行动都是坏事，那么我们就会立即谴责所有的势利感。我认为我们多数人所采取的立场是介于这两个极端之间的某个地方，我们把某些行动看作是好的，某些是无关紧要的，或彻底坏的。我们赞成的只能是那些激起我们认为是较好的行动的势利感，其余的我们只能或容忍，或憎恶。例如，多数专业知识分子会赞成文化势利感（即使他们十分讨厌多数文化势利者个人），因为这迫使市侩庸人们至少对精神上的东西要稍加赞许，因此有助于使世界比没有这一点赞许时对精神可能少一点危险和不安全。另一方面，一个汽车制造商会把财产势利感置于文化势利感之上，他会尽其所能使人们相信，占有东西少的人，特别是在四个轮子上的东西，低于占有东西多的人。依此类推。每一等级的人到头来终有自己具体崇拜的教皇。

[1] philistine  n.市侩庸人

# 我的林园
# My Wood

【英国】E. M. 福斯特

作者简介

E. M. 福斯特 (1879–1970) 是二十世纪英国著名的作家,其作品包括六部小说,两集短篇小说集,几部传记和一些评论文章。福斯特的作品语风清新淡雅,虽然人物的个性很容易被把握,但命运安排往往令人不可预测却又铺叙自然。《印度之行》、《看得见风景的房间》、《天使不敢驻足的地方》、《莫利斯》和《霍华德庄园》都被成功地搬上银幕。虽然反映的都是二十世纪初英国的社会状况,但其间表达的自由、平等与人道的精神对已经走入二十一世纪的人类社会仍有实际的借鉴意义。《我的林园》这篇叙事散文围绕作者自己的林园,诙谐生动地谈了财产对人的品格的影响,剖析了有产者的内心世界。

我的林园
My Wood

A few years ago I wrote a book[1] which dealt in part with the difficulties of the English in India. Feeling that they would have had no difficulties in India themselves, the Americans read the book freely. The more they read it the better it made them feel, and a check to the author was the result. I bought a wood with the check. It is not a large wood—it contains scarcely any trees, and it is intersected, blast it, by a public foot-path. Still, it is the first property that I have owned, so it is right that other people should participate in my shame, and should ask themselves, in accents that will vary in horror, this very important question: What is the effect of property upon the character? Don't let's touch economics; the effect of private ownership upon the community as a whole is another question—a more important question, perhaps, but another one. Let's keep to psychology. If you own things, what's their effect on you? What's the effect on me of my wood?

In the first place, it makes me feel heavy. Property does have this effect. Property produces men of weight, and it was a man of weight who failed to get into the Kingdom of Heaven. He was not wicked, that unfortunate millionaire in the parable, he was only stout; he stuck out in front, not to mention behind, and as he wedged himself this way and that in the crystalline entrance and bruised his well-fed flanks, he saw beneath him a comparatively slim camel passing through the eye of a needle and being woven into the robe of God[2]. The Gospels all through couple stoutness and slowness. They point out what is perfectly obvious, yet seldom realized: that if you have a lot of things you cannot move about a lot, that furniture requires dusting, dusters require servants, servants require insurance stamps, and the whole tangle of them makes you think twice before you accept an invitation to dinner or go for a bathe in the Jordan. Sometimes the Gospels proceed further and say with Tolstoy that property is sinful; they approach the difficult ground of asceticism here, where I cannot follow them. But as to the immediate effects of property on people, they just show straightforward logic. It produces men of weight. Men of weight cannot, by definition, move like the lightning from the East unto the West, and the ascent of a

193

最 散文
Zui Prose

fourteen-stone bishop into a pulpit is thus the exact antithesis of the coming of the Son of Man. My wood makes me feel heavy.

In the second place, it makes me feel it ought to be larger.

The other day I heard a twig snap in it. I was annoyed at first, for I thought that someone was blackberrying, and depreciating the value of the undergrowth. On coming nearer, I saw it was not a man who had trodden on the twig and snapped it, but a bird, and I felt pleased. My bird. The bird was not equally pleased. Ignoring the relation between us, it took flight as soon as it saw the shape of my face, and flew straight over the boundary hedge into a field, the property of Mrs. Henessy, where it sat down with a loud squawk. It had become Mrs. Henessy's bird. Something seemed grossly amiss here, something that would not have occurred had the wood been larger. I could not afford to buy Mrs. Henessy out, I dared not murder her, and limitations of this sort beset me on every side. Ahab[3] did not want that vineyard—he only needed it to round off his property, preparatory to plotting a new curve—and all the land around my wood has become necessary to me in order to round off the wood. A boundary protects. But—poor little thing—the boundary ought in its turn to be protected. Noises on the edge of it. Children throw stones. A little more, and then a little more, until we reach the sea. Happy Canute[4]! Happier Alexander[5]! And after all, why should even the world be the limit of possession? A rocket containing a Union Jack, will, it is hoped, be shortly fired at the moon. Mars. Sirius. Beyond which... But these immensities ended by saddening me. I could not suppose that my wood was the destined nucleus of universal dominion—it is so small and contains no mineral wealth beyond the blackberries. Nor was I comforted when Mrs. Henessy's bird took alarm for the second time and flew clean away from us all, under the belief that it belonged to itself.

In the third place, property makes its owner feel that he ought to do something to it. Yet he isn't sure what. A restlessness comes over him, a vague sense that he has a personality to express—the same sense which, without any vagueness, leads the artist to an act of creation. Sometimes I think I will cut down such trees as remain in the wood, at other times I want to fill up the gaps between them with new trees. Both impulses are pretentious and empty. They are not honest movements towards moneymaking or beauty. They spring from a foolish desire to express myself and from an inability to enjoy what I have got. Creation, property, enjoyment form a sinister trinity in the human mind. Creation and enjoyment are both very, very good, yet they are often unattainable without a material basis, and at such moments property pushes itself in as a substitute, saying, "Accept me instead—I'm good enough for all three." It is not enough. It is, as Shakespeare said of lust, "The expense of spirit in a waste of shame": it is "Before, a joy proposed; behind, a dream." Yet we don't know how to shun it. It is forced on us by our economic system as the alternative to starvation. It is also forced on us by an internal defect in the soul, by the feeling that in property may lie the germs of self-development and of exquisite or heroic deeds. Our life on earth is, and ought to be, material and carnal. But we have not yet learned to manage our materialism and carnality properly; they are still entangled with the desire for ownership, where in the words of Dante "Possession is one with loss."

And this brings us to our fourth and final point: the blackberries.

Blackberries are not plentiful in this meager grove, but they are easily seen from the public footpath which traverses it, and all too easily gathered. Foxgloves, too—people will pull up the foxgloves, and ladies of an educational tendency even grub for toadstools to show them on the Monday in class. Other ladies, less educated, roll down the bracken in the arms of their gentlemen friends. Here is paper, there are tins. Pray, does my wood belong to me or doesn't it? And, if it does, should I not own it best by allowing no one else to walk there? There is a wood near Lyme Regis, also cursed by a public footpath, where the owner has not hesitated on this point. He has built high stone walls each side of the path, and has spanned it by bridges, so that the public circulate like termites while he gorges on the blackberries unseen. He really does own his wood, this able chap. Dives[6] in

Hell did pretty well, but the gulf dividing him from Lazarus shall come to this in time. I shall wall in and fence out until I really taste the sweets of property. Enormously stout, endlessly avaricious, pseudo-creative, intensely selfish, I shall weave upon my forehead the quadruple crown of possession until those nasty Bolshies come and take it off again and thrust me aside into the outer darkness.

几年前我写过一本书,部分地谈到英国人在印度陷入的困境。美国人感到自己在印度不会有困难,于是坦然地阅读那本书。他们愈读愈感到舒畅,结果给作者汇来一张支票。我用这张支票买下一处林园,不是一片大的林园——树木稀少,更倒霉的是,还被一条公共小道穿过。但无论怎样说,它毕竟是我拥有的第一份产业,这一下也该让别人分担我的耻辱,以程度不同的惊骇口气向他们自己提出一个很重要的问题:财产对人的品格会产生什么影响? 咱们别提经济问题,私有制对于整个公众的影响是另一码事——也许是一个更为重要的问题,但是另一码事。咱们从心理上说吧,假若你拥有财产,它对你会产生什么影响? 我的林园对我有什么影响?

　　首先,它使我感到沉重。财产确实会产生这种影响。财产造就出笨重的人,而身体笨重便进不了天堂。《圣经》寓言中那位不幸的富翁并非心术不正,只是身体太粗壮。他前部大腹便便,别提身子后面有多臃肿了。他在水晶般透明的天堂入口侧来转去,擦伤了肥胖的两肋,这时他却看见下边一头身体较为细长的骆驼穿过针眼,到了上帝的身边。四部福音书都把粗壮和缓慢相提并论,它们指出了显而易见却很少意识到的道理:假如你拥有许多财产,你的行动就会很不方便。家具需要打扫,扫帚需要雇人使用,雇人需要给保险金——这一连串事儿够你在接受晚宴请帖时或决定去约旦河游泳之前三思而行。福音书的进一步阐述还表明了与托尔斯泰一致的观点:财产是罪恶。在这里,它接近于苦行主义的艰难领域,我不能亦步亦趋。但谈到财产对人的直接影响,完全符合逻辑,不言而喻。财产产生笨重的人,顾名思义,笨重者不能疾速如闪电,由东至西一瞬而过;

体重将近两万磅的主教登上布道坛,恰好会与耶稣临世形成尖锐的对照。我的林园使我感到沉重。

其次,它使我感到林地还应当更宽阔一些。

不久前的一天,我听见林中树枝啪地一声响。开始我有些恼怒,心想有人在摘黑莓,全然不顾树下的草木。走近一看,踏在树枝上并弄出啪声的不是人,而是一只鸟。我心里坦然了。我的鸟。鸟儿却并不同样坦然,它才不管我们之间的关系呢,一见我露面便展翅而飞,直越过界篱飞进一块地里——赫尼希太太的地产,并歇在那儿尖叫了一声。它现在成了赫尼希太太的鸟儿了,我顿觉怅然若失,林园要再大些就不会出现这等事了。我没钱买下赫尼希太太的地产,也不敢谋害她,这种种局限从四面八方向我袭来。亚哈并不想占那个葡萄园——全是为了使自己的地产完整,他正筹划一条新的地界。而为了使我的林园完整,林园周围的土地都该属于我。有了边界才能有保障。但遗憾的是,新的边界又需要得到保障。否则,喧嚣会越过界墙,小孩子会扔石子。就这样,一大再大,逐步扩张,直到我们与大海接壤。幸运的卡鲁特王!更幸运的亚历山大大帝!这个世界为什么竟成了占有者的极限?但愿载着英国国旗的火箭不久会发射到月球去。到火星,天狼星,再往外……但这样广袤的空间终会令人沮丧失望。我不能设想自己的林园注定会是征服宇宙的核心——太狭小了,没有任何矿产,只结一些黑莓。当赫尼希太太的鸟儿再次受惊飞起,我也很不高兴;它完全飞离了我们,深信它只属于它自己。

第三,财产使它的主人感到应该用它来办点什么事,但他又不清楚究竟要办什么事。不安宁的心情占据了他,他模糊地感到需要表现自己的个性——同样的感觉(但不模糊)驱使艺术家进行创作活动。有时我想砍倒剩余的树,有时又想在树间空地补栽新苗,两种冲动都很矫揉造作和空虚,既没有诚心以此获利,又不打算以此美化林园,都源出于表现自我的愚蠢愿望,出于缺乏享受已有财产的能力。在人的心灵里,创造、财产和享受组成一个邪恶的三位一体。创造和享受两者都不错,但要是没有物质基础,则往往无法办到。这时,作为一种替代选择,财产插了进来自荐:"接受我吧,我于大家都有利。"其实,并不很有利,正像莎士比亚谈到淫念时说的:"精神损耗于羞耻之中。""事前令人感到喜悦,事后恍若一梦。"然而,我们不知道如何避免,它被我们的经济体制作为饥饿的替换物强加给了我们,这也是灵魂深处的内在缺陷所强加于我们的负担,认为财产之中蕴藏着自我发展的胚胎,蕴藏着优雅或英勇行为的根源。我们在世上的生活本是——也应当是——物质的和肉体的存在,但我们还没有学会如何适当地处理物质利益和享受之间的关系,两者仍然同占有欲纠缠在一起,用但丁的话来说:"占有与丧失同一"。

而这把我们领入了第四点,即最后一点:黑莓。

在稀疏的丛林里,黑莓结得并不多,站在横穿林园的公共小道上便可一览无遗,伸手摘取也毫不费力。毛地黄,人们爱攀摘;受过些教育的女人,甚至伸手去采毒菌,以便在星期一的课堂上显示显示。另外一些受教育较少的女人,则搂着男朋友在蕨草地上打滚。这儿扔下纸,那儿留下罐头盒。天哪,我的林园还属不属于我? 倘若属于我的话,我是否最好不让任何人入内? 在林蒙雷基地方有一处林园,不幸也有一条公共小道穿过,但它的主人在这个问题上毫不犹豫。他在路的两旁筑起高大的石墙,墙间以桥横跨。当公众像白蚁般来回走动其间,他却在饱餐黑莓,但谁也看不见他。这个能干的家伙,名副其实地拥有他的林园。戴夫斯在阴间的表现不错,他与拉撒若斯之间的鸿沟能被意念跨越,但这儿什么也无法通过,说不定哪一天,我也会这样做。我将在路边筑起墙,园边围起篱笆,让我能够真正领略拥有财产的甜蜜。身躯庞大,贪得无厌,冒充创造,极端自私,我将为自己编织一顶偌大的财产王冠,直到那些布尔什维克走到跟前,重又把它摘下,然后把我推入黑暗。

---

[1] 指小说《印度之行》(1924),本文写于1926年。

[2] 见《圣经·新约全书》的《马太福音》第十九章二十四节。

[3] 亚哈,公元前九世纪的以色列君王。

[4] 卡鲁特王(994~1035),征服不列颠的丹麦王。

[5] 亚历山大大帝(公元前356~323)马其顿国王,历史上著名的军事征服者。

[6]《圣经》寓言中的富豪。在世时,乞丐拉撒若斯上门乞讨,他让狗驱赶他;死后,两者的命运颠倒过来。

# 怎样发大财
# How to Make a Million Dollars

【加拿大】斯蒂芬·里柯克

作者简介

斯蒂芬·里柯克(1869-1944)，政治经济学教授，加拿大首位获得世界声誉的幽默作家。在美国，他被认为是继马克·吐温之后最受人欢迎的幽默作家。他的作品充满幽默感，他的幽默是一种淡淡的、含蓄的幽默，善于从平淡无奇的日常生活中提炼出一些为大家司空见惯却又往往熟视无睹的可笑的和不合理的东西加以放大后呈现在读者面前，让他们产生共鸣而发出会心的微笑或无奈的苦笑，发人深省。《怎样发大财》用夸大的写法板着脸逗人，艰苦的发财被轻松地幽默之一默。

I mix a good deal with the Millionaires. I like them. I like their faces. I like the way they live. I like the things they eat. The more we mix together the better I like the things we mix.

Especially I like the way they dress, their grey check trousers, their white check waist-coats, their heavy gold chains, and the signet-rings that they sign their cheques with. My! they look nice. Get six or seven of them sitting together in the club and it's a treat to see them. And if they get the least dust on them, men come and brush it off. Yes, and are glad to. I'd like to take some of the dust off them myself.

Even more than what they eat I like their intellectual grasp. It is wonderful. Just watch them read. They simply read all the time. Go into the club at any hour and you'll see three or four of them at it. And the things they can read! You'd think that a man who'd been driving hard in the office from eleven o'clock until three, with only an hour and a half for lunch, would be too fagged. Not a bit. These men can sit down after office hours and read the Sketch and the Police Gazette and the Pink Un, and understand the jokes just as well as I can.

What I love to do is to walk up and down among them and catch the little scraps of conversation. The other day I heard one lean forward and say, "Well, I offered him a million and a half and said I wouldn't give a cent more, he could either take it or leave it—" I just longed to break in and say, "What! what! a million and a half! Oh! say that again! Offer it to me, to either take it or leave it. Do try me once: I know I can: or here, make it a plain million and let's call it done."

Not that these men are careless over money. No, sir. Don't think it. Of course they don't take much account of big money, a hundred thousand dollars at a shot or anything of that sort. But little money. You've no idea till you know them how anxious they get about a cent, or half a cent, or less.

Why, two of them came into the club the other night just frantic with delight: they said wheat had risen and they'd cleaned up four cents each in less than half an hour. They bought a dinner for sixteen on the strength of it. I don't understand it. I've often made twice as much as that writing for the papers and never felt like boasting about it.

One night I heard one man say, "Well, let's call up New York and offer them a quarter of a cent." Great heavens! Imagine paying the cost of calling up New York, nearly five million people, late at night and offering them a quarter of a cent! And yet—did New York get mad? No, they took it. Of course it's high finance. I don't pretend to understand it. I tried after that to call up Chicago and offer it a cent and a half, and to call up Hamilton, Ontario, and offer it half a dollar, and the operator only thought I was crazy.

All this shows, of course, that I've been studying how the millionaires do it. I have. For years. I thought it might be helpful to young men just beginning to work and anxious to stop.

You know, many a man realizes late in life that if when he was a boy he had known what he knows now, instead of being what he is he might be what he won't; but how few boys stop to think that if they knew what they don't know instead of being what they will be, they wouldn't be? These are awful thoughts.

At any rate, I've been gathering hints on how it is they do it.

One thing I'm sure about. If a young man wants to make a million dollars he's got to be mighty careful about his diet and his living. This may seem hard. But success is only achieved with pains.

There is no use in a young man who hopes to make a million dollars thinking he's entitled to get up at 7.30, eat force and poached[1] eggs, drink cold water at lunch, and go to bed at 10 p.m. You can't do it. I've seen too many millionaires for that. If you want to be a millionaire you mustn't get up till ten in the morning. They never do. They daren't. It would be as much as their business is worth if they were seen on the street at half-past nine.

And the old idea of abstemiousness is all wrong. To be a millionaire you need champagne, lots of it and all the time. That and Scotch whisky and soda: you have to sit up nearly all night and drink buckets of it. This is what clears the brain for business next day. I've seen some of these men with their brains so clear in the morning that their faces look positively boiled.

To live like this requires, of course, resolution. But you can buy that by the pint.

Therefore, my dear young man, if you want to get moved on from your present status in business, change your life. When your landlady brings your bacon and eggs for breakfast, throw them out of window to the dog and tell her to bring you some chilled asparagus and a pint of Moselle. Then telephone to your employer that you'll be down about eleven o'clock. You will get moved on. Yes, very quickly.

Just how the millionaires make the money is a difficult question. But one way is this. Strike the town with five cents in your pocket. They nearly all do this; they've told me again and again (men with millions and millions) that the first time they struck town they had only five cents. That seems to have given them their start. Of course, it's not easy to do. I've tried it several times. I nearly did it once. I borrowed five cents, carried it away out of town, and then turned and came back at the town with an awful rush. If I hadn't struck a beer saloon in the suburbs and spent the five cents I might have been rich today.

Another good plan is to start something. Something on a huge scale: something nobody ever thought of. For instance, one man I know told me that once he was down in Mexico without a cent (he'd lost his five in striking Central America) and he noticed that they had no power plants. So he started some and made a mint of money. Another man that I know was once stranded in New York, absolutely without a nickel. Well, it occurred to him that what was needed were buildings ten stories higher than any that had been put up. So he built two and sold them right away. Ever so many millionaires begin in some such simple way as that.

There is, of course, a much easier way than any of these. I almost hate to tell this, because I want to do it myself.

I learned of it just by chance one night at the club. There is one old man there, extremely rich, with one of the best faces of the lot, just like a hyena. I never used to know how he had got so rich. So one evening I asked one of the millionaires how old Bloggs had made all his money.

"How he made it?" he answered with a sneer. "Why he made it by taking it out of widows and orphans."

Widows and orphans! I thought, what an excellent idea. But who would have suspected that they had it?

"And how," I asked pretty cautiously, "did he go at it to get it out of them?"

"Why," the man answered, "he just ground them under his heels, that was how."

Now isn't that simple? I've thought of that conversation often since and I mean to try it. If I can get hold of them, I'll grind them quick enough. But how to get them. Most of the widows I know look pretty solid for that sort of thing, and as for orphans, it must take an awful lot of them. Meantime I am waiting, and if I ever get a large bunch of orphans all together, I'll stamp on them and see.

I find, too, on inquiry, that you can also grind it out of clergymen. They say they grind nicely. But perhaps orphans are easier.

我跟阔佬们一向过从很密。我喜欢他们。我喜欢他们的脸相。我喜欢他们的生活方式。我喜欢他们的饮食。我越跟他们打交道,就越喜欢他们的一切。

我尤其喜欢他们的穿戴:灰色带格子的裤了,白色带格子的坎肩,沉甸甸的表链,以及那可以当作图章使用的戒指——他们就凭那戒指来签发支票。啊,他们打扮得真叫可爱!要是有那么六七位阔佬围坐在俱乐部里,那看起来才过瘾呢。只要他们身上稍微沾上点儿尘土,听差马上就跑过来掸掉。真的,而且做的时候满心欢喜。我恨不得自己也去替他们掸掸呢。

我喜欢他们的饮食,但是我更喜欢他们那一肚子的学问。真是了不起。你留心吧,他们简直时时刻刻都在看书。随便你什么时候跨进俱乐部去,你总会碰上三四位阔佬。瞧他们看的那些东西!你也许会想:一个人在办公室里从早上十一点一直工作到下午三点,中间仅仅花了一个半小时吃午饭,一定疲劳不堪了吧,可是一点儿也不。这些先生们处理完了公事就坐下来看《社会随笔》,看《警察公报》和《桃色》,并且对杂志里的那些笑话领会起来一点儿也不比咱们差。

我很喜欢在他们那堆人中间走来走去,听他们说的一言半语。那天我听到一位阔佬探着身子说:"喏,我已经出到一百五十万,并且告诉他说,再多一分钱也不出啦,要还是不要,全随他——"我满心想插嘴说:"喂,喂,一百五十万!啊,再说一遍吧,要还是不要,你问问我看。你试试看,我准能给你个答复。或者咱们干脆说一百万,就算一言为定吧。"

这些阔佬们对钱财并不马虎。不是的,先生,你可别那么想。他们对于大数目自然是不大在乎的,譬如说,一回花上它百八十万的。他们在乎的是小数目。你简直不能想象他们为了一分半分,甚至比那更小的数目,能着急到怎样的地步。

那天晚上,两位阔佬进了俱乐部,高兴得快发疯。他们说小麦的价格涨啦,不到半个钟头他们就各自赚了四分钱。就凭这一注财,他们叫了十六块钱一客的大菜。我真不懂。我给报馆写稿子,曾经赚过比那多上一倍的钱,可是我从来也没觉得有什么可夸耀的。

又有一天晚上我听到一位阔佬说:"来,咱们给纽约打个电话,告诉他们咱们愿意出两厘五。"好家伙!深更半夜花钱给纽约(差不多有五百万人口啊)打电话,表示愿意出两厘五!可是——纽约见怪没见怪呢?没有,他们要啦。自然,这是高等金融,我也不便滥充内行。后来我也叫叫芝加哥看,我告诉他们我情愿出一分五厘,然后又打电话给安大略省的海密尔顿市,表示我愿意出五毛,结果,电话接线员只当我发了疯。

当然,这一切只不过表明我的确曾经仔细研究过那些阔佬的发财之道。我的确下过一番苦功夫,下过几年的苦功夫啊。我心里想,对于那些刚开始工作就盼着大大捞一笔钱退休的年轻人,这种钻研也许会有好处。

你知道,许多人到晚年才发觉,要是小时候对人生就有了今天的认识,他们也不会干目前干的事,而干起他们当初所不愿意干的事了。可是天下有几个小伙子肯停下来思索一下,要是他们当初晓得现在所不晓得的东西,前途会不会大大两样?这些都是怕人的思想。

不管怎样,我曾经到处搜集他们的成功秘诀。

有一件事我确实知道。一个年轻小伙子要是想发大财,他对于起居饮食得十分当心。这个听起来也许挺难办到,可是成功总是要经过一番艰苦过程的。

年轻人要是打算发大财,就别以为他还有资格早上七点半起床,早饭吃几个煮鸡蛋,午饭的时候喝杯凉水,晚上十点睡觉,那可办不到!阔佬我是见识多了,对这一点我十分清楚。你要是立志想当个阔佬,那么早上十点以前就别起床。阔佬们向来不那么做。他们不敢起来。晚上九点半他们还在街上荡来荡去,那才跟他们的家当相称。

要节制的说法是陈旧的,完全不对头。当了阔佬,你就得喝香槟酒,而且多多地喝,不停地喝。香槟酒以外,还得喝苏格兰威士忌酒加苏打。你差不多得通宵达旦地熬夜,大桶大桶地喝酒,这样才能保持清醒的脑筋,第二天好做生意。我曾经见过阔佬早晨头脑非常清醒,他们的脸肿得像煮过了似的。

自然喽,要照这么生活,必须有毅力。可是毅力这玩意儿现成得很。

所以,亲爱的小伙子,要是你有意从当前在商界的地位再高升一步,那么就改变一下你的生活吧。吃早饭的时候要是房东太太给你端来火腿蛋,就把它从窗口丢出去喂狗,吩咐她给你送凉芦笋和一升葡萄酒来,然后用电话通知你的老板说,你十一点去上班。这样办你一定会步步高升,而且快得很。

阔佬们究竟怎么个发财法儿,这问题可不好回答。可是一条路子是这样的:口袋里只带上五分钱,就奔一个城去打天下。阔佬们都是这么起家的。他们(家私几百万几千万的阔佬)一再告诉我,头回进城打天下的时候,他们口袋里只有五分钱。这似乎就是他们的本钱。自然,办起来这也不那么容易。我试过好几回。有一回我差一点儿成功啦。我向人借了五分钱,我带着它出了城,然后飞快地折了回来。要不是在近郊碰上一家酒馆,把五分钱花掉了,此刻我也许真的发了财呢。

另外一条路子是创办点儿什么,规模大大的,创办点儿从来没人想过的事。譬如说,一个熟人告诉我,有一回他身上一个钱也没有(他到美洲中部打天下的时候,把五分钱丢了),就来到墨西哥。他看到那里没有发电厂,于是,他开办了几所发电厂,赚了一大笔钱。另外一个熟人有一回困在纽约了,身上一文不名。哦,他灵机一动,发现那里需要比现有的高楼大厦更高出十层的建筑。于是,他就盖了两座,转手卖掉了。许许多多的阔佬们就是这么毫不费力发迹起来的。

自然,还有比这些更简便的路子。我几乎舍不得公开出来,因为我自己也正想尝试一下。

这是一天晚上我偶尔在俱乐部里学来的。那儿有个老头儿,他非常非常阔。在阔佬里,他的脸长得算是顶漂亮了,活像条土狼。我一向不晓得他是怎么阔到这个地步的,所以有一天晚上,我就请教一位阔佬,布洛哥这老家伙的财是怎么发的。

"怎么发的?"那个人冷笑了一声说,"他是从孤儿寡妇身上抢来的。"

孤儿寡妇!哦,这真是条高明不过的办法。可是谁料到孤儿寡妇身上会有财可发呢?

"但是,他是怎么发的呀?"我小心翼翼地问,"他是扑到他们身上硬抢过来的吗?"

"很简单,"那个人回答说,"他只不过把他们放在脚后跟下面碾,就这样。"

瞧,这多省事呀!从那以后,我时常思索这段谈话,并且有意试它一试。要是我能弄到些孤儿寡妇,我会很快就把他们碾碎的。可是怎么把他们弄到手呢?我所认识的寡妇,看来大半都很壮实,不好碾;至于孤儿,那得弄到一大群才成呢。我目前还在等待着。要是我能弄到一大批孤儿,我一定要碾碾他们看。

后来一打听,原来牧师身上也碾得出东西来。据说他们的汁水还特别多。可是,也许孤儿们更容易碾一些哩。

---

[1] poach  vt.水煮

# 流动的盛宴
# A Moveable Feast

【美国】欧内斯特·海明威

作者简介

　　欧内斯特·海明威( 1899-1961)美国小说家。1954年度的诺贝尔文学奖获得者、"新闻体"小说的创始人。他作为"迷惘的一代"的代表,写了反战小说《永别了,武器》,小说中惯用象征写法,塑造"硬汉"形象,写作风格为"冰山原则"。

Then there was the bad weather. It would come in one day when the fall was over. We would have to shut the windows in the night against the rain and the cold wind would strip the leaves from the trees in the Place Contrescarpe. The leaves lay sodden in the rain and the wind drove the rain against the big green autobus at the terminal and the Café des Amateurs was crowded and the windows misted over from the heat and the smoke inside. It was a sad, evilly run café where the drunkards of the quarter crowded together and I kept away from it because of the smell of dirty bodies and the sour smell of drunkenness. The men and women who frequented the Amateurs stayed drunk all of the time, or all of the time they could afford it, mostly on wine which they bought by the half-liter or liter. Many strangely named apéritifs were advertised, but few people could afford them except as a foundation to build their wine drunks on. The women drunkards were called poivrottes which meant female rummies.

The Café des Amateurs was the cesspool of the rue Mouffetard, that wonderful narrow crowded market street which led into the Place Contrescarpe. The squat toilets of the old apartment houses, one by the side of the stairs on each floor with the two cleated cement shoe-shaped elevations on each side of the aperture so a locataire would not slip, emptied into cesspools which were emptied by pumping into horse-drawn tank wagons at night. In the summer time, with all windows open, we would hear the pumping and the odor was very strong. The tank wagons were painted brown and saffron color and in the moonlight when they worked the rue Cardinal Lemoine their wheeled, horse-drawn cylinders looked like Braque[1] paintings. No one emptied the Café des Amateurs though, and its yellowed poster stating the terms and penalties of the law against public drunkenness was as flyblown and disregarded as its clients were constant and ill-smelling.

All of the sadness of the city came suddenly with the first cold rains of winter, and there were no more tops to the high white houses as you walked but only the wet blackness of the street and the closed doors of the small shops, the herb sellers, the stationery and the newspaper shops, the midwife—second class—and the hotel where Verlaine had died where I had a room on the top floor where I worked.

It was either six or eight flights up to the top floor and it was very cold and I knew how much it would cost for a bundle of small twigs, three wire-wrapped packets of short, half-pencil length pieces of split pine to catch fire from the twigs, and then the bundle of half-dried lengths of hard wood that I must buy to make a fire that would warm the room. So I went to the far side of the street to look up at the roof in the rain and see if any chimneys were going, and how the smoke blew. There was no smoke and I thought about how the chimney would be cold and might not draw and of the room possibly filling with smoke, and the fuel wasted, and the money gone with it, and I walked on in the rain. I walked down past the Lycée Henri Quatre and the ancient church of St.-étienne-du-Mont and the windswept Place du Panthéon and cut in for shelter to the right and finally came out on the lee side of the Boulevard St.-Michel and worked on down it past the Cluny and the Boulevard St.-Germain until I came to a good café that I knew on the Place St.-Michel.

It was a pleasant café, warm and clean and friendly, and I hung up my old waterproof on the coat rack to dry and put my worn and weathered felt hat on the rack above the bench and ordered a café au lait. The waiter brought it and I took out a notebook from the pocket of the coat and a pencil and started to write. I was writing about up in Michigan and since it was a wild, cold, blowing day it was that sort of day in the story. I had already seen the end of fall come through boyhood, youth and young manhood, and in one place you could write about it better than in another. That was called transplanting yourself, I thought, and it could be as necessary with people as with other sorts of growing things. But in the story the boys were drinking and this made me thirsty and I ordered a rum St. James. This tasted wonderful on the cold day and I kept on writing, feeling very well and feeling the good Martinique rum warm me all through my body and my spirit.

A girl came in the café and sat by herself at a table near the window. She was very pretty with a face fresh as a newly minted coin if they minted coins in smooth flesh with rain-freshened skin, and her hair was black as a crow's wing and cut sharply and diagonally across her cheek.

I looked at her and she disturbed me and made me very excited. I wished I could put her in the story, or anywhere, but she had placed herself so she could watch the street and the entry and I knew she was waiting for someone. So I went on writing.

The story was writing itself and I was having a hard time keeping up with it. I ordered another rum St. James and I watched the girl whenever I looked up, or when I sharpened the pencil with a pencil sharpener with the shavings curling into the saucer under my drink.

I've seen you, beauty, and you belong to me now, whoever you are waiting for and if I never see you again, I thought. You belong to me and all Paris belongs to me and I belong to this notebook and this pencil.

Then I went back to writing and I entered far into the story and was lost in it. I was writing it now and it was not writing itself and I did not look up nor know anything about the time nor think where I was nor order any more rum St. James. I was tired of rum St. James without thinking about it. Then the story was finished and I was very tired. I read the last paragraph and then I looked up and looked for the girl and she had gone. I hope she's gone with a good man, I thought. But I felt sad.

I closed up the story in the notebook and put it in my inside pocket and I asked the waiter for a dozen portugaises and a half-carafe of the dry white wine they had there. After writing a story I was always empty and both sad and happy, as though I had made love, and I was sure this was a very good story although I would not know truly how good until I read it over the next day.

As I ate the oysters with their strong taste of the sea and their faint metallic taste that the cold white wine washed away, leaving only the sea taste and the succulent texture, and as I drank their cold liquid from each shell and washed it down with the crisp taste of the wine, I lost the empty feeling and began to be happy and to make plans.

Now that the bad weather had come, we could leave Paris for a while for a place where this rain would be snow coming down through the pines and covering the road and the high hillsides and at an altitude where we would hear it creak as we walked home at night. Below Les Avants there was a chalet where the pension was wonderful and where we would be together and have our books and at night be warm in bed together with the windows open and the stars bright. That was where we could go. Traveling third class on the train was not expensive. The pension cost very little more than we spent in Paris.

I would give up the room in the hotel where I wrote and there was only the rent of 74 rue Cardinal Lemoine which was nominal. I had written journalism for Toronto and the checks for that were due. I could write that anywhere under any circumstances and we had money to make the trip.

Maybe away from Paris I could write about Paris as in Paris I could write about Michigan. I did not know it was too early for that because I did not know Paris well enough. But that was how it worked out eventually. Anyway we would go if my wife wanted to, and I finished the oysters and the wine and paid my score in the café and made it the shortest way back up the Montagne Ste. Geneviève through the rain, that was now only local weather and not something that changed your life, to the flat at the top of the hill.

"I think it would be wonderful, Tatie," my wife said. She had a gently modeled face and her eyes and her smile lighted up at decisions as though they were rich presents. "When should we leave?"

"Whenever you want."

"Oh, I want to right away. Didn't you know?"

"Maybe it will be fine and clear when we come back. It can be very fine when it is clear and cold."

"I'm sure it will be," she said. "Weren't you good to think of going, too."

　　随着秋天的远去，不知哪一天坏天气就会不期而至。夜晚，我们得紧闭窗户，以防雨水飘进来。壕沟外护墙广场上，寒风把树上的叶子纷纷吹落。落叶浸泡在雨水中，风携着雨敲打着终点站上那辆绿色的大公共汽车。可是爱好者咖啡馆中却人头攒动，里面的热气和烟雾给窗子蒙上水汽，显得模糊不清。那是家可悲的、丑形恶状的咖啡馆，里面挤满了当地的酒鬼，他们污秽不堪，醉醺醺地吐着酒气，令我望而却步。经常光顾这里的男男女女们总是烂醉如泥，或者说，只要他们买得起醉，就准会喝得酩酊大醉。他们多半成半升或一升地买葡萄酒来喝。许多名字稀奇古怪的开胃酒在做着广告，但是没有几个人能喝得起，除非在狂饮葡萄酒前喝一点垫底。那些女酒客被称为poivrottes，也就是女酒鬼的意思。

　　爱好者咖啡馆是穆费塔路上的藏污纳垢之处。那条奇特的商业街狭窄而拥挤，一直通向壕沟外护墙广场。老式公寓房内的蹲式厕所都安置在每层楼的楼梯旁边，蹲坑两边有两个隆起的防滑鞋形踏脚，由水泥浇制而成，以防房客滑倒。厕所内的粪便排入污水池，再于夜间由污水池抽泵到马拉的运粪罐车里。夏天，因为窗户都开着，我们能听到这种抽泵的声音，而且还臭气熏天。这些运粪车被漆成了棕色和橘黄色，当它们在月光下沿着勒穆瓦纳红衣主教路缓缓前行时，那些装上了轮盘的、由马牵拉着的罐筒看起来就像是布拉克的画。可是没人给爱好者咖啡馆排污清秽。它那发了黄的布告上写着禁止在公共场合酗酒的法律条文及惩罚规定，但根本没人理会，它的那些顾客仍一如既往照喝不误，永远散发着一身酒气。

　　伴随着冬天里的最初几场冷雨，这座城市突然显得凋敝和肃杀。当你走在街上，再也看不到那些高大的白色房子的屋顶，迎面看到的只是湿漉漉的黑色路面，和那些关门打烊的小店铺、草药店、文具店和报刊亭，还有助产士（二流的）和魏尔伦驾鹤西游的旅馆——就在那旅馆的顶层还有我的一个工作间。

　　走到顶层要经过六段或是八段楼梯，天气又很冷。我知道要生火取暖的话，得买一捆捆树枝，三包金属丝绑着的半枝铅笔长短的松木片——用来从细树枝上引火，外加一捆半干的硬木块，这可得花多少钱啊。于是，我走到大街深处，抬起头看着雨中的屋顶，看看是否有烟囱在冒烟，这烟又是往什么方向吹的。但天空中并没有烟飘出来，我想到了烟囱可能是冷的，也许不通风，又想到房间内可能正烟雾弥漫，燃料白白浪费掉了，钱也随之付诸东流，就又继续在雨中走着。一路经过亨利四世公立中学、古老的圣艾蒂山教堂、大风掠过的先贤祠广场，然后向右拐去躲避风雨，最后，我来到圣米歇尔大街的背风一侧，沿街继续走着，经过克鲁尼和圣日耳曼大街，直至来到圣米歇尔广场上一家我熟悉的不错的咖啡馆。

这是家舒适的咖啡馆，温暖、洁净而且使人感到十分亲切。我把旧雨衣挂在衣架上晾干，把那饱受雨淋的旧毡帽放在长凳上方的架子上，然后叫了一杯牛奶咖啡。服务员端来了咖啡，我从上衣口袋里拿出一本笔记簿和一支铅笔，开始写作。我写的是发生在密歇根北部的故事，因为那天天气很糟，风雨交加，而且很冷，正巧和我故事里的场景十分吻合。从少年、青年一直到长大成人，我早就见识过这种秋末的景致；至于说到要记录下这样的场景，你会觉得一个地方比另一个地方更合适。我想，这就是所谓的自我移植吧。自我移植对其他的生长性动植物固然必不可少，对于人也莫不如此。不过，因为故事里的男孩们在喝酒，我也感到口渴起来，于是，就要了一份圣詹姆斯朗姆酒。这种酒在天冷的时候喝，口感尤其好。我继续奋笔疾书，内心感觉良好，感到这上好的马提尼克朗姆酒温暖着我的整个身心。

一位姑娘走进咖啡馆，独自一人在靠窗的桌边坐下。她十分漂亮，脸色娇嫩，宛若一枚刚刚铸就的钱币，一枚由顺滑的肌肉和因雨水而鲜亮的皮肤铸就的"硬币"。她的头发像乌鸦的翅膀一样黑亮，修剪得丝缕分明，斜斜地掠过她的面颊。

我看着她，她搅乱了我的心神，使我异常激动。我但愿能把她写进这个故事，或者别的什么故事，但她已经选好了位置，她坐在那儿，既能看到大街又能注视入口，我知道她是在等人。于是，我继续写作。

故事的情节在逐渐展开，可我却已经有点赶不上它的节奏了。我又要了一份圣詹姆斯朗姆酒。每当我抬起头来，或用卷笔刀削着铅笔，任凭那木屑旋入酒杯下的浅碟时，我都会注视那姑娘。

我对着自己说，不管你在等谁，不管我将来再也见不到你，我已经看到你了，美人儿，现在你是我的。你是我的，整个巴黎也都是我的，而我则属于这本笔记本和这支铅笔。

接着，我又写了起来。我深深地沉入了这个故事，迷失在其中。现在是我在主导着这个故事，而不是任由它自己展开故事情节。我没有再抬头，全然忘却了时间和地点，也没有再要圣詹姆斯朗姆酒。我不想喝酒的时候，就会讨厌圣詹姆斯朗姆酒。然后，故事写完了。我也累了。我读完最后一段，抬起头来寻找那姑娘，可她已经走了。我想，我希望她是跟一个好男人走的。但我还是感到难过。

我把写好的故事合在笔记簿里，再把笔记簿放在里面的口袋。我叫来服务员，要了一打他们那儿特有的葡萄牙牡蛎和半瓶干白葡萄酒。写完一个故事之

后，我内心总感到空荡荡的，既悲伤又幸福，好像刚和别人亲热过似的。我相信这是一个很不错的故事。尽管等第二天读过一遍之后，我才会知道这个故事有多好。

我吃着牡蛎，它们带有浓浓的海腥气和淡淡的金属味。冰冷的白葡萄酒冲散了金属味，只留下大海的味道和鲜美多汁的牡蛎肉。当我从贝壳中吸取牡蛎那冰冷的汁液，再就着爽口的葡萄酒把它咽下肚时，空落落的感觉消失了。我开始高兴起来，开始做计划了。

既然糟糕的天气已经到来，我们可以离开巴黎一阵子，去一个不下雨却有雪的地方。雪从松枝间飘落下来，覆盖了马路和高高的山坡。在那样一个地势颇高的地方，夜间走回家的时候，我们会听到雪在脚下嘎吱作响。在前锋山下就有一处小屋，那里的膳宿好极了，我们可以一起住在那儿，看我们的书，晚上一起躺在床上，暖暖的，窗户开着，明亮的星星闪烁着。那是我们可以去的地方。乘火车坐三等车厢旅行并不很贵。那里的膳宿费用也不比巴黎贵多少。

我会退掉旅馆里那间我用来写作的房间，这样就只需要付勒穆瓦纳红衣主教路74号的房租了，那是很便宜的。我曾给多伦多方面写过报道，那些支付稿费的支票也到了。我可以在任何地方、任何情况下开出支票，我们有钱来进行这次旅行。

也许离开了巴黎我就能写巴黎，就像在巴黎我能写密歇根一样。我没有意识到写巴黎实际上时机还不成熟，因为我还不够了解这座城市。不过，最终我还是做到了。不管怎么说，如果我太太想去，我们就去。于是，我吃完了牡蛎，喝干了酒，付清了咖啡馆的账，冒着雨——此刻的雨不过是在这儿下，并不足以改变你的生活——沿圣热奈维埃弗山而上，抄近路回到位于山顶的那套公寓房。

"我想这太棒了，塔迪！"我太太说道。她有一张圆润柔和的脸，每当听到合心意的决定，她就像收到了一份大礼，眼睛里和脸上都会放出光芒。"我们什么时候动身？"她问道。

"随时都可以。"

"啊，我想马上就走。你早就知道我的心意了吧？"

"也许，等我们回来天就晴好了。如果天气寒冷还能够放晴，这儿会很不错。"

"我相信会有这样的日子，"她说，"你能想到去旅行不也很好吗？"

---

[1] Braque n. 领导立体派运动的法国画家布拉克 (1882–1963)。

# 第六卷

奇谈杂论
Miscellaneous Arguments

# 论爱
# On Love

【英国】珀西·比西·雪莱

**作者简介**

　　珀西·比西·雪莱(1792-1822)，英国诗人及社会改革家，是英格兰最伟大的浪漫主义诗人之一。他最有名的作品是《西风颂》、《云》以及《致云雀》，它们堪称是抒情诗歌中的极品。《阿多尼斯》被公认为英国文学史上最伟大的挽歌之一。雪莱的诗歌象征意义很强，他选用的意象(大部分取于自然)准确而鲜明。雪莱的散文作品具有唯美、敏感、诙谐、讽刺的特点。《论爱》以诗意的笔触恣情讴歌了唯美的爱，给人以力量和希望，是值得背诵的佳作。

What is Love? Ask him who lives, what is life; ask him who adores, what is God?

I know not the internal constitution of other men, nor even thine, whom I now address. I see that in some external attributes they resemble me, but when, misled by that appearance, I have thought to appeal to something in common, and unburthen my inmost soul to them, I have found my language misunderstood, like one in a distant and savage land. The more opportunities they have afforded me for experience, the wider has appeared the interval between us, and to a greater distance have the points of sympathy been withdrawn. With a spirit ill fitted to sustain such proof, trembling and feeble through its tenderness, I have everywhere sought sympathy, and have found only repulse and disappointment.

Thou demandest what is Love. It is that powerful attraction towards all we conceive, or fear, or hope beyond ourselves, when we find within our own thoughts the chasm of an insufficient void, and seek to awaken in all things that are, a community with what we experience within ourselves. If we reason, we would be understood; if we imagine, we would that the airy children of our brain were born anew within another's; if we feel, we would that another's nerves should vibrate to our own, that the beams of their eyes should kindle at once and mix and melt into our own; that lips of motionless ice should not reply to lips quivering and burning with the heart's best blood. This is Love. This is the bond and the sanction which connects not only man with man, but with every thing which exists. We are born into the world, and there is something within us which, from the instant that we live, more and more thirsts after its likeness. It is probably in correspondence with this law that the infant drains milk from the bosom of its mother; this propensity developes itself with the developement of our nature. We dimly see within our intellectual nature a miniature as it were of our entire self, yet deprived of all that we condemn or despise, the ideal prototype of every thing excellent and lovely that we are capable of conceiving as belonging to the nature of man. Not only the portrait of our external being, but an

217

最散文
Zui Prose

assemblage[1] of the minutest particles of which our nature is composed; a mirror whose surface reflects only the forms of purity and brightness; a soul within our own soul that describes a circle around its proper Paradise, which pain and sorrow and evil dare not overleap. To this we eagerly refer all sensations, thirsting that they should resemble or correspond with it. The discovery of its antitype; the meeting with an understanding capable of clearly estimating our own; an imagination which should enter into and seize upon the subtle and delicate peculiarities which we have delighted to cherish and unfold in secret; with a frame whose nerves, like the chords of two exquisite lyres, strung to the accompaniment of one delightful voice, vibrate with the vibrations of our own; and of a combination of all these in such proportion as the type within demands; this is the invisible and unattainable point to which Love tends; and to attain which, it urges forth the powers of man to arrest the faintest shadow of that, without the possession of which there is no rest nor respite to the heart over which it rules. Hence in solitude, or in that deserted state when we are surrounded by human beings, and yet they sympathize not with us, we love the flowers, the grass, the waters, and the sky. In the motion of the very leaves of spring, in the blue air, there is then found a secret correspondence with our heart. There is eloquence in the tongueless wind, and a melody in the flowing brooks and the rustling of the reeds beside them, which by their inconceivable relation to something within the soul, awaken the spirits to a dance of breathless rapture, and bring tears of mysterious tenderness to the eyes, like the enthusiasm of patriotic success, or the voice of one beloved singing to you alone. Sterne says that if he were in a desert he would love some cypress. So soon as this want or power is dead, man becomes the living sepulchre of himself, and what yet survives is the mere husk of what once he was.

什么是爱？要回答这个问题，让我们先问那些活着的人，什么是生活？问那些虔诚的教徒，什么是上帝？

我不知其他人的内心结构，也不知你们——我正与之讲话的你们的内心；我看到在有些外在属性上，别人同我相像；惑于这种形似，当我诉诸某些应当共通的情感并向他们吐露灵魂深处的心声时，我发现我的话语遭到了误解，仿佛它是一个遥远而野蛮的国度的语言。人们给我体验的机会越多，我们之间的距离越远，理解与同情也就愈离我而去。带着无法承受这种现实的情绪，在温柔的颤栗和虚弱中，我在海角天涯寻觅知音，而得到的却只是憎恨与失望。

你垂询什么是爱吗？当我们在自身思想的幽谷中发现一片虚空，从而在天地万物中呼唤，寻求与身内之物的通感对应之时，受到我们所感、所惧、所奢望的事物的那种情不自禁的、强有力的吸引，就是爱。倘使我们推理，我们总希望能够被人理解；倘若我们遐想，我们总希望自己头脑中逍遥自在的孩童会在别人的头脑里获得新生；倘若我们感受，那么，我们祈求他人的神经能和我们的一起共振，他人的目光和我们的交融，他人的眼睛和我们的一样炯炯有神；我们祈愿默然麻木的冰唇不要对另一颗心的火热、颤抖的唇讯诮嘲讽。这就是爱，这就是那不仅连接了人与人而且联结了人与万物的神圣的契约和债券。我们降临世间，我们的内心深处存在着某种东西，自我们存在那一刻起，就渴求着与它相似的东西。也许这与婴儿吮吸母亲乳房的奶汁这一规律相一致。这种与生俱来的倾向随着天性的发展而发展。在思维能力的本性中，我们影影绰绰地看到的仿佛是完整自我的一个缩影，它丧失了我们所蔑视、嫌厌的成分，而成为尽善尽美的人性的理想典范。它不仅是一幅外在肖像，更是构成我们天性的最精细微小的粒子组合。它是一面只映射出纯洁和明亮的形态的镜子；它是在其灵魂固有的乐园外勾画出一个为痛苦、悲哀和邪恶所无法逾越的圆圈的灵魂。这一灵魂同渴求与之相像或对应的知觉相关联。当我们在大千世界中寻觅到了灵魂的对应物，在天地万物中发现了可以无误地评估我们自身的知音（它能准确地、敏感地捕捉我们所珍惜，并怀着喜悦悄悄展露的一切），那么，我们与对应物就好比两架精美的竖琴上的琴弦，在一个快乐的声音的伴奏下发出音响，这音响与我们自身神经组织的震颤相共振。这——就是爱所要达到的无形的、不可企及的目标。正是它，驱使人的力量捕捉

其淡淡的影子;没有它,为爱所驾驭的心灵就永远不会安宁,永远不会歇息。因此,在孤独中,或处在一群毫不理解我们的人群中(这时,我们仿佛遭到遗弃),我们会热爱花朵、小草、河流以及天空。就在蓝天下,在春天的树叶的颤动中,我们找到了秘密的心灵的回应:无语的风中有一种雄辩;流淌的溪水和河边瑟瑟的苇叶声中,有一首歌谣。它们与我们灵魂之间神秘的感应,唤醒了我们心中的精灵去跳一场酣畅淋漓的狂喜之舞,并使神秘的、温柔的泪盈满我们的眼睛,如爱国志士胜利的热情,又如心爱的人为你独自歌唱之音。因此,斯泰恩说,假如他身在沙漠,他会爱上柏树枝的。爱的需求或力量一旦死去,人就成为一个活着的墓穴,苟延残喘的只是一副躯壳。

[1] assemblage  n. 集会, 集合, 装配

# 论羞涩
# On Being Shy

【英国】杰罗姆·K·杰罗姆

**作者简介**

　　杰罗姆·K·杰罗姆(1859-1927),为英国现代最杰出的幽默小说家、散文家和剧作家。其作品以幽默睿智见长,饱含对人生的感悟,后期作品较为严肃深沉。幽默杰作《三人同舟》和《懒人懒思录》至今仍是英语世界广受欢迎的名作,也奠定了作者在世界文坛的独特地位。其视作小技的散文随笔百年来却从未停止印行。《论羞涩》足以见证其小技之大成。此文幽默、睿智,写作手法不拘一格,遣词造句信手拈来,不避俚俗。如果以中国现代作家比之,杰罗姆可说是兼有林语堂、梁实秋的闲适与鲁迅的幽默和讽刺。

All great literary men are shy. I am myself, though I am told it is hardly noticeable.

I am glad it is not. It used to be extremely prominent at one time, and was the cause of much misery to myself and discomfort to every one about me—my lady friends especially complained most bitterly about it.

A shy man's lot is not a happy one. The men dislike him, the women despise him, and he dislikes and despises himself. Use brings him no relief, and there is no cure for him except time; though I once came across a delicious recipe for overcoming the misfortune. It appeared among the "answers to correspondents" in a small weekly journal and ran as follows—I have never forgotten it: "Adopt an easy and pleasing manner, especially toward ladies."

Poor wretch! I can imagine the grin with which he must have read that advice. "Adopt an easy and pleasing manner, especially toward ladies," forsooth! Don't you adopt anything of the kind, my dear young shy friend. Your attempt to put on any other disposition than your own will infallibly result in your becoming ridiculously gushing and offensively familiar. Be your own natural self, and then you will only be thought to be surly and stupid.

The shy man does have some slight revenge upon society for the torture it inflicts upon him. He is able, to a certain extent, to communicate his misery. He frightens other people as much as they frighten him. He acts like a damper upon the whole room, and the most jovial spirits become in his presence depressed and nervous.

This is a good deal brought about by misunderstanding. Many people mistake the shy man's timidity for overbearing arrogance and are awed and insulted by it. His awkwardness is resented as insolent carelessness, and when, terror-stricken at the first word addressed to him, the blood rushes to his head and the power of speech completely fails him, he is regarded as an awful example of the evil effects of giving way to passion.

But, indeed, to be misunderstood is the shy man's fate on every occasion; and whatever impression he endeavors to create, he is sure to convey its opposite. When he makes a joke, it is looked upon as a pretended relation of fact and his want of veracity much condemned. His sarcasm is accepted as his literal opinion and gains for him the reputation of being an ass, while if, on the other hand, wishing to ingratiate himself, he ventures upon a little bit of flattery, it is taken for satire and he is hated ever afterward.

These and the rest of a shy man's troubles are always very amusing to other people, and have afforded material for comic writing from time immemorial. But if we look a little deeper we shall find there is a pathetic, one might almost say a tragic, side to the picture. A shy man means a lonely man—a man cut off from all companionship, all sociability. He moves about the world, but does not mix with it. Between him and his fellow-men there runs ever an impassable barrier—a strong, invisible wall that, trying in vain to scale, he but bruises himself against. He sees the pleasant faces and hears the pleasant voices on the other side, but he cannot stretch his hand across to grasp another hand. He stands watching the merry groups, and he longs to speak and to claim kindred with them. But they pass him by, chatting gayly to one another, and he cannot stay them. He tries to reach them, but his prison walls move with him and hem him in on every side. In the busy street, in the crowded room, in the grind of work, in the whirl of pleasure, amid the many or amid the few—wherever men congregate together, wherever the music of human speech is heard and human thought is flashed from human eyes, there, shunned and solitary, the shy man, like a leper, stands apart. His soul is full of love and longing, but the world knows it not. The iron mask of shyness is riveted before his face, and the man beneath is never seen. Genial words and hearty greetings are ever rising to his lips, but they die away in unheard whispers behind the steel clamps. His heart aches for the weary brother, but his sympathy is dumb. Contempt and indignation against wrong choke up his throat, and finding no safety-valve whence in passionate utterance they may burst forth, they only turn in again and harm him. All the hate and scorn and love of a deep nature such as the shy man is ever cursed by fester and corrupt within, instead of spending themselves

abroad, and sour him into a misanthrope and cynic.

Yes, shy men, like ugly women, have a bad time of it in this world, to go through which with any comfort needs the hide of a rhinoceros. Thick skin is, indeed, our moral clothes, and without it we are not fit to be seen about in civilized society. A poor gasping, blushing creature, with trembling knees and twitching hands, is a painful sight to every one, and if it cannot cure itself, the sooner it goes and hangs itself the better.

The disease can be cured. For the comfort of the shy, I can assure them of that from personal experience. I do not like speaking about myself, as may have been noticed, but in the cause of humanity I on this occasion will do so, and will confess that at one time I was, as the young man in the Bab Ballad says, "the shyest of the shy," and "whenever I was introduced to any pretty maid, my knees they knocked together just as if I was afraid." Now, I would—nay, have—on this very day before yesterday I did the deed alone and entirely by myself (as the school-boy said in translating the "Bellum Gallicum") did I beard a railway refreshment-room young lady in her own lair. I rebuked her in terms of mingled bitterness and sorrow for her callousness and want of condescension. I insisted, courteously but firmly, on being accorded that deference and attention that was the right of the traveling Briton, and at the end I looked her full in the face. Need I say more? True, immediately after doing so I left the room with what may possibly have appeared to be precipitation and without waiting for any refreshment. But that was because I had changed my mind, not because I was frightened, you understand.

One consolation that shy folk can take unto themselves is that shyness is certainly no sign of stupidity. It is easy enough for bull-headed clowns to sneer at nerves, but the highest natures are not necessarily those containing the greatest amount of moral brass. The horse is not an inferior animal to the cock-sparrow, nor the deer of the forest to the pig. Shyness simply means extreme sensibility, and has nothing whatever to do with self-consciousness or with conceit, though its relationship to both is continually insisted upon by the poll-parrot school of philosophy.

Conceit, indeed, is the quickest cure for it. When it once begins to dawn upon you that you are a good deal cleverer than any one else in this world, bashfulness becomes shocked and leaves you. When you can look round a roomful of people and think that each one is a mere child in intellect compared with yourself you feel no more shy of them than you would of a select company of magpies or orang-outangs.

Conceit is the finest armor that a man can wear. Upon its smooth, impenetrable surface the puny dagger-thrusts of spite and envy glance harmlessly aside. Without that breast-plate the sword of talent cannot force its way through the battle of life, for blows have to be borne as well as dealt. I do not, of course, speak of the conceit that displays itself in an elevated nose and a falsetto voice. That is not real conceit—that is only playing at being conceited; like children play at being kings and queens and go strutting about with feathers and long trains. Genuine conceit does not make a man objectionable. On the contrary, it tends to make him genial, kind-hearted, and simple. He has no need of affectation—he is far too well satisfied with his own character; and his pride is too deep-seated to appear at all on the outside. Careless alike of praise or blame, he can afford to be truthful. Too far, in fancy, above the rest of mankind to trouble about their petty distinctions, he is equally at home with duke or costermonger. And valuing no one's standard but his own, he is never tempted to practice that miserable pretense that less self-reliant people offer up as an hourly sacrifice to the god of their neighbor's opinion.

The shy man, on the other hand, is humble—modest of his own judgment and over-anxious concerning that of others. But this in the case of a young man is surely right enough. His character is unformed. It is slowly evolving itself out of a chaos of doubt and disbelief. Before the growing insight and experience the diffidence recedes. A man rarely carries his shyness past the hobbledehoy period. Even if his own inward strength does not throw it off, the rubbings of the world generally smooth it down. You scarcely ever meet a really shy man—except in novels or on the stage, where, by the bye, he is much admired, especially by the women.

There, in that supernatural land, he appears as a fair-haired and saintlike young man—fair hair and goodness always go together on the stage. No respectable audience would believe in one without the other. I knew an actor who mislaid his wig once and had to rush on to play the hero in his own hair, which was jet-black, and the gallery howled at all his noble sentiments under the impression that he was the villain. He—the shy young man—loves the heroine, oh so devotedly (but only in asides, for he dare not tell her of it), and he is so noble and unselfish, and speaks in such a low voice, and is so good to his mother; and the bad people in the play, they laugh at him and jeer at him, but he takes it all so gently, and in the end it transpires that he is such a clever man, though nobody knew it, and then the heroine tells him she loves him, and he is so surprised, and oh, so happy! and everybody loves him and asks him to forgive them, which he does in a few well-chosen and sarcastic words, and blesses them; and he seems to have generally such a good time of it that all the young fellows who are not shy long to be shy. But the really shy man knows better. He knows that it is not quite so pleasant in reality. He is not quite so interesting there as in the fiction. He is a little more clumsy and stupid and a little less devoted and gentle, and his hair is much darker, which, taken altogether, considerably alters the aspect of the case.

The point where he does resemble his ideal is in his faithfulness. I am fully prepared to allow the shy young man that virtue: he is constant in his love. But the reason is not far to seek. The fact is it exhausts all his stock of courage to look one woman in the face, and it would be simply impossible for him to go through the ordeal with a second. He stands in far too much dread of the whole female sex to want to go gadding about with many of them. One is quite enough for him.

Now, it is different with the young man who is not shy. He has temptations which his bashful brother never encounters. He looks around and everywhere sees roguish eyes and laughing lips. What more natural than that amid so many roguish eyes and laughing lips he should become confused and, forgetting for the moment which particular pair of roguish eyes and laughing lips it is that he belongs to, go off making love to the wrong set. The shy man, who never looks at anything but his own boots, sees not and is not tempted. Happy shy man!

Not but what the shy man himself would much rather not be happy in that way. He longs to "go it" with the others, and curses himself every day for not being able to. He will now and again, screwing up his courage by a tremendous effort, plunge into roguishness. But it is always a terrible fiasco, and after one or two feeble flounders he crawls out again, limp and pitiable.

I say "pitiable," though I am afraid he never is pitied. There are certain misfortunes which, while inflicting a vast amount of suffering upon their victims, gain for them no sympathy. Losing an umbrella, falling in love, toothache, black eyes, and having your hat sat upon may be mentioned as a few examples, but the chief of them all is shyness. The shy man is regarded as an animate joke. His tortures are the sport of the drawing-room arena and are pointed out and discussed with much gusto.

"Look," cry his tittering audience to each other. "he's blushing!"

"Just watch his legs," says one.

"Do you notice how he is sitting?" adds another: "right on the edge of the chair."

"Seems to have plenty of color," sneers a military-looking gentleman.

"Pity he's got so many hands," murmurs an elderly lady, with her own calmly folded on her lap. "They quite confuse him."

"A yard or two off his feet wouldn't be a disadvantage," chimes in the comic man, "especially as he seems so anxious to hide them."

And then another suggests that with such a voice he ought to have been a sea-captain. Some draw attention to the desperate way in which he is grasping his hat. Some comment upon his limited powers of conversation. Others remark upon the troublesome nature of his cough. And so on, until

227

最 散
Zui 文
Prose

his peculiarities and the company are both thoroughly exhausted.

His friends and relations make matters still more unpleasant for the poor boy (friends and relations are privileged to be more disagreeable than other people). Not content with making fun of him among themselves, they insist on his seeing the joke. They mimic and caricature him for his own edification. One, pretending to imitate him, goes outside and comes in again in a ludicrously nervous manner, explaining to him afterward that that is the way he—meaning the shy fellow—walks into a room; or, turning to him with "This is the way you shake hands," proceeds to go through a comic pantomime with the rest of the room, taking hold of every one's hand as if it were a hot plate and flabbily dropping it again. And then they ask him why he blushes, and why he stammers, and why he always speaks in an almost inaudible tone, as if they thought he did it on purpose. Then one of them, sticking out his chest and strutting about the room like a pouter-pigeon, suggests quite seriously that that is the style he should adopt. The old man slaps him on the back and says: "Be bold, my boy. Don't be afraid of any one." The mother says, "Never do anything that you need be ashamed of, Algernon, and then you never need be ashamed of anything you do," and, beaming mildly at him, seems surprised at the clearness of her own logic. The boys tell him that he's "worse than a girl," and the girls repudiate the implied slur upon their sex by indignantly exclaiming that they are sure no girl would be half as bad.

They are quite right; no girl would be. There is no such thing as a shy woman, or, at all events, I have never come across one, and until I do I shall not believe in them. I know that the generally accepted belief is quite the reverse. All women are supposed to be like timid, startled fawns, blushing and casting down their gentle eyes when looked at and running away when spoken to; while we man are supposed to be a bold and rollicky lot, and the poor dear little women admire us for it, but are terribly afraid of us. It is a pretty theory, but, like most generally accepted theories, mere nonsense. The girl of twelve is self-contained and as cool as the proverbial cucumber, while her brother of twenty stammers and stutters by her side. A woman will enter a concert-room late, interrupt the performance, and disturb the whole audience without moving a hair, while her husband follows her, a crushed heap of apologizing misery.

The superior nerve of women in all matters connected with love, from the casting of the first sheep's-eye down to the end of the honeymoon, is too well acknowledged to need comment. Nor is the example a fair one to cite in the present instance, the positions not being equally balanced. Love is woman's business, and in "business" we all lay aside our natural weaknesses—the shyest man I ever knew was a photographic tout[1].

所有伟大的文学家都害羞。就拿我来说,我就是这样,不过有人曾说过,我的羞涩几乎是看不出来的。

对这样的说法我感到很高兴。要知道有一阵子它曾经表现得十分明显,以至于成为我诸多痛苦的根源之一,并且,也给我周围的人——尤其是女性朋友,带来不便。对此她们颇有抱怨。

一个羞涩的男人,其命运通常不容乐观。男人讨厌他,女人瞧不起他,而他对自己,则是即讨厌又瞧不起。作为一个有用之人并不能使他解脱,除了时间之外,再也没有其他好的方法了。虽然说是这样说,我倒是有一个克服这种毛病的妙方。它是在一本小周刊的"来信问答"栏中刊登的,是这样写的(我一直都没有忘记):"举止要从容优雅,尤其是对女士,这种态度能够讨人喜欢。"

可怜的人!我能想像得出,他读到这句时脸上的苦笑。"举止要从容优雅,这种态度能够讨人喜欢,尤其是对待女士。"这真是太对了!我亲爱的、年轻羞涩的朋友,你难道不正是这样做的吗?你装作热情大方,刻意掩饰自己的羞怯,结果却因为过分的亲热和滔滔不绝而显得荒唐可笑,令人觉得讨厌。但是,如果你率性自然,腼腆害羞,又会被认为粗鲁无礼和傻里傻气。

爱羞涩的人,对于社会加给自己的折磨,也的确还以轻微的报复。从某种角度来说,他的痛苦可以传染。他害怕别人,但别人因为他所受的惊吓并不比他少。只要他出场,他能使一屋子人都兴趣索然,就连现场最活泼热情的家伙也会立马变得神态沮丧,表情尴尬。

造成这种麻烦多半是误解。许多人把羞涩者的胆怯误以为是盛气凌人的傲慢自大,因而觉得畏惧,并觉得受到了侮辱。他的笨拙行为也被看做是一种傲慢无礼,从而招致人的怨恨。只要一听到别人开口对他说话,他就感到莫名的恐惧,血一下子冲上头顶,头脑一片空白。他本人,就会被看做是喜欢大动肝火的模板。

坦白地说,害羞的人在任何场合都遭人误解,这的确是他们的宿命。无论他怎样努力想给别人留下什么印象,其结果往往是与他料想的相反。他要是开个玩笑,就会被认为是对事实的虚编乱造,并因为缺乏真诚而受到责难。他的讽刺挖苦,却被视作他真实的观点,于是,他理所当然地为自己赢得了大傻瓜的美誉。另一方面,他有时想抱着讨好别人的愿望,便试着向人恭维了几句,却不幸被人家认为那是冷嘲热讽,从此让人家恨一辈子。

上面所说的这些,在局外人看来,爱害羞的人连同其他的烦恼,都被看作是十分好玩的,自古以来这些成为写作滑稽喜剧的首选素材。但是,假使我们的眼光稍稍往深里看一些,就会发现这幕喜剧有它不幸的、甚至可以说是悲惨的一面。一个爱害羞的人意味着他终将是一个孤独者———一个被友谊拒之门外、断绝了所有社会交往的人。他在世界上独来独往,却不能融入其中。在他与他的同胞之间,有堵坚固而无形的墙,永远横亘着,这是一道无法逾越的屏障。他试图攀越它,但无疑是徒劳的,最后只会摔得鼻青脸肿。他看得见墙另一边那愉快的笑容,听得见那欢乐的歌声,却无法伸出自己的手,去握住墙那边的手。他站在那里,注视着那一群群快乐的人,很想和他们说说话,想告诉他们,自己是他们的朋友。然而,人们互相闲聊着愉快地从他身边飘然而过,他无法让他们停下来。他想追上他们,但他却迈不开他的脚,那监狱一样的高墙从四面八方包围着他。在喧嚣的大街上,在拥挤的房间里,在艰辛的劳作中,在欢乐的漩涡里,不管是人多还是人少,无论哪里都有人聚集在一起,无论哪里都能听到人们的欢声笑语,思想的光芒在人们的眼中闪烁着。而这边,爱害羞的人总是孤独地徘徊着,形影相吊,像个被人避之不及的麻风病人。他们内心中充满了爱与渴望,而世人却不知晓。他的脸上罩着羞怯的铁面具,人们从来不知道面罩下的真实面目是什么样子。亲切的话语和由衷的祝福,不时涌到嘴边,却化为喃喃低语,没有人听见在那钢铁夹板后面的话,它就那样消失了。他渴望靠近那些疲惫的兄弟,但他的同情却哑口无言。

对坏事要表示轻蔑或者愤慨，他义愤填膺的语言却找不到可以喷发而出的闸门，最后只能烂在心里，伤害自己。所有源自于一种深邃秉性的仇恨、轻蔑以及爱恋，在这些被人诅咒的爱害羞的人的心中，都在溃烂腐败，却怎么也不能发泄出来，他满心酸楚，成为一个遁世和愤世的人。

是的，容易害羞的人就像容貌丑陋的女人，在这个世界上，日子颇不好过。用犀牛皮那么厚的面具来伪装才能活得稍稍轻松舒适一点。的确，厚皮是我们的精神外套，没有它，我们就不能在文明社会里立足。一个气喘吁吁、面红耳赤的可怜虫，两腿战战兢兢，双手哆哆嗦嗦，谁看了都不舒服，要是自己不能治愈，那还不如找根绳子赶紧上吊好了。

对于羞怯的缓解，我可以用亲身经历向你们保证，这种病是能治好的。完全可以。我并不喜欢谈论自己，这个读者可能已经注意到了，但出于人道主义方面的原因，我还是愿意借此机会交代一下。我得老实承认，我自己曾经是，就像《巴伯谣》里所提到的那个年轻人一样，是"爱害羞的人中的那个最害羞的人"，而且，"把我介绍给某位漂亮姑娘，无论在什么时候。我的两只膝盖就会打颤，像是害怕得发抖"。好了，废话少说，我会做——不，我曾经——在前天已经做了这么一件事。当时，我独自一人（就像翻译《高卢战记》的小学生所说的），使一个在火车点心车厢的小姐陷入一种尴尬的境地。我用酸楚和哀痛相互掺杂着的话，指责她的冷漠和傲慢。我礼貌但坚决地向她指出：英国人在旅行中同样有权利得到尊重和关心。到了最后，我把目光完全落在她的脸上。还要我继续说下去吗？真的，这么做了以后，我马上离开了那里，几乎是慌不择路，一副急急忙忙的样子，顾不上吃点儿东西。你知道，这并不是因为我害怕了，而是因为我改变了主意。

害羞的家伙给他们自己的一个安慰是：羞怯并不一定是愚蠢的代名词。虽说冥顽不灵的小丑的冷嘲热讽，总是那么游刃有余，但最高贵的本性亦并不必然都是那些厚脸皮的人。把马和自比公鸡的麻雀相比，它不算是更低一等的动物，森林里的鹿与猪相比也是同样的道理。羞怯只不过表示极度敏感而已，和忸怩作态没有什么联系，羞怯更不能与狂妄自大相提并论，虽说鹦鹉派哲学总是强调羞怯与这两方面有密切的关系。

毫无疑问，治疗羞涩的最好的药方就是自负。当自负在你身上稍微那么一露头，你就会觉得自己比世界上的任何人都要聪明很多，难为情也就悄然离你而去。当你环视一屋子的人，你认为他们的智力与你相比最多只能算是小孩，你鹤立鸡群，自然不会比他们更感到羞怯。

　　自负是一个人所能穿戴的最精良的盔甲。恶意与嫉妒之剑的轻刺也难以穿透它的光滑表面，只会闪落一旁，你却毫发无伤。只有天才的利剑，而没有自负的护胸铠甲，在生活的战斗中就无法杀开一条路来，因为你在主动进攻时还要防止被动挨打。当然，那些趾高气扬和装腔作势，并不在我所说的自负的行列，那些并不是真正的自负，而只是自负的表演而已。就像孩子们玩扮演国王和王后的游戏，插上凌乱的翎毛，拖着长袍，趾高气扬地走着。真正的自负不会使人觉得讨厌，恰恰相反，它常常使人变得亲切、善良、坦诚。他对自己的性格深感满意，没有必要装模作样，他的骄傲深植于内心，从外表是一点也看不出来的。无论是赞美还是责难，他都淡然处之。他的诚实足够让他受到信任。他内心的幻想比起其它的人不知要高出多少倍，因此对他人的细微差别他总是不屑分辨。公爵或小贩，在他看来没有什么不同。对一个人和一件事的评价，都是依照自己内心的想法；为了让街坊邻居作出好评而做一些虚伪的事情，在他这里是绝不会发生的。

　　另一方面，爱害羞的人又很谦虚——他的谦卑一方面是由自己的判断得来的，另一方面源自于他对别人的看法过于在乎。不过，这对于一个年轻人来说，这样是完全正确的。他的性格还没有完全定型，而是正从多疑而缺乏信任的混沌中慢慢形成，随着观察力和阅历的增长，他们的胆怯会一点点地减少。很少人在青年以后还会爱害羞，即使他自己的内在力量不能完全摆脱它，但社会的磨砺，通常会使它慢慢失去棱角。除了在小说里，或是舞台上，你几乎很难遇到一个真正羞涩的男人——顺便插一句，在那种地方，他们倒是备受推崇，尤其是受女人的爱慕。

　　在那片神奇的场所，他的形象常以圣洁的金发圣人的形象出现——在那里，金发总是隐匿着善良。如果二者中只出现单独的一个，任何有常识的观众恐怕都不肯相信了。我知道一位演员，偶尔有一次，因为他忘记把假发放到了什么地方，而不得不顶着自己的黑头发匆忙上台饰演主角。结果，观众席上对于他的每一次饱含情感的表演，都报以一片嘘声，因为他的这个样子在观众眼里根本就是一个反面角色。他——羞涩的年轻人——爱着女主人公，爱得那样深（只通过旁边表达，因为他不敢当面告诉她）。他那么高尚，那么无私，说话的声音低沉而有磁性，对母亲那么恭顺，戏里的坏人嘲笑他、捉弄他，他却平静地承受一切。最后的结局表明，他是个极聪明的人，虽然没有人理解这一点。然后，女主人公告诉他，她也爱他。他那么惊讶，而且，噢，那么幸福！每个人都爱他，请求他的原谅，他则以几句恰到好处而略带挖苦的话，接受了他们的道歉，并祝福他们。好像他一直都是这样的快乐幸福,弄得那些以前并不羞涩的年轻人全都希望自己变得羞涩起来。可真正羞涩的男人对此却并不这样想,他知道现实并不如此让人愉快。他的生活就远不如虚构里的主人公的生活那么有趣,与戏剧中的主人公比较起来,他的手笨脚也笨,脑子也不如人家灵活。爱情的真挚和宽容的心胸似乎稍逊一筹,并且,他的头发也未免太黑了点。所有这些加到一起,其结果就使生活与戏剧不大一样了。

在现实中和他的偶像相一致的,是他的忠诚。爱害羞的青年对爱情的专一这一美德,我要加以赞美和肯定,那就是他。当然,要找到其原因并不困难。事实情况是,他和一个女人四目相对时,就已经耗尽了全部的勇气储备。简直没有可能再让他去经受第二个女人的残酷考验。他对于整个女性有着深深的恐惧感。根本不敢与更多女人作周旋。一个对他来说已经够他受的了。

可对于那些脸皮较厚的年轻人则完全不是这样的。他所受到的诱惑,实在是他羞羞答答的兄弟压根就没遇见过的。他环顾四周,到处都是挑逗的眼睛和微笑的嘴唇。置身于这么多挑逗的眼睛和微笑的嘴唇之中,他自己搞不清究竟自己属于哪一双挑逗的眼睛,哪两片微笑的嘴唇,因而向错误的女孩求爱,这是再自然不过的事。而爱害羞的人,除了自己的鞋子,是从来都不看任何其他的东西,真可谓是眼不见心不烦。由此可见真正有福的是爱害羞的人!

不过,爱害羞的人自己倒宁可不要这样的福气,他更希望能和别人一样"刺激刺激",每天因为自己不谙此道而臭骂自己。有时候用尽全力地鼓足勇气,想要投身潇洒哥们儿的队伍当中去,但结果总是不理想。一两次无力挣扎之后,他有气无力而又可怜地再次爬上来。

我虽然说"可怜",但恐怕从没有人可怜他。一些不幸给受害者带来巨大的痛苦,却并没有得到他们应该得到的同情。弄丢雨伞、坠入情网、牙疼、鼻青脸肿、别人坐在了自己的帽子上。这里所提到的可能是极少数的几个例子,不过,羞怯的人还应在这里受冲击。爱害羞的人被当作可以随时消遣的笑料。他的痛苦就像是客厅竞技场上的娱乐活动,观看的人兴致盎然,对他指指点点,谈笑风生。

"瞧啊,"他们窃笑着对彼此说,"他脸红啦!"

"快瞧他的两条腿。"一个家伙说。

"您看到他是怎么坐的吗?"另一个补充道,"坐到了椅子边沿上啦。"

"看上去还挺爱脸红嘛。"一位军人模样的先生讥讽道。

"他不知道该把手放在什么地方,真可怜,"一位老太太低声道,她自己的手

安静地交叉在腿上，"他的手把自己给弄糊涂了！"

"截下一两码他的腿不会有什么损害吧，"喜欢乱起哄的家伙插嘴道，"你看他似乎正急着想把它们藏起来。"

接着，对于他那样的嗓音有人建议他应该去当船长；他抓起帽子时有人注意到他那股发狠的劲儿；还有人对他的不善言辞大加议论；还有一些人则对他不停地咳嗽感到十分厌烦。诸如此类，不用枚举，直到他的这些毛病都被——数落为止。而那群家伙这时也都筋疲力尽了。

在亲戚朋友那儿，这个可怜的孩子情况更让人不满（和其他人比起来，亲戚朋友对他更有讨厌的权利）。他们不满足于在他背后一起取笑他，而且还非得让他亲自明白自己的可笑之处不可。他们故意模仿、丑化他，以为这样是为了教诲、开导他。其中有一位假扮成他，先走到外面，接着再用滑稽而紧张的方式走进来，然后向他解释说：他（那个脑腴的家伙）就是这么走进房间的。再不然就转身对他说："你和人家握手时是这样的。"然后和屋里的其他人——握手，他们一起演出这场滑稽哑剧，他们握着每一个人的手就像是握着一个滚烫的盘子，摸一摸再无力地放下。接下来，他们追问他为什么要脸红，为什么要结结巴巴，为什么他讲起话的声音总是那样的小，几乎让人听不见，他们似乎觉得他是故意这么做的。再后来，他们其中一位挺起胸脯，像只大肚鸽子那样在屋子里大摇大摆地走起来，然后很认真地对他说：他应该这样走路。老头在他背上拍了一下说："大胆些，孩子，谁也别怕。"母亲对他说："阿尔杰农，千万别做任何会让你丢脸的事，这样你就永远不必为你做过的任何事而羞愧。"她对着他和蔼地微笑，似乎惊讶于自己如此清晰的逻辑。男孩们说他"还不如一个女孩子"；而姑娘们则愤怒地给予还击——因为这样的话有对自己性别的暗示性诋毁。她们有把握的反驳，肯定没有哪个姑娘有他这样的一半糟。

她们没有错，确实没有哪个女孩会这样。依据我所知道的，世界上从来就没有"羞涩女人"这一说。当然，或许有，可我不知道，但无论如何我是从未碰见过，我是不肯相信这个世界有她们的存在，除非你带过来一个让我看看。我知道，普遍被接受的东西恰好是相反的。所有女人都被认为应该是胆小羞怯，像惊慌失措的小鹿。被人家看的时候，她们应当低下头，脸色绯红地垂下她们温柔的双眼。人家和她们说话时，她们应当一溜烟地跑开。而男人则被认为应该是大胆的、爱嬉笑打闹的一类。可怜又可爱的小女人为此崇拜我们，但对我们又怕得要命。此种理论固然很能让人接受，但正如大多数被普遍接受的理论一样，这只不过是信口开河、胡说八道罢了。一个十二岁女孩很早就学会了自作主张,镇定自若,而她二十岁的哥哥却唯唯诺诺地站在她身旁。在音乐会上如果一个女人迟到了,即使她打断演出、搅扰全体观众而丝毫不会脸红心跳;而她的丈夫,则弯腰弓背、缩头缩脑,跟在她身后,诚惶诚恐地连声道歉。

从第一次抛媚眼到蜜月结束,女人们在一切与爱情有关的事情上,全都艺高胆大,这是世人皆知的事情,没有必要在这儿啰嗦了。前面所举实例当然会有不公平的地方,因为男女没有得到一视同仁的对待。爱情是女人的事业,我们在对待事业时,要把自己的天生弱点理所当然放置在一旁——我所认识的最害羞的男人的事业就是给照相馆招揽顾客。

最 散文
Zui Prose

[1] tout  n. 兜售者,侦察者

# 饱学者无知论
# On the Ignorance of the Learned

【英国】威廉·赫兹列特

**作者简介**

  威廉·赫兹列特(1778–1830)是浪漫主义时期英国大散文家,与兰姆齐名。他主张民主共和,同情法国革命。其文体气势磅礴,感情洋溢。他重感性和想象,张扬个性,反对权威和陈规陋习。是19世纪浪漫主义运动中的一位重要代表。散文,是赫兹列特一生主要的文学成就。他没有写过小说、剧本或诗歌。他的散文主要分为评论和随笔两大类。在他的随笔写作中,以《燕谈录》、《直言集》影响最大。《饱学者无知论》以飞扬的言辞和狂飙突进的气势讽刺了徒有虚名、不顾实际的迂腐书虫。

"For the more languages a man can speak,

His talent has but sprung the greater leak;

And, of the industry he has spent upon't,

Must full as much some other way discount.

The Hebrew, Chaldee, and the Syriac

Do, like their letters, set men's reason back,

And turn their wits that strive to understand it

(Like those that write the characters) left-handed.

Yet he that is but able to express

No sense at all in several languages,

Will pass for learneder than he that's known

To speak the strongest reason in his own."

Butler ( Samuel)

237

最 散文
Zui Prose

The description of persons who have the fewest ideas of all others are mere authors and readers. It is better to be able neither to read nor write than to be able to do nothing else. A lounger who is ordinarily seen with a book in his hand is (we may be almost sure) equally without the power or inclination to attend either to what passes around him or in his own mind. Such a one may be said to carry his understanding about with him in his pocket, or to leave it at home on his library shelves. He is afraid of venturing on any train of reasoning, or of striking out any observation that is not mechanically suggested to him by passing his eyes over certain legible characters; shrinks from the fatigue of thought, which, for want of practice, becomes insupportable to him; and sits down contented with an endless, wearisome succession of words and half-formed images, which fill the void of the mind, and continually efface one another. Learning is, in too many cases, but a foil to common sense; a substitute for true knowledge. Books are less often made use of as "spectacles" to look at nature with, than as blinds to keep out its strong light and shifting scenery from weak eyes and indolent dispositions. The book-worm wraps himself up in his web of verbal

generalities, and sees only the glimmering shadows of things reflected from the minds of others Nature puts him out. The impressions of real objects, stripped of the disguises of words and voluminous roundabout descriptions, are blows that stagger him; their variety distracts, their rapidity exhausts him; and he turns from the bustle, the noise, and glare, and whirling motion of the world about him (which he has not an eye to follow in his fantastic changes, nor an understanding to reduce to fixed principles), to the quite monotony of the dead languages, and the less startling and more intelligible combinations of the letters of the alphabet. It is well, it is perfectly well. "Leave me to my repose", is the motto of the sleeping and dead. You might as well ask the paralytic to leap from his chair and throw away his crutch, or, without a miracle, to "take up his bed and walk", as expect the learned reader to throw down his book and think for himself. He clings to it for his intellectual support; and his dread of being left to himself is like the horror of a vacuum. He can only breathe a learned atmosphere, as other men breath common air. He is a borrower of sense. He has no ideas of his own, and must live on those of other people. The habit of supplying our ideas from foreign sources "enfeebles all internal strength of thought" as a course of dram drinking destroys the tone of the stomach. The faculties of the mind, when not exerted, or when cramped by custom and authority, become listless, torpid, and unfit for the purposes of thought or action. Can we wonder at the languor and lassitude which is thus produced by a life of learned sloth and ignorance; by poring over lines and syllables that excite little more idea or interest than if they were the characters of an unknown tongue, till the eye closes on vacancy, and the book drops from the feeble hand! I would rather be a wood-cutter, or the meanest hind, that all day "sweats in the eye of Phoebus, and at night sleeps in Elysium", than wear out my life so, 'twixt dreaming and awake. The learned author differs from the learned student in this, that the one transcribes what the other reads. The learned are mere literary drudges. If you set them upon original compositions their heads turn, they don't know where they are. The indefatigable readers of books are like the everlasting copiers of pictures, who, when they attempt to do anything of their own, find they want an eye quick enough, and hand steady enough, and colours bright enough, to trace the living forms of nature.

Anyone who has passed through the regular gradations of a classical education, and is not made a fool by it, may consider himself as having had a very narrow escape. It is an old remark, that boys who shine at school do not make the greatest figure when they grow up and come out into the world. The things, in fact, which a boy is set to learn at school, and on which his success depends, are things which do not require the exercise either of the highest or the most useful faculties of the mind. Memory (and that of the lowest kind) is the chief faculty called into play in conning over and repeating lessons by rote in grammar, in languages, in geography, arithmetic, etc., so that he who has the most of this technical memory, with the least turn for other things, which have a stronger and more natural claim upon his childish attention, will make the most forward school-boy. The jargon containing the definitions of the parts of speech, the rules for casting up an account, or the inflections of a Greek verb, can have no attraction to the tyro of ten years old, except as they are imposed as a task upon him by others, or from his feeling the want of sufficient relish or amusement in other things. A lad with a sickly constitution and no very active mind, who can just retain what is pointed out to him, and has neither sagacity to distinguish, nor spirit to enjoy for himself, will generally be at the head of his form. An idler at school, on the other hand, is one who has high health and spirits, who has the free use of his limbs, with all his wits about him, who feels the circulation of his blood and the motion of his heart, who is ready to laugh and cry in a breath, and who had rather chase a ball or a butterfly, feel the open air in his face, look at the fields or the sky, follow a winding path, or enter with eagerness into all the little conflicts and interests of his acquaintances and friends, than doze over a musty spelling-book, repeat barbarous distichs after his master, sit so many hours pinioned to a writing-desk, and receive

his reward for the loss of time and pleasure in paltry prize-medals at Christmas and Midsummer. There is indeed a degree of stupidity which prevents children from learning the usual lessons, or ever arriving at these puny academic honours. But what passes for stupidity is much often a want of interest, of a sufficient motive to fix the attention and force a reluctant application of the dry and unmeaning pursuits of school learning. The best capacities are as much above this drudgery as the dullest are beneath it. Our men of the greatest genius have not been most distinguished for their acquirements at school or at the university.

Th' enthusiast Fancy was a truant ever.

Gray and Collins were among the instances of this wayward disposition. Such persons do not think so highly of the advantages, nor can they submit their imaginations so servilely to the trammels of strict scholastic discipline. There is a certain kind and degree of intellect in which words take root, but into which things have not power to penetrate. A mediocrity of talent, with a certain slenderness of moral constitution, is the soil that produces the most brilliant specimens of successful prize-essays and Greek epigrammatists. It should not be forgotten that the least respectable character among modern politicians was the cleverest boy at Eton.

Learning is the knowledge of that which is not generally known to others, and which we can only derive at second-hand from books or other artificial sources. The knowledge of that which is before us, or about us, which appeals to our experience, passions, and pursuits, to the bosom and businesses of men, is not learning. Learning is the knowledge of that which none but the learned know. He is the most learned man who knows the most of what is farthest removed from common life and actual observation, that is of the least practical utility, and least liable to be brought to the test of experience, and that, having been handed down through the greatest number of intermediate stages, is the most full of uncertainty, difficulties and contradictions. It is seeing with the eyes of others, hearing with their ears, and pinning our faith on their understandings. The learned man prides himself in the knowledge of names and dates, not of men or things. He thinks and cares nothing about his next-door neighbours, but is deeply read in the tribes and castes of the Hindoos and Calmuc Tartars. He can hardly find his way into the next street, though he is acquainted with the exact dimensions of Constantinople and Pekin. He does not know whether his oldest acquaintance is a knave or a fool, but he can pronounce a pompous lecture on all the principal characters in history. He cannot tell whether an object is black or white, round or square, and yet he is a professed master of the laws of optics and rules of perspective. He knows as much of what he talks about as a blind man does of colours. He cannot give a satisfactory answer to the plainest question, nor is he ever in the right in any one of his opinions upon any one matter of fact that really comes before him, and yet he gives himself out for an infallible judge on all those points, of which it is impossible that he or any other person living should know anything but by conjecture. He is expert in all the dead and in most of the living languages; but he can neither speak his own fluently, nor write it correctly. A person of this class, the second Greek scholar of his day, undertook to point out several solecisms in Milton's Latin style; and in all its own performance there is hardly a sentence of common English. Such was Dr. — Such is Dr. —. Such was not Porson [Richard Porson (1759–1808)]. He was an exception that confirmed the general rule, —a man that, by uniting talent and knowledge with learning, made the distinction between them more striking and palpable.

A mere scholar, who knows nothing but books, must be ignorant even of them. "Books do not teach the use of books." How should he know anything of a work who knows nothing of the subject of it? The learned pedant is conversant with books only as they are made of other books, and those again of others, without end. He parrots those who have parroted others. He can translate the same word into ten different languages, but he knows nothing of the thing which it means in any one of them. He stuffs his head with authorities built on authorities, with quotations quoted from

241

quotations, while he locks up his senses, his understanding, and his heart. He is unacquainted with the maxims and manners of the world; he is to seek in the characters of individuals. He sees no beauty in the face of nature or of art. To him "the mighty world of eye and ear" is hidden; and "knowledge", except at one entrance, "quite shut out". His pride takes part with his ignorance, and his self-importance rises with the number of things of which he does not know the value, and which he therefore despises as unworthy of his notice. He knows nothing of pictures, —"of the colouring of Titian, the grace of Raphael, the purity of Domenichino, the corregioscity of Correggio, the learning of Poussin, the airs of Guido, the taste of the Caracci, or the grand contour of Micheal Angelo", —of all those glories of the Italian and miracles of the Flemish school, which have filled the eyes of mankind with delight, and to the study and imitation of which thousands have in vain devoted their lives. These are to him as if they had never been, a mere dead letter, a by-word; and no wonder, for he neither sees nor understands their prototypes in nature. A print of Rubins' Watering place, or Claude's Enchanted Castle, may be hanging on the walls of his rooms for months without his once perceiving them; and if you point them out to him he will turn away from them. The language of nature, or of art (which is another nature), is one that he does not understand. He repeats indeed the names of Apelles and Phidias, because they are to be found in classic authors, and boasts of their works as prodigies, because they no longer exist; or when he sees the finest remains of Grecian art actually before him in the Elgin Marbles, takes no other interest in them than as they lead to a learned dispute, and (which is the same thing) a quarrel about the meaning of a Greek particle. He is equally ignorant of music; he "knows no touch of it", from the strains of the all-accomplished Mozart to the Shepherd's pipe upon the mountain. His ears are nailed to his books; and deadened with the sound of the Greek and Latin tongues, and the din and smithery of school-learning. Does he know anything more of poetry? He knows the number of feet in a verse, and of acts in a play; but of the soul or spirit he knows nothing. He can turn a Greek ode into English, or a Latin epigram into Greek verse; but whether either is worth the trouble he leaves to the critics. Does he understand 'the act and practique part of life' better than 'the theorique'? No. He knows no liberal or mechanic art, no trade or occupation, no game of skill or chance. Learning "has no skill in surgery", in agriculture, in building, or in working in wood or in iron; it cannot make any instrument of labour, or use it when made; it cannot handle the plough or the spade, or the chisel or the hammer; it knows nothing of hunting or hawking, fishing or shooting, of horses or dogs, of fencing or dancing, or cudgel-playing, or bowls or cards, or tennis, or anything else. The learned professor of all arts and sciences cannot reduce any one of them to practice, though he may contribute an account of them to an Encyclopedia. He has not the use of his hands or of his feet; he can neither run, nor walk, nor swim; and he considers all those who actually understand and can exercise any of these arts of body or mind as vulgar and mechanical men,— though to know almost any one of them in perfection requires long time and practice, with powers originally fitted, and a turn of mind particularly devoted to them. It does not require more than this to enable the learned candidate to arrive, by painful study, at a doctor's degree and a fellowship, and to eat, drink and sleep the rest of his life!

The thing is plain. All that men really understand is confined to a very small compass; to their daily affairs and experience; to what they have an opportunity to know and motives to study or practise. The rest is affectation and imposture. The common people have the use of their limbs; for they live by their labour or skill. They understand their own business and the characters of those they have to deal with; for it is necessary that they should . They have eloquence to express their passions, and wit at will to express their contempt and provoke laughter. Their natural use of speech is not hung up in monumental mockery, in an obsolete language; nor is there sense of what is ludicrous, or readiness at finding out allusions to express it, buried in collections of Anas. You will hear more good things on the outside

of a stage-coach from London to Oxford than if you were to pass a twelvemonth with the undergraduates, or heads of colleges, of that famous university; and more home truths are to be learnt from listening to a noisy debate in an ale house than from attending to a formal one in the House of Commons. An elderly country gentlewoman will often know more of character, and be able to illustrate it by more amusing anecdotes taken from the history of what has been said, done, and gossiped in a country town for the last fifty years, than the best blue-stocking of the age will be able to glean from that sort of learning which consists in an acquaintance with all the novels and satirical poems published in the same period. People in towns, indeed are woefully deficient in a knowledge of character, which they see only in the bust, not as a whole-length. People in the country not only know all that has happened to a man, but trace his virtues or vices, as they do his features, in their descent through several generations, and solve some contradiction in his behaviour by a cross in the breed half a century ago. The learned know nothing of the matter, either in town or country. Above all, the mass of society have common sense, which the learned in all ages want. The vulgar are in the right when they judge for themselves; they are wrong when they trust to their blind guides. The celebrated nonconformist divine, Baxter, was almost stoned to death by the good women of Kidderminster, for asserting from the pulpit that 'hell was paved with infants' skulls'; but, by the force of argument, and of learned quotations from the Fathers, the reverend preacher at length prevailed over the scruples of his congregation, and over reason and humanity.

Such is the use which has been made of human learning. The labourers in this vineyard seem as if it was their object to confound all common sense, and the distinctions of good and evil, by means of traditional maxims and preconceived notions taken upon trust, and increasing in absurdity with increase of age. They pile hypotheses on hypotheses, mountain high, till it is impossible to come to the plain truth on any question. They see things, not as they are, but as they find them in books, and 'wink and shut their apprehension up', in order that they may discover nothing to interfere with their prejudices or convince them of their absurdity. It might be supposed that the height of human wisdom consisted in maintaining contradictions and rendering nonsense sacred. There is no dogma, however fierce or foolish, to which these persons have not set their seals, and tried to impose on the understandings of their followers, as the will of Heaven, clothed with all the terrors and sanctions of religion. How little has the human understanding been directed to find out the true and useful! How much ingenuity has been thrown away in defense of creeds and systems! How much time and talents have been wasted in theological controversy, in law, in politics, in verbal criticism, in judicial astrology and in finding out the art of making gold! What actual benefit do we reap from the writings of a Laud or Whitgift, or of Bishop Bull or Bishop Waterland, or Prideaux' Connections or Beausobre, or Calmet, or St Augustine, or Puffendorf, or Vattel, or from the more literal but equally learned and unprofitable labours of Scaliger, Cardan, and Scioppius? How many grains of sense are there in their thousand folio or quarto volumes? What would the world lose if they were committed to the flames tomorrow? Or are they not already 'gone to the vault of all the Capulets'? Yet all these were oracles in their time, and would have scoffed at you or me, at common sense and human nature, for differing with them. It is our turn to laugh now.

To conclude this subject, the most sensible people to be met with in society are men of business and of the world, who argue from what they see and know, instead of spinning cobweb distinctions of what things ought to be. Women have often more of what is called good sense than men. They have fewer pretensions; are less implicated in theories; and judge of objects more from their immediate and involuntary impression on the mind, and, therefore, more truly and naturally. They cannot reason wrong; for they do not reason at all. They do not think or speak by rule; and they have in general more eloquence and wit, as well as sense, on that account. By their wit, sense and eloquence together, they generally contrive to govern their husbands. Their style, when they write to their friends (not for the booksellers), is better than that of most authors. —Uneducated people have most exuberance of invention and the greatest freedom from prejudice. Shakespeare was evidently an uneducated mind, both in the freshness of his imagination and the variety of his views; as Milton was scholastic, in the texture both of his thoughts and feelings. Shakespeare had not been accustomed to write themes at school in favour of virtue or against vice. To this we owe the unaffected but healthy tone of his dramatic morality. It we wish to know the force of human genius we should read Shakespeare. If we wish to see the insignificance of human learning we may only study his commentators.

一个人会讲的语言愈多，
愈益暴露其才学的漏洞。
这儿那儿把心血呕，
总免不了大打折扣。
希伯来文、加尔蒂文和叙利亚文，
一如其写法，让人理智颠倒，
若要竭力研读它，就像用左手写字，
令人心智左右颠倒。
然而，若要表达超前，
根本不用几种语言，
用母语发出最强音，
通常被认为更有学问。

——巴特勒

　　人群中对周围事物了解最少的是那些只会写和读的人。不会读又不会写，比起只会读和写，倒要好一些。整日手捧书本而不务世事的人——我们几乎可以肯定——既无力也无心去关心他周围或脑子里的事物。像这样的人,或许有人会说,已经把自己的理解力装在了口袋里,或遗在家里的书架上了。他不敢做深思;他不敢做任何评论,除非他亲眼看到的文字机械地提议他这样做;他害怕苦思冥想,因为他缺少实践,无从可想;他整日独坐,满足于和那些冗长乏味的词句以及模糊不清的形象为伴。这些东西填充着他空虚的头脑,同时也不停地彼此磨损、消失。在很多情况下,书本只是常识的陪衬,真知的替补。与其说书本是用来观察自然的"眼睛",还不如说它会遮蔽那些弱视和怠懒的人的眼睛,使他们看不到大自然炫目的光线和变幻的美景。书呆子把自己包裹在其织就的文字之网中,只能看见别人脑中反映出来的事物的微弱阴影。大自然让他目眩。真实物体的印象,一旦被剥去文字的伪装和各种迂回的描述,对他简直就是迎头痛击,令他脚步踉跄,站立不稳;它们的丰富多彩令他无所适从,它们的飞速变化令他筋疲力尽;他转身离开这个喧闹、嘈杂、使人头晕目眩的世界(他既不关注其巨大的变化,也不懂得如何归纳出固有的规律),转向那些单调的已经没有生气的语言,以及那些乏味的、不太令人吃惊的、不太难懂的字母单词组合。这没什么不好,非常可取。"让我安宁吧!"这是睡者和死者的箴言。期望学问人能放下书本去独立思考,就像让一个偏瘫病人撒开拐杖从椅子上跳起来,或者不靠什么奇迹就能收起床铺迈步走一样,是不可能的。他紧抱书本不放,把它作为自己的知识支柱;他害怕被独自遗下,就像害怕真空一样。他仅能呼吸学术空气,就像别人呼吸自然空气一样。他的感觉都借自别人,没有自己的思想,必须靠别人的思想为生。这种依靠外界资源给自己提供思想的习惯会"削弱一切内在思维力量",就像长期地少量饮酒也会慢慢地损坏肠胃一样。思维器官被弃置不用,或受到习俗或者权威的束缚时,就会变得倦怠、麻木,不再适合支配行动和思考。学问人苦心钻研空洞无聊的字句和音节,直到两眼发黑,书本从无力的手中滑落下来。对学问人这种倦怠和无聊的生活人们已经习以为常,这种盲从而慵懒的生活使人精神倦怠,身心疲惫。我宁愿做一个伐木工人,或地位卑微的农夫,整日在"太阳底下挥汗劳作,夜晚就在逍遥世界里美美地睡觉",也不愿意这样半睡半醒,耗费我的生命。有学问的作者和读者之间的区别在于:一个抄书,另一个读书。做学问的人只是文字长工。如果你让他们真正自己写一篇文章,他们会觉得头昏脑胀,不知自己身处何处。孜孜不倦地读书就像那些不停地临摹别人画的人,在他们自己尝试作画时,却发现自己的眼睛不够快,手不够稳健,用色不够鲜艳,而无法描绘大自然的生动形态。

凡是经过正规传统教育的人，即使若没有被教成一个傻瓜，也会有劫后余生之感。学校里的尖子学生长大进入社会后却不是最突出的，这已经是老生常谈了。事实是，孩子在学校里学习的东西，即他们成功所在，往往不需要运用大脑中最有用的功能。在学习语法、语言、地理、算术等科目时，依靠的主要是以最低级层次的功能去糊弄，去记忆。因此，那些机械记忆力最强却很少关注其他事情——那些事情能激起儿童更强的兴趣——的学生会名列前茅。对于一个十多岁的初学者来说，包含语言成分定义的术语、运算的法则、希腊语动词的曲折变化，这些都没有任何吸引力，除非是作为任务强加给他们或者他们对其他事情没有浓厚兴趣。身体羸弱、思维不活的孩子，刚好能记住老师指定的功课，他虽然没有明辨是非的智慧，也没有自娱自乐的精神，往往会是年级的尖子。另一方面，学校里的那些懒学生，他们有健康的体魄和充沛的精力，四肢灵活、头脑敏捷，他们可以感觉到体内血液的流动和心脏的跳动；他们恣意哭笑；他们宁愿追逐皮球和蝴蝶，感受户外空气的吹拂，或瞩目原野和天空，或信步于蜿蜒的小径，或急切地与朋友争论或讨论，也不愿意面对陈腐的课本而昏昏欲睡，或者跟着老师重复那些格格不入的句子，或久久地被栓在课桌旁；不愿意为了在圣诞节和施礼约翰节上得到一些无足轻重的奖励而失去时间和乐趣。确实，他们学不会学校的普通课程，或得不到那些寥寥的学习荣耀在一定程度上是因为他们笨，但往往是因为他们没有兴趣，缺乏学习动机，不愿花力气到枯燥而且无聊的学业中去，而这却往往被错认为是愚笨。人类最高的能力远高于读书这个苦差事，就像最笨的学生的能力要远远低于它一样。我们最伟大的天才在小学或大学里的成绩并不都是最好的：

爱幻想的学生都曾经逃过学。

格雷和柯林斯就是这种任性的例证。他们这些人对学校严格的纪律不以为然，更不会让他们的想象力受其束缚。确实有某些智力在一定程度上是文句的来源，但是客观事物却无法渗透进去。那些道德欠佳的平庸天才正是产生奖章作家和希腊语讽刺诗人的沃土。我们不要忘了现代政客中最不体面的家伙曾经是伊顿公学中最聪明的学生。

学问是不为常人所知只能间接地从书本或其他人为的来源中获得的知识。我们眼前的、周围的需要我们用经验、情感、追求或需要我们心灵和事业的知识不是学问。学问只有有学问的人知道而其他人一概不知。最有学问的人只知道那些远离日常生活和实际观察的知识，而这些知识是最没有实际作用，最经不起实验检验，再加上历经数不清的中间阶层的层层相传，其中充满了疑难、矛盾和不确定性。他用别人的眼睛看,用别人的耳朵听,完全相信和依赖别人的理解。有学问的人为他们知道的名字和历史日期而感到骄傲,而不懂得人和事本身。他无心考虑也不关心邻家之事,却精通印度人和鞑靼卡尔马克人的等级制度和部落群体。他不知道临街的道路如何走,却准确地知道君士坦丁堡和北京有多大。他不知道他的老朋友是一个无赖还是一个傻瓜,但却可以就历史上所有重要人物夸夸其谈。他辨不清物体是黑还是白,是方还是圆,但却是光学定律和透视法则的资深专家。他对所谈对象一无所知,就像瞎子谈论色彩一样。对于最简单的问题,他也不能给予满意的答复;对于他遇见的实际问题,他的意见从未正确过,然而,他对其本人或旁人都不可能知道,只能揣测一二的事情却总是宣称他是绝对正确的权威。他精通所有已经湮没的语言以及大多数还在使用的语言;但他既不能流利地讲,也不能正确地写其母语。有这样一个二流的希腊语学者,曾指出弥尔顿拉丁文中存在的一些语法错误,但在他自己的文章中,却几乎没有一句规范的英语句子。以前的某某博士是这样,现在的某某博士是这样,波尔森(1759～1808)却不是这样。他这个例外则证实了这条通则——它把学问和才能结合起来,使它们之间的区别更加鲜艳夺目。

一个懂书本知识的纯粹学者,对书本上的知识甚至也无法领会。"书不会告诉你如何使用书本。"对书中所讲的事物不理解,又如何能懂得书呢?那些书呆子精通书本,只是因为这些书源于另外一些书,而另外一些书又源自其他的书,如此循环不尽。他鹦鹉学舌一样模仿别人,而别人也是在重复其他的人。他可以把同一个词翻译成十种不同的语言,但却全然不知这些词语的意思。他头脑里填满了权威的权威,引语的引语,却锁起自己的感觉、领悟和心智。他不谙为人处世之道,他对个人的不同性格茫然无知。他看不到自然界和艺术的美。对于他,"可以耳闻目见的现实世界"避而不见,而"知识",除了读书这个途径,都被排斥在门外。其自傲伴着其无知而生,他对事物价值不知晓得越多就越使他的自大增长得更甚。他不懂绘画——不知道提香的用色、拉斐尔的典雅、多梅尼基诺的纯洁、柯雷吉欧的柯雷吉欧技法、普桑的渊博、圭多的风韵、卡拉齐兄弟的格调、米开朗基罗的雄奇线条——他全然不知意大利画派的辉煌以及弗兰德斯流派创造的奇迹,尽管所有这些都让人类欢欣雀跃,尽管有千千万万的人耗尽毕生心血去模仿和研究它们。但对他,所有这些都仿佛不存在,都只是已经湮没的字母和人云亦云之语;这不足为奇,因为他没有看过也不理解它们在自然界中的原型。他房间的墙上可能会挂一幅鲁本斯的《海滨浴场》或克劳德的《鬼堡》,但他也许数月都不

249

曾看它一眼;你若向他指出,他准会转而言他。自然和艺术(另一种自然)的语言他是不能理解的。他确实会反复提到阿佩莱斯和菲迪亚斯的名字,但那只是因为他们出现在古典著作里;他把他们的作品捧为天才之作,只是因为它们都已不复存在;或者,当他亲眼看到埃尔金大理石雕像这些古希腊艺术精品的遗迹时,他感兴趣的只是这些遗迹导致的学术争论或者关于某个希腊语小品词意义的争论,这两者其实是一回事。他对音乐也同样无知,无论听到完美的莫扎特乐曲还是山坡上牧人的笛声,他都无动于衷。他的耳朵已钉在书本之中,已让希腊语和拉丁语以及学校里的嘈杂声吵得失了聪。至于诗歌,他是不是懂得要多一些呢? 他知道一首诗有多少韵脚,一出戏有多少幕;但对于它们的灵魂和精神却一无所知。他可以把一首希腊颂诗译成英文诗,或者把拉丁短诗译成希腊文。但他的辛苦有何价值,他从未想过,他把它留给了批评家们。那么他对于"生活的实践部分"比"理论"理解得是否要深入一些呢? 不,他不懂得艺术和技术,不会经商,不会工作,也不懂得玩任何智力游戏和运气游戏。学问人"不懂外科医术",不会农业、建筑业、木工和铁匠等技术;他不会制造也不会使用任何劳动工具;他扶不好犁,挥不了锹,也用不好锤和凿;他不懂狩猎,不会驯鹰,不懂得钓鱼和射箭,不懂得马术和驯狗、击剑和跳舞,不懂得棍法、纸牌和网球,他什么也不懂。有学问的文理科教授们虽然能为百科全书增加一些词条,但他们不肯把他们的知识付诸实践。他们四肢不勤,走不好,跑不好,还不会游泳;他们认为这些体力和心力技艺都是那些粗鄙、呆板之人要去了解和学习的——虽然要精通其中任何一门都需要长时间地不懈练习,需要天赋和全身心地投入。相对来说,做一个有学问的人无须这么刻苦,他们只要努力学习,便可获得博士或职称,便可衣食无忧、一劳永逸。

道理很明显,人真正能理解的知识仅限于一个很小的范围之内,仅限于他们的日常事物和经验,仅限于他们有机会认识,并促使他们去研究和实践的事情。其他的知识只不过是不懂装懂,冒充内行而已。老百姓要动手,因为他们靠劳动或技术维生。他们得懂得自己的行业,也了解和他们打交道的人的性格;因为这很必要。他们既有足够的口才表达他们的情感,又有足够的机智传达他们的不屑而又能让人大笑。他们不会处处模仿,引用过时的语言,而忘了如何自然地说话;他们自然的语言中没有荒谬感,也不会准备随时地引经据典。坐在从伦敦开往牛津的驿车上你听到的趣事比你和著名的牛津大学的学生或院长呆上12个月听到的还要多;你从酒店里乱哄哄的吵闹中学到的浅显而真切的道理,比你在下议院的正式辩论中学到的还要多。乡下老太太对人物的性格比与其同龄的最出色的女学者要了解得多,因为她能从近50年里在村镇里的所见所闻以及各种流言碎语这些往事中找出非常有趣的轶事去论证她的看法,而女学者只能从同时期发表的小说、讽刺诗里搜集相关的知识去阐明。实际上,城里人对人物性格的了解少之又少,因为他们看人只看到部分。乡下人不仅知道一个人的经历,而且可以像研究其长相一样,把他的优缺点追溯到他数代之前的先人,还可以用半个世纪前的一次异族的婚姻来解释他矛盾的行为。而无论是城里还是乡下的事情,有学问的人都一概不知。更重要的是,公众都有常识,历代有学问的人却没有。老百姓自行判断,他们的结果往往是正确的;但若听信盲目的指导,往往会步入歧途。著名的非国教教会牧师巴克斯特因为在布道时曾宣称"地狱由婴儿的头颅铺就"而差点被肯德明斯特善良的妇女们扔石头砸死;但他的雄辩及援引的教父们的学说使他最终打消了教民们的顾虑,也胜过了理智和人性。

这就是人类学问的用武之地。在学问圈里的这些人的目标似乎就是用传统的箴言和先入为主的观点去混淆所有的常识与善恶之别,而且年事愈高愈荒谬。他们把假说堆到像山高,直到看不到任何问题的本相。他们不从事物本身,而是从书本上看事物。他们闭上眼睛,停止思考,以保证他们的偏见不受什么干扰,对自己的荒谬深信不疑。似乎可以说,人类的最高智慧在于维持矛盾,在于使谬论神圣化。他们把所有的教条——不管他们有多么严厉或荒唐——都打上自己的印章,给它们披上宗教的恐惧和戒律外衣,并竭力使门徒接受天意。人类在寻求真实而有用的事物上付出的心智何其少! 为了维护教义和体制,有多少智士能人被弃置不用? 又有多少时间和俊杰白白地浪费在辩论、法律、政治、文学评论、占星术和炼金术中呀? 从劳德或惠吉夫的著作中,从布尔主教或沃特兰主教的大作中,从波瑞杜可斯的《关系》中,从波索波、卡尔梅、圣·奥古斯丁、普芬道夫、瓦特尔等人的著作中,或从斯卡利杰、卡尔旦和西奥皮乌斯的虽更具书卷气却没有多大实际意义的名著中,我们究竟能得到什么实际的益处呢? 那上千卷的对开本和四开本的书籍中到底有着多大的意义呢? 即使明天把这些书籍都付之一炬,全世界又会有什么损失呢? 它们不是早已尘封土埋、被人遗忘了吗? 虽然当时它们曾经是神语圣言,稍有不同意见,就会对你我,常识以及人性加以嘲笑。但现在,该我们嘲笑它们了。

总而言之,社会上最理智的人莫过于从事事业的脚踏实地的人。他们总是从其所见所知出发,而不会拘泥于事物细枝末节之差别。女人比男人具有更多正确的感觉。她们很少自命不凡,很少受理论的束缚;她们根据事物在其头脑中直接的、自然的印象去判断它们，因而其判断就更真实，更自然。她们的推理不会出错，因为她们根本不推理。她们不按常理思考和表达，故就此而言，她们一般更善于雄辩，更有智慧，更有感觉。她们综合运用这三者，设法统治自己的丈夫。她们写信给朋友时(不是给书商)，文笔比大多数作家都要好——没有受过高等教育的人往往是最富有创造力，最不受偏见摆布。莎士比亚显然没有受过教育，所以他才有新颖的想象力和各种多姿多彩的观点；而弥尔顿是个学者，无论其思想特征还是情感特征都透露出学者气息。莎士比亚在学校里不习惯写那些惩恶扬善的文章。正因为如此，才有了他健康而自然的不朽喜剧。若要了解人类天才的力量，我们就该去读莎士比亚的作品；若要领略人类学问的无聊空洞，我们也许只有研究对其作品的注释了。

# 论美
# Beauty

【美国】拉尔夫·瓦尔多·爱默生

　　拉尔夫·瓦尔多·爱默生（1803－1882），美国思想家、散文作家、诗人。有人称其为"美国的孔子"。著名的《论文集》为爱默生赢得了巨大的声誉，他的思想被称为超验主义的核心，他本人则被冠以"美国文艺复兴的领袖"之美誉。《论美》以哲学家的角度探讨了人类文明中这一深刻的话题，让人回味无穷。

A nobler want of man is served by nature, namely, the love of Beauty.

The ancient Greeks called the world "kosmos", beauty. Such is the constitution of all things, or such the plastic power of the human eye, that the primary forms, as the sky, the mountain, the tree, the animal, give us a delight in and for themselves; a pleasure arising from outline, color, motion, and grouping. This seems partly owing to the eye itself. The eye is the best of artists. By the mutual action of its structure and of the laws of light, perspective is produced, which integrates every mass of objects, of what character soever, into a well colored and shaded globe, so that where the particular objects are mean and unaffecting, the landscape which they compose, is round and symmetrical. And as the eye is the best composer, so light is the first of painters. There is no object so foul that intense light will not make beautiful. And the stimulus it affords to the sense, and a sort of infinitude which it hath, like space and time, make all matter gay. Even the corpse has its own beauty. But besides this general grace diffused over nature, almost all the individual forms are agreeable to the eye, as is proved by our endless imitations of some of them, as the acorn, the grape, the pine-cone, the wheat-ear, the egg, the wings and forms of most birds, the lion's claw, the serpent, the butterfly, sea-shells, flames, clouds, buds, leaves, and the forms of many trees as the palm.

For better consideration, we may distribute the aspects of Beauty in a threefold manner.

1. First, the simple perception of natural forms is a delight. The influence of the forms and actions in nature, is so needful to man, that, in its lowest functions, it seems to lie on the confines of commodity and beauty. To the body and mind which have been cramped by noxious work or company, nature is medicinal and restores their tone. The tradesman, the attorney comes out of the din and craft of the street, and sees the sky and the woods, and is a man again. In their eternal calm, he finds himself. The health of the eye seems to demand a horizon. We are never tired, so long as we can see far enough.

But in other hours, Nature satisfies by its loveliness, and without any mixture of corporeal benefit. I see the spectacle of morning from the hill-top over against my house, from day-break to sun-rise, with emotions which an angel might share. The long slender bars of cloud float like fishes in the sea of crimson light. From the earth, as a shore, I look out into that silent sea. I seem to partake its rapid transformations: the active enchantment reaches my dust, and I dilate and conspire with the morning wind. How does Nature deify us with a few and cheap elements! Give me health and a day, and I will make the pomp of emperors ridiculous. The dawn is my Assyria; the sun-set and moon-rise my Paphos, and unimaginable realms of faerie; broad noon shall be my England of the senses and the understanding; the night shall be my Germany of mystic philosophy and dreams.

Not less excellent, except for our less susceptibility in the afternoon, was the charm, last evening, of a January sunset. The western clouds divided and subdivided themselves into pink flakes modulated with tints of unspeakable softness; and the air had so much life and sweetness that it was a pain to come within doors. What was it that nature would say? Was there no meaning in the live repose of the valley behind the mill, and which Homer or Shakspeare could not reform for me in words? The leafless trees become spires of flame in the sunset, with the blue east for their background, and the stars of the dead calices of flowers, and every withered stem and stubble rimed with frost, contribute something to the mute music.

The inhabitants of cities suppose that the country landscape is pleasant only half the year. I please myself with the graces of the winter scenery, and believe that we are as much touched by it as by the genial influences of summer. To the attentive eye, each moment of the year has its own beauty, and in the same field, it beholds, every hour, a picture which was never seen before, and which shall never be seen again. The heavens change every moment, and reflect their glory or gloom on the plains beneath. The state of the crop in the surrounding farms alters the expression of the earth from week to week. The succession of native plants in the pastures and

roadsides, which makes the silent clock by which time tells the summer hours, will make even the divisions of the day sensible to a keen observer. The tribes of birds and insects, like the plants punctual to their time, follow each other, and the year has room for all. By water-courses, the variety is greater. In July, the blue pontederia or pickerel-weed blooms in large beds in the shallow parts of our pleasant river, and swarms with yellow butterflies in continual motion. Art cannot rival this pomp of purple and gold. Indeed the river is a perpetual gala, and boasts each month a new ornament.

But this beauty of Nature which is seen and felt as beauty, is the least part. The shows of day, the dewy morning, the rainbow, mountains, orchards in blossom, stars, moonlight, shadows in still water, and the like, if too eagerly hunted, become shows merely, and mock us with their unreality. Go out of the house to see the moon, and it is mere tinsel; it will not please as when its light shines upon your necessary journey. The beauty that shimmers in the yellow afternoons of October, who ever could clutch it? Go forth to find it, and it is gone: it is only a mirage as you look from the windows of diligence.

2. The presence of a higher, namely, of the spiritual element is essential to its perfection. The high and divine beauty which can be loved without effeminacy, is that which is found in combination with the human will. Beauty is the mark God sets upon virtue. Every natural action is graceful. Every heroic act is also decent, and causes the place and the bystanders to shine. We are taught by great actions that the universe is the property of every individual in it. Every rational creature has all nature for his dowry and estate. It is his, if he will. He may divest himself of it; he may creep into a corner, and abdicate his kingdom, as most men do, but he is entitled to the world by his constitution. In proportion to the energy of his thought and will, he takes up the world into himself. "All those things for which men plough, build, or sail, obey virtue;" said Sallust. "The winds and waves," said Gibbon, "are always on the side of the ablest navigators." So are the sun and moon and all the stars of heaven. When a noble act is done,—perchance in a scene of great natural beauty; when Leonidas and his three hundred martyrs

consume one day in dying, and the sun and moon come each and look at them once in the steep defile of Thermopylae; when Arnold Winkelried, in the high Alps, under the shadow of the avalanche, gathers in his side a sheaf of Austrian spears to break the line for his comrades; are not these heroes entitled to add the beauty of the scene to the beauty of the deed? When the bark of Columbus nears the shore of America;—before it, the beach lined with savages, fleeing out of all their huts of cane; the sea behind; and the purple mountains of the Indian Archipelago around, can we separate the man from the living picture? Does not the New World clothe his form with her palm-groves and savannahs as fit drapery? Ever does natural beauty steal in like air, and envelope great actions. When Sir Harry Vane was dragged up the Tower-hill, sitting on a sled, to suffer death, as the champion of the English laws, one of the multitude cried out to him, "You never sat on so glorious a seat." Charles II., to intimidate the citizens of London, caused the patriot Lord Russel to be drawn in an open coach, through the principal streets of the city, on his way to the scaffold. "But," his biographer says, "the multitude imagined they saw liberty and virtue sitting by his side." In private places, among sordid objects, an act of truth or heroism seems at once to draw to itself the sky as its temple, the sun as its candle. Nature stretcheth out her arms to embrace man, only let his thoughts be of equal greatness. Willingly does she follow his steps with the rose and the violet, and bend her lines of grandeur and grace to the decoration of her darling child. Only let his thoughts be of equal scope, and the frame will suit the picture. A virtuous man is in unison with her works, and makes the central figure of the visible sphere. Homer, Pindar, Socrates, Phocion, associate themselves fitly in our memory with the geography and climate of Greece. The visible heavens and earth sympathize with Jesus. And in common life, whosoever has seen a person of powerful character and happy genius, will have remarked how easily he took all things along with him,—the persons, the opinions, and the day, and nature became ancillary to a man.

3. There is still another aspect under which the beauty of the world may

be viewed, namely, as it becomes an object of the intellect. Beside the relation of things to virtue, they have a relation to thought. The intellect searches out the absolute order of things as they stand in the mind of God, and without the colors of affection. The intellectual and the active powers seem to succeed each other, and the exclusive activity of the one, generates the exclusive activity of the other. There is something unfriendly in each to the other, but they are like the alternate periods of feeding and working in animals; each prepares and will be followed by the other. Therefore does beauty, which, in relation to actions, as we have seen, comes unsought, and comes because it is unsought, remain for the apprehension and pursuit of the intellect; and then again, in its turn, of the active power. Nothing divine dies. All good is eternally reproductive. The beauty of nature reforms itself in the mind, and not for barren contemplation, but for new creation.

All men are in some degree impressed by the face of the world; some men even to delight. This love of beauty is Taste. Others have the same love in such excess, that, not content with admiring, they seek to embody it in new forms. The creation of beauty is Art.

The production of a work of art throws a light upon the mystery of humanity. A work of art is an abstract or epitome of the world. It is the result or expression of nature, in miniature. For, although the works of nature are innumerable and all different, the result or the expression of them all is similar and single. Nature is a sea of forms radically alike and even unique. A leaf, a sun-beam, a landscape, the ocean, make an analogous impression on the mind. What is common to them all,—that perfectness and harmony, is beauty. The standard of beauty is the entire circuit of natural forms, —the totality of nature; which the Italians expressed by defining beauty "il piu nell' uno." Nothing is quite beautiful alone: nothing but is beautiful in the whole. A single object is only so far beautiful as it suggests this universal grace. The poet, the painter, the sculptor, the musician, the architect, seek each to concentrate this radiance of the world on one point, and each in his several work to satisfy the love of beauty which stimulates him to produce. Thus is Art, a nature passed through the alembic of man. Thus in art, does nature work through the will of a man filled with the beauty of her first works.

The world thus exists to the soul to satisfy the desire of beauty. This element I call an ultimate end. No reason can be asked or given why the soul seeks beauty. Beauty, in its largest and profoundest sense, is one expression for the universe. God is the all-fair. Truth, and goodness, and beauty, are but different faces of the same All. But beauty in nature is not ultimate. It is the herald of inward and eternal beauty, and is not alone a solid and satisfactory good. It must stand as a part, and not as yet the last or highest expression of the final cause of Nature.

人有一个更崇高的需求,为自然所满足,即爱美。

古希腊人称世界为"kosmos",即"美"之意。此为万物之构形,或颇具塑造性的人眼所致;因此凡基本形体,如天空、高山、树木、动物,本身即令我们赏心悦目,其轮廓、色彩、运动与组合使我们感到欣喜。这似乎部分归功于眼睛本身。眼乃是最优秀的艺术家,以其构造加上光律的相互作用,使美景产生;任何东西无论特征如何,均构成一个色彩完美的整体,所以单个物体虽微不足道,但一经组合便呈现出丰满匀称的景色。眼睛既然最善于组合,光线亦最能描绘。再丑陋的东西,强有力的光亦会使之变得妩媚。它带来感官的刺激,它所具有的像空间和时间的那种无限性,使一切呈现欢乐色彩。即便尸体也有其美之处。不过,除大自然显现出的整体美外,几乎一切个体都悦人眼目,这已为我们不断模仿它们所证实,诸如橡树子、葡萄、松果、麦穗、蛋、许多鸟的翅膀和体型、狮爪、蛇、蝴蝶、海贝壳、火焰、云块、蓓蕾、叶子,许多如棕榈那种树的形状。

为细加思考,我们不妨把美一分为三:

一、首先,只需感知自然之形体,即是一种快乐。人颇离不开自然形体和运动的影响,以致它最低微的作用,似乎局限于实用和美观的范畴。人的身心为讨

厌的工作或交往所累，而自然则有益健康，使其恢复正常。街上不乏烦扰和骗术，商人、律师将其摆脱，看见天空和树林，从而恢复本我。置身大自然永恒的静谧，他方发现自己。眼睛若要康健，似乎需有广阔视域。只要能极目远眺，我们便绝无困乏之时。

但在其余时候，自然则以其可爱令人惬意，而与消除疲乏无关。我从黎明到日出，站在房后的山顶上观赏壮丽的晨景，心情犹如天使的一般。那些细长的云块，像漂浮在泛着红光的大海里的鱼儿。站在地上，一如站在岸边，我遥望静静的海洋。它瞬息万变，我似乎参与其中；它富有生机的魔力，触及我身心，我感到生命扩张，与晨风一道飞舞。自然用几许廉价之物，就使我们有神圣之感！给我以健康之躯、明媚之日，我便觉得赫赫皇帝亦荒唐可笑。黎明是我的亚述；日落月出是我的帕福斯和无法想象的仙境；明朗的中午将是我富有理智的英国；夜晚将是我充满神秘哲学和梦想的德国。

时值一月，昨日傍晚我见日落同样妩媚之极，只是每到下午我们的感觉没那么灵敏而已。西方云散，成粉红薄片，色调之柔和难以形容；空气中充满生机，温和无比，此时进屋实在会让人不快。那自然美景会说什么？磨坊后的山谷虽一片宁静，但却生气勃勃，即使荷马或莎士比亚也无法用语言为我再现，难道这毫无意义？光秃的树，在霞光里像燃烧的尖塔，衬托在东方蓝蓝的背景里；花朵已谢，然而点点犹如繁星；败枝残干，布上霜迹，无不为这无声的音乐增添美妙情调。

城市居民以为，一年中乡村景色只有一半时间才悦人心目。而对于冬景之美，我却自得其乐，以为它给我们的美感并不亚于温和宜人的夏季。只要细心观察，每时每刻都有其美；即便在同一田野，每一小时你都能看见从未见过、并且再不会见到的画面。天空也在时刻变化，因此大地或光辉灿烂，或阴沉昏暗。周围农场的庄稼，一周又一周地呈现新貌。牧场或路边土生的植物相继生长，成为无声的时钟，人们由此可知四季光阴，敏锐的人甚至可觉察到一天的变易。各种鸟虫也像植物一样准时，相继出现——凡天地生物无不有成长之机会。河水边，变化更是丰富多彩。每当7月，河流欢快，浅水处蓝色的梭子鱼草大片盛开，大群大群的黄蝴蝶翩翩起舞。金紫相交，辉映出其壮丽景色，艺术怎能企及。的确，河流是一个永恒的节目，每月均有新装展现。

但此种为我们所见所感的自然之美，实在微不足道。一日奇观，诸如清新的早晨、彩虹、高山、盛开的果园、星星、月光、水中静影等等，若求之太切，则只成为虚饰之物，以其虚无缥缈令我们失望。步出屋外去看月，它不过华而不实，征途旅人行进于月光下的快乐你不会获得。10月下午,金光闪闪,其美何人能捕捉? 你跨步向前,将其寻觅,而它已不复存在;从车窗观之,它不过一片幻景而已。

二、美若要达到至善至美境地,必须有一个更崇高的因素,即精神。崇高神圣的美,能为人所爱而无娇柔之气,与人的意志密不可分。美是上帝印在美德上的标记。凡自然的行为皆美好。凡英勇行为皆体面,它让所在之地与那里的人亦生光彩。我们从伟人的作为中得知,世界为人人所有。每个有理性的人,均可把一切自然视为个人财产。只要他有此心愿,即会如此。他可以将其放弃,躲进一个角落,不要自己的王国,一如许多人那样;但他既立身于世,即有资格享有世界。他占据世界多少,全凭自己的心志而定。"人为之耕耘、建造或航行的一切,无不唯善是从,"萨卢斯特说。吉本说,"风浪总有利于最杰出的航海家。"日月、星辰无不如此。当某人有高尚之举——或许在风光美极之地;当莱奥尼达斯及其300名战士于一日中壮烈牺牲,日月相继而出,作别葬身德摩比利深谷中的英雄;在高高的阿尔卑斯山上,面临雪崩的危险,阿诺德·温克尔里德以血肉之躯挡住奥地利军队的长矛,为战友们冲破防线——这些英雄们,难道不能以自然之美,为其献身之美增添光彩? 当哥伦布的船靠近美洲海岸——当时海滩上站满土人,他们从茅屋里飞奔而出;后面是大海;周围耸立着印第安群岛呈现紫色的高峰——难道我们能将这举世英雄与活生生的画面截然分开? 难道新大陆没以其棕榈树和大平原,为其贵体披上美丽的盛装? 自然之美总像空气一般悄然而入,为豪行壮举穿上新衣。当亨利·范内爵士为维护英国法律的尊严,坐着雪橇被拖上塔山处死时,众人中一人高喊:"你以前从未坐过如此荣耀的宝座!"爱国者罗素勋爵在被送上绞刑架前,查理二世将其送上一辆敞蓬马车,使之穿过伦敦大街以便示众。"但是,"他的传记作者说,"众人心想他们看见自由和美德就在他身旁。"即便在隐僻之地,肮脏之处,只要有正直或英勇行为,似乎天空立即成为其圣堂,太阳成为其烛光。自然伸出双臂将人拥抱,只为让他有同样伟大的思想。她带着玫瑰和紫罗兰,心甘情愿护随其后,以优美富丽之线条,打扮自己可爱的孩子。只要其思想影响深远,身躯又何不与美景相融。一位德善之人,是与自然杰作互为协调的,并成为大地的中心。我们记得,荷马、品达、苏格拉底和福基翁,均与希腊的地理和气候完美地融为一体。而耶稣也与天同广,与地同厚。在平常生活中,谁见到一位德才非凡之人,都会说他多么事事顺心——不管待人、持论还是度日,连自然也从属于他。

三、世上之美,尚另有一面可予考察,即它成为心智研究的对象。事物除与

德善相联,亦与思想相关。在上帝心中,它们处于何种绝对位置,均为心智所探究,而毫无感情色彩。人的思考能力与活动能力似乎相继而生,一者先独占其身,随后被另一者取代。它们彼此虽有所抵触,但正如动物时而吃食时而干活,双方都准备着被接替。因此,与行为相关之美已如我们所见,会不寻自来,而正因为不寻自来,它便期待着心智的理解和探寻;继而又激发行动。凡神圣者均不会死亡。一切善美之物再生不断。自然之美再现于人的心中,非为贫乏之思考,而为崭新之创造。

任何人,都或多或少为世界景色所感动,有的甚至为之欣喜。此种爱美曰"情趣"。更有他人,爱美有过之而无不及,不仅满足于赞美,而且力求以新的形式再现。此为创造美,谓之"艺术"。

艺术品产生,使人性的秘密有所揭示。一件艺术品,即是世界的一种概括或缩影。它产生于自然,又为自然之表现,不过是其微形罢了。因为尽管自然之作数不胜数,各不相同,但因之而生的艺术,或其在艺术上的表现却单纯专一。自然虽有无数形体,但却基本相同,甚至十分独特。树叶阳光,山水海洋,给人以相似之感。它们有一种共同点——完美与协调,即美。美之标准,即是自然形体的总和——亦即自然之整体;意大利人解释美时,将其表述为"一中见多"。任何东西,单独时都不甚美,唯置于整体方显出其美。单个物体,当显示出普遍之美时,方美丽之至。诗人、画家、雕刻家、音乐家、设计师,均力求将世界的光辉集中于一点,在各自的工作中满足爱美之心——此心激发着他去创作。因此艺术是经过人提炼的自然;艺术家的心中,满怀着自然之美,继而他便以其意志将自然转化为艺术。

所以世界之存在,意在满足爱美之心。此种要素,我谓之根本目的。心何以求美,既无法问及,亦难以作答。美,以其最深广意义而论是宇宙之表现。上帝是至美。真、善、美,为同一整体的三个方面。但自然之美并非根本,它是内在永恒之美的使者,单独并非充实圆满。自然之美只为一部份,并非自然之最终目标的最权威或最崇高的表现。